THE REALITY OF ESP

THE REALITY OF ESP

A Physicist's Proof of Psychic Abilities

Russell Targ

Foreword by **Stephan A. Schwartz**

QUEST

BOOKS

Theosophical Publishing House
Wheaton, Illinois * Chennai, India

Cover design by Drew Stevens
Typesetting by Wordstop Technologies, Inc.

Illustration credits:
Page 211, drawings by Dr. Elizabeth Rauscher

Library of Congress Cataloging-in-Publication Data

Targ, Russell.

The reality of ESP: a physicist's proof of psychic abilities / Russell Targ: foreword by Stephan A. Schwartz—1st Quest ed.

      p. cm.

Includes bibliographical references and index.
ISBN 978-0-8356-0884-8
1. Extrasensory perception. I. Title.
BF1321.T366 2012
133.8—dc23   2011041948

5 4 3 2 1 * 12 13 14 15 16

Printed in the United States of America

For Ingo Swann,
and for all who cherish our capacity
for unobstructed awareness

If the doors of perception were cleansed,
every thing would appear to man as it is, infinite.
For man has closed himself up,
till he sees all things through narrow chinks of his cavern.
—William Blake

Skepticism is not *unanswerable, but obviously nonsensical,*
when it tries to raise doubts where no question can be asked.
—Ludwig Wittgenstein

CONTENTS

Illustrations

Illustrations

Tables

Foreword

A Matter of Proof

In a book that claims to present proof, it is worth considering what proof means exactly. Russell Targ's version, which he presents in the preface of this book, is as follows:

> Scientists usually define *proof* as overwhelming evidence, so strong that it would be logically or probabilistically unreasonable to deny the supported argument. Proof establishes knowledge or the truth of a conclusion—such as aspirin preventing heart attacks, in which case the evidence was so strong that the National Institutes of Health stopped the experiments to avoid killing off the untreated controls.
>
> What I present here is not a mathematical proof but rather published experimental evidence from Stanford Research Institute (SRI) and from laboratories across the country. Based on all these decades of data, I believe it would be logically and empirically incoherent to deny the existence of *some kind* of human ability for direct awareness or experience of distant events that are blocked from ordinary perception, such experience being commonly known as ESP. I say this while fully recognizing that all scientific knowledge is provisional and never immune from subsequent revision . . .

Is the overwhelming evidence Targ requires actually present in this book? You will read it and make your own determination, but consider this assessment of just the remote-viewing work of which Targ himself was co-investigator with fellow physicists Harold Puthoff and Edwin May:

In 1995 the US Congress commissioned the American Institutes for Research (AIR), a not-for-profit think tank based in Washington, D.C. with a long history of work in human performance and close government ties, to assess the reality of remote viewing in research the US government had previously funded.

To make the assessment, AIR selected the nationally recognized statistics professor Jessica Utts of the University of California, Davis, and the well-known skeptic Ray Hyman, a psychology professor at the University of Oregon and a fellow of the Committee for the Scientific Investigation of Claims of the Paranormal (now the Committee for Skeptical Inquiry). Both had previously written on this topic and were notably sophisticated in the issues involved. Utts, in 1991, had already addressed the question that Congress was asking in a paper published in the journal *Statistical Science*.

AIR asked both Hyman and Utts to produce an independent report by a fixed date. Utts complied and submitted her report by the deadline. Hyman did not. As a result, he was able to see her report before writing his own; and the approach he chose to take, when he did write, was largely a commentary on her analysis. To compensate for this inequity, AIR allowed Utts to write a response that was incorporated into the final document submitted to Congress. It is in this unplanned form of exchange that the essence of the two positions is revealed. Utts's initial statement is remarkable for its clarity. She wrote:

> Using the standards applied to any other area of science, it is concluded that psychic functioning has been well established. The statistical results of the studies examined are far beyond what is expected by chance. Arguments that these results could be due to methodological flaws in the experiments are soundly refuted. Effects of similar magnitude have been replicated at a number of laboratories across the

world. Such consistency cannot be readily explained by claims of flaws or fraud. The magnitude of psychic functioning exhibited appears to be in the range between what social scientists call a small and medium effect. That means that it is reliable enough to be replicated in properly conducted experiments, with sufficient trials to achieve the long-run statistical results needed for replicability.[1]

In responding to Utts's report, Hyman wrote:

> I want to state that we agree on many [other] points. We both agree that the experiments [being assessed] were free of the methodological weaknesses that plagued the early . . . research. We also agree that the . . . experiments appear to be free of the more obvious and better known flaws that can invalidate the results of parapsychological investigations. We agree that the effect sizes reported . . . are too large and consistent to be dismissed as statistical flukes.[2]

This acknowledgment is important because what Hyman is conceding is that the way in which the kinds of laboratory experiments described in the AIR report had been conducted, and the way in which they were analyzed, is no longer a matter for dispute. In other words, the nonlocal perception required to carry out a remote viewing successfully cannot be explained away as some artifact resulting from how the data were collected or evaluated.

Consider also that universities and labs all over the world are now using four different protocols experimentally, those protocols being Remote Viewing, the Ganzfeld, Random Number Generation Perturbations, and Presentiment. The results collectively, by protocol, each show a six-sigma effect. Basically, that means that the odds are one in a billion that the results could have occurred by chance. The importance of this statistic becomes clear when we realize that one in a mere *twenty* is the threshold of significance.

So, that being true, why doesn't everyone embrace the reality of ESP? The effects are, for instance, considerably larger than the effect size for 81 mg aspirin therapy.[3] Millions of men take without hesitation a small aspirin on a much smaller level of evidence, while many of those pills takers, particularly if they are scientists, would dispute the reality of ESP, even though the evidence of its reality is much better established. Why is this? The answer of course, as Targ discusses, is that it is not facts alone that change minds, particularly when accepting change requires accepting a new world view.

Max Planck, one of the towering physicists of the twentieth century who became a Nobel Laureate in 1918 for his seminal work on quantum theory, said, in an interview published in the British *Observer*, October 25, 1931: "A new scientific truth does not triumph by convincing its opponents and making them see the light, but rather because its opponents eventually die, and a new generation grows up that is familiar with it." That is the blunt *realpolitik* view of a veteran scientific pioneer who, himself, faced harsh criticism when he first advanced the concept of quantum mechanics—an insight now fundamental to modern physics. As Planck learned in his own life, facts do not always change minds, even when they are overwhelming.

It is not that materialist scientists oppose ESP because the evidence is flawed. In many cases they don't even know the research. In her very fine book, *Science, God, and the Nature of Reality: Bias in Biomedical Research*, biomedical science Professor Sarah S. Knox of the West Virginia University School of Medicine clearly frames this issue:

> Since [critics contend] there is no plausible mechanism within a materialist frame of reference to explain them, paranormal phenomena can't possibly be valid. This is the same reasoning that the learned men of Galileo's day used when they refused to look in the telescope. This attitude is nowhere more evident than in the number of scientists who

are willing to volunteer as "expert" commentators on television programs about paranormal phenomena, astonishingly undeterred and unembarrassed by their complete lack of knowledge concerning the existing experimental data. These "experts" smile condescendingly as they explain that the phenomena under discussion can be explained by chance occurrence, brain abnormality, etc., depending on the topic at hand. Since the belief that causality can only be found in matter reigns supreme, there doesn't seem to be any requirement that these "experts" support their claims with actual data. They need only introduce the possibility that the same outcome might have been achieved through some other means, to convince their naïve audience that it is all "hocus pocus."[4]

Along with Ed May, I once debated with Daniel Dennett, a prominent critic of ESP research, at an event produced by ABC News for station news staffs and station managers. We debated along for about thirty minutes, with Dennett making dismissive and disparaging remarks to anything Ed or I said, but always in generalities. Finally I said to him: "Let's pick an experiment we both know, and you tell me what is wrong with it, and I will respond." Without a moment's hesitation he shot back in the most deliberately condescending act I have ever witnessed, saying, "You don't think I actually read this stuff, do you?" There was a moment's silence, then laughter began, first as giggles, then as chuckles, and, finally, as guffaws. It suddenly dawned on Dennett what he had said. He blushed and sat down, and left as soon as he could.

As the British Society for Psychical Research puts it, "Opposition to psychical research is often against its implications and not the quality of its evidence."[5]

Physicist Douglas Hofstadter of Indiana University makes the materialist point very explicitly. Speaking of a recent ESP study conducted by Cornell University psychology professor Daryl Bem, which Targ discusses at length, he said, "If any of [Bem's] claims were true, then all of the bases underlying contemporary science would be toppled, and we would have to rethink everything about the nature of the universe."[6] This is the core materialist objection. It is not, however, the view of physicists as a group, although the deniers would have you believe it is.

Physicist Olivier Costa de Beauregard observes, "Today's physics allows for the existence of so-called 'paranormal' phenomena. . . . The whole concept of 'non-locality' in contemporary physics requires this possibility."[7] Physicist Henry Margenau concurs, saying, "Strangely, it does not seem possible to find the scientific laws or principles violated by the existence of [psi phenomena]. We can find contradictions between [their occurrence] and our culturally accepted view of reality—but not—as many of us have believed—between [their occurrence] and the scientific laws that have been so laboriously developed."[8]

J. P. Schwartz, Henry Stapp, and Olivier Costa de Beauregard, writing in *Philosophical Transactions of the Royal Society of Biological Sciences*, give a sense of where they see science moving, and it is not consistent with the materialist view Hofstadter proposes at all:

> Neuropsychological research on the neural basis of behavior generally posits that brain mechanisms will ultimately suffice to explain all psychologically described phenomena. This assumption stems from the idea that the brain is made up entirely of material particles and fields, and that all causal mechanisms relevant to neuroscience can therefore be formulated solely in terms of properties of these elements. Thus, terms having intrinsic mentalistic and/or experiential content (e.g. "feeling," "knowing" and "effort") are not included as primary causal factors. This theoretical restriction is motivated primarily by ideas about the natural world that have been known to be fundamentally incorrect for more than three-quarters of a century.[9]

Princeton physicist and philosopher of science Thomas Kuhn, generally acknowledged to be the leading philosopher and historian of science in the twentieth century, coined the term *paradigm*, by which he meant the philosophical and theoretical framework within which a scientific discipline builds its theories, laws, and generalizations and conducts the experiments that test those theories and formulations. A paradigm is, in essence, the worldview of the discipline; when a consensus emerges, paradigm is achieved, and that discipline becomes, in Kuhn's terms, a science.

In his classic book *The Structure of Scientific Revolutions*, Kuhn explains that those who are drawn to science and who become scientists are members of a special community dedicated to solving certain very restricted and self-defined problems, *all of which are defined by the prevailing, accepted worldview or paradigm*. He defines the power of paradigms in their character as "universally recognized scientific achievements [in a given field] that *for a time* provide model *problems and solutions* to a community of practitioners" [emphasis added].[10] For scientists who are immersed in it, a paradigm is their worldview. Its boundaries outline for them both what the universe contains and, equally important, *what it does not contain*. The paradigm explains how this universe operates. But Kuhn recognized that paradigms can and should change, because eventually they simply fail to explain observed phenomena. In time, anomalies accumulate that the paradigm cannot encompass, and these inadequacies force the paradigm into crisis. Kuhn saw this process of change as revolutionary—not evolutionary—saying, "Successive transition from one paradigm to another via revolution is the usual developmental pattern of mature science."[11]

There is nothing theoretical about what Kuhn is saying. It has happened. In 1900, Sir William Thomson, admitted to British peerage as Baron Kelvin in 1892 and one of the most important physicists of the nineteenth century, is reported to have said in an address to the

British Association for the Advancement of Science: "There is nothing new to be discovered in physics now. All that remains is more and more precise measurement." But a mere five years later, Albert Einstein published his paper on special relativity, and the simple rules of Newtonian mechanics used to describe force and motion for more than two hundred years were quickly discarded. Why? Because Einstein's worldview better described the observed universe.

This sense of paradigm shift comprises the essence of Targ's book. He recounts the accumulated anomalies that cannot be subsumed within the old materialist paradigm, which looks something like this:

- The mind is solely the result of physiologic processes.
- Each consciousness is a discreet entity.
- No communication is possible except through the defined physiologic senses.
- Consciousness dwells entirely within the time-space continuum.

In contrast, the emerging consciousness paradigm, which now more accurately describes our world, looks like this:

- Only certain aspects of the mind are the result of physiologic processes.
- Consciousness is causal, and physical reality is its manifestation.
- All consciousnesses, regardless of their physical manifestation, are part of a network of life that they not only inform and influence but also are informed and influenced by.
- Some aspects of consciousness are not limited by the space-time continuum.

In the end, though, you will read Targ's proofs and make up your own mind, giving your weight to both facts and beliefs. If you come down on the side of facts, then the real importance of what Targ is saying can come through. Planck wrestled with the issues Targ discusses and in the British newspaper *The Observer* of January 25, 1931 said, "I regard consciousness as fundamental. I regard matter as derivative from consciousness. We cannot get behind consciousness. Everything that we talk about, everything that we regard as existing, postulates consciousness."

This research, with all the proof Targ has assembled (and there is more, besides), suggests that all life is interconnected and interdependent. There is an aspect of human consciousness that exists independent of time and space that is susceptible to volitional control; and there is an interconnection between all life forms that must be understood if the universal impulse humans feel toward the spiritual component of their lives is to mature properly. This assertion is not just a scientific fact, it is a worldview. If you accept it, you will make different life choices. Targ's proof is a beginning, not an end.

—Stephan A. Schwartz
Senior Samueli Fellow
The Samueli Institute
October 2011

Preface

Perhaps you are surprised that I assert *proof* in the subtitle of this book. Scientists usually define *proof* as overwhelming evidence, so strong that it would be logically or probabilistically unreasonable to deny the supported argument. Proof establishes knowledge or the truth of a conclusion—such as aspirin preventing heart attacks, in which case the evidence was so strong that the National Institutes of Health stopped the experiments to avoid killing off the untreated controls.

What I present here is not a mathematical proof but rather published experimental evidence from Stanford Research Institute (SRI) and from laboratories across the country. Based on all these decades of data, I believe it would be logically and empirically incoherent to deny the existence of *some kind* of human ability for direct awareness or experience of distant events that are blocked from ordinary perception, such experience being commonly known as ESP. I say this while fully recognizing that all scientific knowledge is provisional and never immune from subsequent revision and that we probably misconstrue the fundamental nature of ESP—and of space-time as well.

In 1905, Albert Einstein proved that even Newton's venerable laws of motion are incomplete and not immune to change. In 1921, the great logician Ludwig Wittgenstein concluded his crystalline *Tractatus Logico-Philosophicus* with the admonition that "the solution to the riddle of life in space and time lies *outside* space and time." And in 1964, theoretical physicist John Stewart Bell proved mathematically that the results predicted by quantum mechanics could not be explained by *any* theory that preserves our usual ideas of locality. I discuss this nonlocal connectivity further in the introduction. Finally, statistics professor Jessica Utts, at the University of California Davis (UC Davis), began her detailed 1995 CIA-commissioned assessment of our SRI remote viewing research by writing, "Using the standards applied to any other area of science, it is concluded that psychic functioning has been well established. The statistical results of the studies examined are far beyond what is expected by chance. Effects of similar magnitude have been replicated in laboratories across the world."

If it is possible for facts alone to convince a skeptical investigator of the reality of ESP, then I believe this book should do it.

The written material here is new except for chapter 8 on distant healing, which is revised and updated from my earlier book, *Limitless Mind*. And while many of the photographs and their introductions from my personal participation in SRI experiments have been published previously, they have never been organized all together as they are here.

As the cofounder of the SRI remote-viewing program, I consider this book to be the soundest and most thorough summary that anyone is likely to write about the work we did in that pioneering investigation. My intention is to provide a source book for future researchers trying to find out why we were so successful in the early decades of that research.

I hope that readers will find this book to be new and inspiring. Since it is likely to be my last book on the subject, I have tried to make it strong, comprehensive, and unapologetic and to use all the best available data.

—Russell Targ
Palo Alto, California
October 2011
www.espresearch.com

Acknowledgments

Because I am now concluding my eighth decade as a sentient being, I am sorry to report that most of the people whom I sincerely wish to thank for their contributions to my work have already preceded me into a new and different realm. I hope they approve of my physical and metaphysical construal of the world they helped me to put together.

First and foremost, I want to thank my father, William Targ, editor and publisher extraordinaire—editor-in-chief of G. P. Putnam's Sons and publisher of Mario Puzo's *The Godfather* and of other authors such as Simone de Beauvoir, MacKinlay Kantor, and James T. Farrell. He had a lifelong interest in the fringes of the knowable—from stage magic to the teachings of Helena Petrovna Blavatsky, the founder of Theosophy, whose biography he published in 1980. He introduced these to me and encouraged me to explore them and everything else. And he kindled my interest in science fiction from his large and eclectic library. Many times he took me to see the world's most famous magicians, including Henry Blackstone, Sr. known as the Great Blackstone, and he got us front row seats so that I could be appropriately mystified by the miracles occurring on stage in spite of my very poor vision.

My first spiritual teacher, Mollie Walker Margliotti, was in charge of the drafting room at Columbia University, where I was a graduate student in physics in 1954. She encouraged me to look for *prana*, bursts of vital life-sustaining energy in the sunbeams shining through her thirteenth-floor loft in the Pupin physics building, but I never saw any. She also took me—her twenty-year-old protégé—to meet the luminaries at the New York Theosophical Society, where I met Dora Kunz, the famous spiritual healer, co-creator of Therapeutic Touch, and president of the society. And then, thirty years later, Mollie reached out to me when I was in the hospital recovering from cancer surgery. She had just finished her PhD dissertation on the great Buddhist logician Nagarjuna, who wrote at the time of Christ. He is considered by many to be the second Buddha. He created a type of four-valued logic in which most things we believe are revealed as neither true nor not-true, in exact contradiction to Aristotle and in complete agreement with modern physics. His thought is the basis of my book *The End of Suffering*.

Shortly after joining Stanford Research Institute in 1972, I met Dean Brown, nuclear physicist, computer pioneer, mystic, and Sanskrit scholar. My beloved friend Dean introduced me to the ancient magic in *The Yoga Sutras of Patanjali*, which he translated, and to the transcendent and unique wisdom on emptiness, known as *sunyata*, described in the *Prajnaparamita* (teachings of Buddha). Dean introduced me to a world of mysticism and scholarship that I would never have found without him.

It was my daughter and fellow researcher, Elisabeth Targ, who showed me the light of the fourteenth-century dharma master Longchen Rabjam, who directly propels the reader, including me, into the experience of *timeless awareness* in his book *The Precious Treasury of the Basic Space of Phenomena*. This was my first experience of a direct transmission from any source. I am sorry to say that Longchenpa was Elisabeth's last gift to me. She was a psychiatrist and gifted researcher, publishing her groundbreaking and successful investigations into distant healing for her AIDS patients in *The Western Journal of Medicine* in 1999. Elisabeth tragically left us in July of 2002.

My most significant experience of a direct transmission has been the flow of loving awareness made available to me by my peerless teacher Gangaji. She is a renowned American spiritual teacher in the tradition of Ramana Maharshi. She has had a pivotal influence on my life through her strong emphasis on self-enquiry and hence finally accomplished an insuperable task: teaching a New York Jew to be quiet—the kind of quiet described in *advaita vedanta*. Gangaji is not to be considered as necessarily supporting or agreeing with any spiritual of metaphysical ideas expressed in this book, except perhaps that self-enquiry is a good idea.

This book would not have been written were it not for the stimulating conversations I recently had with Dr. Leonard Levine, my study partner and best friend from high school and college and now a computer science professor at the University of Wisconsin, Milwaukee. After a sixty-year friendship, we became reconnected on the very sad occasion of the death of his wife, Marilyn Gordon Levine, who also happened to be my birthday mate. On the phone to me, Leonard expressed amazement that "after all these years you are still involved with that ESP stuff." He suggested that, if there were really something to ESP, why didn't I write a book for nonbelievers? I have attempted to do that here. Thanks!

I also want to thank my friend and colleague Dr. Jane Katra, with whom I wrote two previous books. Her insights and understanding have stimulated my treatment of many ideas in this book as well. And thanks, too, to Professor Elizabeth Rauscher for her major contribution to our formulation of the eight-space geometric model describing a space-time metric in which psychic phenomena might occur.

In addition, I wish to express thanks to my good friend and editor Phyllis Butler for editing my original manuscript so that I might submit it for publication, as well as to Sharron Dorr, my tireless and meticulous editor and publisher at Quest Books, for seeing me through the painstaking task of getting this complicated book ready for publication. I also want to acknowledge Quest's acquisitions editor, Richard Smoley, for his support in preparing this book and selecting it for publication.

Finally, it is with deep gratitude that I want to acknowledge the tireless support and significant encouragement of my loving and patient

Acknowledgments

wife, Patricia Kathleen. I am very grateful for her cheerful generosity in putting aside her brushes and oil paints from time to time to keep me well fed and well loved during the many months I was chained to my keyboard writing and editing this book.

I shall not commit the fashionable stupidity
of regarding everything I cannot explain as a fraud.
—C. G. Jung

Introduction

Why I Believe in ESP and
Why You Should, Too

This book is about psychic abilities. These abilities—which we all possess—offer a spacious mind that can change your life and your view of reality. Buddhists and Hindus have known this truth since before the time of Christ. The scientific evidence for it is now overwhelming, and modern physics has the means and tools to embrace it. Such abilities have many names: Psi, metaphysics, clairvoyance, and ESP (extrasensory perception)—the last being most familiar.

This book is for people who don't believe in ESP, as well as for those who are already familiar with psychic experiences. I will not ask you to accept anything for which there isn't excellent evidence. As a laser physicist with forty years experience in psychic research, I am convinced that most people can learn to move from their ordinary, ego-based mind-set to a much more interesting perspective—one that is not obstructed by conventional barriers of space and time. Eighth-century Buddhists understood this meditative skill as moving from *conditioned awareness* to *spacious* or *naked awareness*. Who would not want to try that?

In this book, I will show you how to take some surprising steps in the direction of this skill. It is what we in the twenty-first century call *remote viewing*. This ability is about learning how to quiet your mind and separate the visual images of the psychic signal from the uncontrolled chatter of the mind. I describe the laboratory data, the military applications, and the personal experiences of many remote viewers. I also cover perspectives from Buddhism to quantum physics. However, I will not be talking about having faith or devotion; eating porridge at the feet of your guru is not required here.

My firm conclusion from decades of ESP research is that we significantly misapprehend the physical and psychological nature of the interconnected space-time in which we live. As I sit on my deck in Portola Valley looking out across San Francisco Bay, I feel that I can reliably experience the beautiful and spacious scene before me. But on reflection I realize that this conviction is unfortunately based neither on a complete perception nor a correct understanding of what I am viewing. The internalized perception of nature before me is created, obstructed, and obscured by mental noise.

Mental noise is the ongoing chatter in our mind, together with our desire to name and concretize everything we see or experience. The great psychic Ingo Swann calls this noise *analytical overlay* (AOL) and says it comprises memory, imagination, and analysis—all of which we use to color and reconfigure our sights and experiences. The idea is that we give everything we experience all the meaning it has for us. Our assumption is that the outer world has no meaning inherent to itself. This illusion is what Buddhists call *maya* or *samsara*—and it can cause a lot of unnecessary suffering. In fact, it usually does. It is this misperception that makes me want to write a book about questioning reality and examining our potential for nonlocal awareness regarding both time and space.

Introduction

Remote viewing is not a spiritual path. However, living in a spacious and interconnected world such as I'm describing, one tends to be more open and compassionate than in a state of mind that is isolated and insulated. In exploring what physicists call our *nonlocal* universe, we begin to feel that the Buddhists have it right as they say again and again that "separation is an illusion," that all is connected. In this world of entangled or extended minds, compassion seems to me to be a natural conclusion. It's an idea whose time has come— teaching that when one person suffers we all suffer, because the data show that our minds are frequently telepathically connected to one another. And today, there are more than two million Google pages devoted to information about "remote viewing," so at least some people are catching on to the idea that it is not difficult to do.

When I was first working on the development of the laser, about fifty years ago, I read a well-known psychology text that dealt briefly with psychic abilities, which was already a passionate interest of mine. The book was called *Human Behavior: An Inventory of Scientific Findings*. With regard to my favorite subject it said:

> The state of research in parapsychology can be summarized as follows: A small number of investigators, roughly thirty or forty, who have done a large number of studies, are convinced that there is such a thing as extrasensory perception (telepathy, clairvoyance, etc). Whereas, the majority of psychologists, *most of whom have not studied the subject*, are not convinced. [emphasis mine].[1]

When I first read this analysis, I thought it was some kind of sardonic joke. But unfortunately, it still pretty well represents the view of much of the contemporary scientific community with regard to psychic abilities. In this book I hope to remedy that situation with analytical statistical data and first-hand laboratory observations. Some people like to read about miracles. Others prefer double-blind, published experiments showing at least five standard deviations from chance expectation (meaning that a particular event would happen by chance less often than one time in a million). I am offering here a manifesto from my personal experience with *both* kinds of evidence for ESP, based on two decades of government-supported investigations at Stanford Research Institute (SRI). I cofounded this program with laser physicist Dr. Harold Puthoff in 1972.

I believe in ESP because I have seen psychic miracles day after day in our government-sponsored investigations. It is clear to me, without any doubt, that many people can learn to look into the distance and into the future with great accuracy and reliability. This is what I call *unobstructed awareness* or *remote viewing* (RV). To varying degrees, we all have this spacious ability. I do not believe that ESP has metaphysical origins. I believe that it is just a kind of ability we strengthen by expanding our awareness to think nonlocally. It will become less mysterious as more of us become more skillful.

For example, while working for the CIA program at our lab in Menlo Park, California, our psychic viewers were able to find a downed Russian bomber in Africa, to describe the health of American hostages in Iran, and to locate a kidnapped American general in Italy. We also described Soviet weapons factories in Siberia and a Chinese atomic-bomb test three days before it occurred and performed countless other amazing tasks—all using the ability that our colleague Ingo Swann dubbed *remote viewing.*

My background is in experimental physics, psychology, and, as a young man, stage magic. In the 1950s, I was a graduate student in physics at Columbia University and became a pioneer in the development of the laser. However, one of the reasons I didn't complete that degree was that I was spending too much time hanging around the magic shops on Forty-Second Street, studying mental magic and ESP—all compelling pastimes for me. Since then, I have published more than a hundred refereed technical papers dealing with lasers, laser applications, and ESP research in some of the best scientific journals. In addition, I was a senior staff scientist and project manager for more than two decades at Lockheed Missiles and Space Co. and at GTE Sylvania, where I specialized in laser communications and atmospheric windshear measurements with lasers, seeing what no man had seen before.

As a mid-course correction between these two laboratories (Lockheed and GTE), I was cofounder of the above-mentioned ESP research program at SRI. This twenty-million dollar, twenty-three year program launched during the Cold War was supported by the CIA, NASA, the Defense Intelligence Agency, Army and Air Force Intelligence, and many other government agencies. We developed the psychic perception technique we called remote viewing, which proved to allow a person to quiet his or her mind of mental chatter and accurately describe and experience places and events blocked from ordinary perception by distance or time. We published our highly significant psychic findings in *Nature*,[2] *The Proceedings of the Institute of Electronic and Electrical Engineers (IEEE)*,[3] and *Frontiers of Time: Retrocausation Experiment and Theory*, published by the American Institute of Physics.[4] Our research has been replicated worldwide. And remote viewing is so easy to do that it has become a cottage industry. Hundreds of people are teaching it. Many of them are from the Army Psychic Corps that we created at Fort Meade, Maryland, in the 1980s. (This has little to do with the recent film *The Men who Stare at Goats*—in which a goat is psychically killed—although in one of our experiments a healer did accidentally kill a hypertensive rat while trying to lower its blood pressure psychically at a hospital in San Francisco.)

My psychic career involved two further outstanding events: First, my little post-SRI research group, Delphi Associates, made $120,000 by psychically forecasting *for nine weeks in a row* the direction and amount of changes in the silver commodity futures market—without error. This successful forecasting of "December Silver" made the front page of the *Wall Street Journal*[5] and led to a *NOVA* film in 1983.[6] The other notable success was that our SRI lab was the first to identify and name the kidnapper of San Francisco heiress Patricia Hearst, who had been abducted from her home in Berkeley. At the Berkeley police station, I stood with psychic policeman Pat Price as he put his finger on the face of a man his ESP chose as Hearst's kidnapper. He did this from a police loose-leaf mug book of hundreds of photos. He then told the police where to go to find the kidnap car. When the kidnapper and the car were confirmed the following day, I knew I had just seen a "miracle." In all of these cases—as I will describe as we go along—there is absolutely no chance that it was just our lucky day!

There are presently four classes of published and carefully examined ESP experiments that are independently significant, with a probability of chance occurrence of less than one time in a million. In the course of the book I will present the data for these explorations as it occurred in these four classes:

1. *Remote Viewing*: Princeton University Professor Robert Jahn (Dean of Engineering) and his associate Brenda Dunn oversaw two decades of remote-viewing experiments with Princeton students as subjects. Students in the laboratory were asked to describe their mental impressions of what they saw at a site where someone was hiding at a randomly chosen distant location. These remote-viewing students had to fill out a thirty-item questionnaire to quantify their perceptions in this game of psychic hide-and-go-seek. Their findings—spanning several years and comprising a series of 411 trials—showed

that it is no harder to remote view hundreds of miles in the distance than it is to describe a person around the corner. Furthermore, it is no harder to describe a randomly chosen hiding place to be selected in the next hour, day, or week than it is to describe a hidden event underway at the same moment. Modern physics would describe these phenomena as *nonlocal*, in that they are experimentally found to be *independent of space and time*. Nonlocality and *entanglement*, which were first described by Erwin Schrödinger in the late 1920s, are now hot research topics in modern physics. This intriguing phenomenon is explained very clearly and amusingly by Anton Zeilinger, one of the world's leading experimentalists in quantum optics, in his 2010 book, *Dance of the Photons: From Einstein to Teleportation*. Zeilinger writes:

> Entanglement describes the phenomenon that two particles may be so intimately connected to each other that the measurement of one instantly changes the quantum state of the other, no matter how far away it may be. . . . This nonlocality is exactly what Albert Einstein called 'spooky'; it seems eerie that the act of measuring one particle could instantly influence the other one.[7]

Robert Jahn's highly significant results were published in the *Proceedings of the Institute of Electrical and Electronics Engineers (IEEE)* in 1982[8] as a replication of our original SRI remote-viewing experiments published in the same journal six years earlier. These data show odds greater than a billion-to-one (1.8×10^{-11}) against chance expectation, strong evidence for the existence of nonlocal mind..

2. *Distant Mental Influence*: In the 1970s and 1980s William Braud and Marilyn Schlitz carried out nineteen successful experiments in what they called Distant Mental Influence on Living Systems (DMILS).[9] In these experiments, a precursor to other distant-healing experiments

supported by the National Institutes of Health (NIH), the researchers showed convincingly that the thoughts of one person can affect the physiology (heart rate, skin resistance, etc.) of a distant person in another laboratory. Braud was able psychically to calm or excite the physiology of a person hundreds of feet away. Marilyn Schlitz is now the president of the Institute of Noetic Sciences in Petaluma, California. Braud, who is now teaching at the Institute for Transpersonal Psychology (ITP) in Palo Alto, California, has published twelve of his highly significant formal experiments in an excellent book called *Distant Mental Influence.*[10]

3. *The Ganzfeld*: Over a span of thirty years several researchers at five different laboratories here and abroad carried out telepathy experiments in which one person was in a situation of sensory isolation called the *ganzfeld*, which is German for "whole field isolation." This person was asked to describe his or her ongoing mental impressions of an interesting video clip being watched *by a friend* in a separate part of the lab. In a published meta-analysis of seventy-nine studies comprising hundreds of individual trials, the probability that the results of the experiments were chance was almost one in a billion (2×10^{-8}), meaning that the isolated receiver was extraordinarily successful in describing what his distant friend was seeing.[11]

4. *Feeling the Future*: Recently, Professor Daryl Bem at Cornell University carried out a series of nine precognition experiments. In this remarkable five-year study, he showed that the future can affect the past in surprising ways. That is, the elephant you see on television in the morning can be the cause of your having dreamed about elephants the *previous* night: Saturday morning's elephant caused Friday's dream. We call that phenomenon *retrocausality*. For example, students in Bem's experiments reliably favor and choose one of four possible pictures of people, even though they are shown that one only *after* they

have made their conscious choice, and even though the one shown has been randomly selected only after the students have chosen.

In 2010, Bem's sixty-page paper presenting his meta-analysis of these retrocausal experiments was accepted for publication.[12] This meta-analysis shows a statistical significance of more than six standard deviations from chance expectation (1.3×10^{-11}), which equals odds of more than a *billion to one* against chance. I am entirely convinced by this analysis—and so is distinguished statistics professor Jessica Utts from the University of California, Davis. In all his experiments, Bem's one thousand Cornell-student participants find themselves making free choices, guided again and again by the material they will see or experience in the future—*but only after they have made their selection.* Many people believe that precognition is the dominant phenomenon in all psychic functioning. All of Bem's experiments have been carried out and published since the 1962 publication of the annoying *Inventory of Scientific Findings* that I mentioned earlier. From his recent precognition experiments at Cornell and my own successful forecasting of silver commodity markets, it appears that we have the ability to expand our perceived "now" to include as much of the future as we choose to accommodate.

During one experiment at SRI, the psychic Pat Price did not arrive for the scheduled trial. In this series of ten trials, we were trying to describe the day-to-day activities of Hal Puthoff as he traveled through Colombia in South America. Price had thus far been describing churches, harbors, markets, and volcanoes. We wouldn't receive any feedback until Hal returned, so I had no clues at all with regard to what he was doing. But, in Price's absence, and in the spirit of "the show must go on," I decided to undertake the remote viewing myself. Until then, I had been only an interviewer and facilitator for such trials. So, this was in fact my first remote viewing.

Introduction

I closed my eyes and immediately had an image of an island airport. The surprisingly accurate sketch I drew is shown below in figure 0.1. A photo of the airport site is shown in figure 0.2.

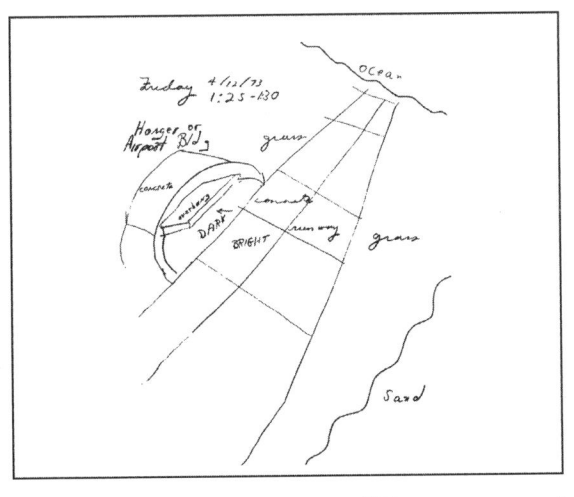

Figure 0.1. Sketch produced by physicist Russell Targ as a remote viewer in the absence of psychic Pat Price. Targ correctly saw and described "sand and grass on the right, an airport building on the left, and ocean at the end of a runway."

Figure 0.2. This photograph shows the target, which was an airport on an island in San Andres, Colombia.

Introduction

What we learned from this trial is that even a scientist can be psychic when the necessity level is high enough. I am not making any claims for my own psychic prowess in this demonstration. If I have any ability in that direction, it is the same as that of anyone else who will sit in a chair and quiet his or her mind. Artists and musicians are generally much better at remote viewing than physicists or engineers, probably because the latter favor analysis, while artists are accustomed to using the nonanalytic right side of the brain—which greatly facilitates *psi,* a nonanalytic ability.

The term *psi* is derived from the Greek, Ψ *(psi),* the twenty-third letter of the Greek alphabet, and means "psyche" or "soul." *Psi* was coined in a parapsychological sense by biologist Bertold P. Wiesner and first used in print in 1942 by Robert Thouless. Parapsychologists prefer *psi* to ESP, because the term *extrasensory perception* implies the use of a sense that we don't normally have—an *extra* sense, whereas in actuality there is nothing extra about psi, even though it is often repressed and even though, in fact, it transcends our usual ideas of the limitations posed by time and space. Psi is a gift we all have. It represents an amazing and unique opportunity for spaciousness that I am happy to share with all who will join me in this great adventure.

I have a brilliant friend named Dan Kubert, now deceased, who was a great polymath and a retired Harvard math professor. He was for some years a shut-in because of his poor physical health, but he would call me several times a week to chat. A year ago he called to talk about a new proof for Fermat's Last Theorem—the subject of a book we had both read. I told him I was sorry but I couldn't talk with him that day because I was finishing a book I was reading for my book club. He immediately said, "That must be *Anna Karenina*"—a book which we had never discussed. I asked him why he named that particular book. He told me that, as soon as I mentioned I was reading a book, he had a clear mental picture of the alluring Vivian Leigh as she appeared in the movie *Anna Karenina*. That was of course the book I was indeed reading. Dan was often startlingly psychic with regard to events in my life, both public and private. I attribute it to his very quiet lifestyle and his ability to focus his attention.

My point in telling this anecdote is that I believe each of us has the potential for vast psychic awareness that fills all of space-time. Not only does Hindu and Buddhist literature of the past two millennia describe the naturalness and availability of these abilities (see chapter 12), but also numerous laboratory experiments indicate that we have the opportunity to know anything upon which we fix our attention. In my experience and according to most other researchers, it appears that *an experienced psychic can answer any question that has an answer*. I cannot wait to see what the future holds when we fully open the doors of our perception!

When I say that I believe in ESP, it's not as if I am saying that I believe in life on other planets elsewhere in the universe, which, although a statistical probability, remains unproven. Nor is it like saying that I believe in the ideal of social democracy. For in this latter case—while I affirm the desirability of freeing people from fear, poverty, and injustice and the inalienable right of all people to food, education, and health care—I am aware that many educated people seem to think otherwise. I may believe them to be profoundly mistaken, but it's very hard to prove. To the contrary, however, when I say that *I believe in ESP*, it is as if I am saying that I believe in Maxwell's equations (relating electromagnetism and light), quantum mechanics, or lasers—all of which are surprising and hard to believe but nonetheless absolutely true and scientifically provable. Indeed, the experimental evidence for ESP from a century of research is so strong and overwhelming that reasonable people simply should no longer doubt its reality. That powerful and undeniable evidence for extrasensory perception from laboratories around the world is the subject of this book.

For me, questioning reality and the exploration of psychic abilities is the essential next step in the greatest opportunity we have as a species—the evolution of consciousness.

I believe that we have completed our physical growth; our brains are big enough. I am proposing that transcending our own species is the next evolutionary step for us to take. We started first as animals looking for food; then we advanced to moderately self-aware humans trying to understand nature; and now we are finally ready to meet our destiny as beings aware of our spacious and nonlocal consciousness, transcending space and time and accepting the gift of psychic abilities. The suffering, wars, and confused search for meaning we are experiencing as a species are all manifestations of our inner selves sensing but not yet quite grasping our true nature. Our hardware is fine; it's our awareness of our psychic software that must be upgraded—and quickly, given the critical state of affairs. When we accomplish that, we will realize that, in consciousness, we are all one. That realization will make our stirrings of compassion feel much more natural than waging war and stealing from the poor.

In the next few pages I will sketch out what you will find in the rest of this book. Although there are more than a hundred active researchers in the Parapsychological Association, I have chosen to dwell principally on research for which I have a direct connection with the findings. That's not to slight anyone else's research. But over the years, what have convinced me are the miracles that I have personally seen in the lab, and so that's what I report on here. When we scientists get to see miracles often enough—week after week—we tie them up with a ribbon, call the package *data*, and publish it. I start with the origin of the SRI program on a wind-swept barrier island. And I end with the best model I have for the physics underlying world-spanning psychic abilities.

My first chapter describes how the remote viewing program got started at SRI. It required the vision and imagination of Ingo Swann, the New York artist whose prodigious psychic ability spanned the solar system and helped develop our two-decade-long secret CIA program. At SRI, Swann taught us how to experience our psychic selves—our nonlocal awareness. He now lives in his spacious studio in New York City, surrounded by his extraordinary visionary paintings.

Chapter 2 describes my meeting at a NASA conclave on St. Simons Island with rocket-pioneer Wernher von Braun, astronaut Edgar Mitchell, and the NASA director Jim Fletcher. I had been invited to talk about Soviet research in parapsychology, and I took the opportunity to interest these luminaries in helping me initiate an ESP research program at SRI, where my friend Hal Puthoff worked, although there was not yet an ESP program in place. I had already built an ESP teaching machine, which I brought to the island. Von Braun scored excellently on the machine, and Mitchell encouraged Director Fletcher to give us some money to start our program. I proposed to teach astronauts how to get psychically in touch with their spacecraft. I further describe this program in chapter 5 and tell how the ESP Trainer became a free iPhone app.

Although it was Ingo Swann who taught us how to do remote viewing, it was the incredible psychic policeman Pat Price who identified Patricia Hearst's kidnapper and who later described a Soviet weapons factory and read Secret National Security Agency (NSA) files from a distance of 5000 km. Chapter 3 describes our work with Price and his remarkable exploits that drew the attention of the CIA, which funded our program for two decades.

My dear friend Hella Hammid was both a compassionate woman of the world and a hard-working *Life* magazine photographer. In chapter 4, I explain how she joined our program as a "control" subject, after her promise that she had never done anything like psychic viewing. (The CIA wanted to see what inexperienced people could do with such psychic viewing.) For more than a decade, Hella turned out to be our most reliable practitioner, and I learned to teach remote viewing with her patient help.

After six years of research and applications at SRI, Army Intelligence wanted us to set up an East Coast Psychic Army Corps at Fort Meade, Maryland. In chapter 6, I describe the six inexperienced army volunteers to whom we taught remote viewing of distant locations. We accomplished this feat in one week each, with success at odds greater than one in ten thousand as compared with chance expectation.

The most successful remote viewer from Army Intelligence was Joe McMoneagle. He has written several books himself describing his prodigious, new-found psychic abilities. Chapter 6 illustrates some of his great successes in our program. Among many other things, Joe located a downed Soviet bomber in Africa and described the secret construction of a 500-foot Soviet Typhoon-class submarine in Russia. For his contribution to excellence in intelligence, Joe received a Legion of Merit award from the Army.

It is very difficult to *read* anything psychically, let alone stock-market numbers. But using "associative remote viewing," we were able to help a viewer forecast changes in the commodity market nine times in a row. Chapter 7 describes how we did this at odds of better than a quarter-million to one, eventually making $120,000; I will also explain the procedure, so that you can do it (or at least try to do it), too.

William Braud pioneered laboratory research in distant mental influence. And my daughter, Elisabeth Targ, gained national attention for her successful medical research into distant healing of her AIDS patients. Chapter 8 covers a wide range of distant mental influences from Elisabeth's compassionate healing to the Russian experiments in distant strangulation!

Everyone wants to know what survives bodily death. In chapter 9, I will set the stage and then tell you about two very convincing "ghost stories"—the subjects with which I had a peripheral connection and about the reality of which I am convinced.

How does it all work? Chapter 10 presents a physicist's view of psychic abilities. The evidence suggests that who we truly are is nonlocal eternal awareness, manifesting for a few years as a physical body in nonlocal space-time. I will present a comprehensive mathematical model of this nonlocal space-time that allows psychic functioning to occur, agrees with all the data, and does not generate any weird or nonexistent physics. This agreement holds true even as our nonlocal awareness transcends both space and time with equal ease.

This model should be contrasted with string theory, which is a model for subatomic physics that is presently hanging by a thread. String theory predicts that elementary particles are one-dimensional in extent, rather than zero-dimensional points in space. However, science is an empirical subject, meaning that all accepted theories must be based on evidence to support them. And after forty years of investigation by thousands of physicists, to date no version of string theory has ever made an experimentally verifiable prediction that could not be explained with another, simpler theory. By contrast, ESP rests on more than a century of experimental research from laboratories all over the planet. Thus, in my opinion, string theory is more airy-fairy than ESP.

Since starting the SRI program, I have been teaching remote viewing for almost forty years. I can hardly believe how successful the process is—worldwide—from fashionably dressed Italian women in Milan to American dowsers in bibbed overalls in Vermont. In chapter 11, I will offer simple instruction about how you and a friend can get in touch with the part of your awareness that is psychic. I will tell you how to quiet your mind and learn to separate psychic signals from the mental noise of memory and imagination. You already have the ability—I'll help you use it.

Finally, chapter 12 will explore *naked awareness*, a term in Buddhism and Hinduism for that contemplative, meditative state most conducive to psychic experiences. The Buddhists and Hindus have known about all the psychic abilities discussed in this book for millennia. Centuries ago they described the power and importance of these abilities as part of a meditation practice or spiritual path—but warned us not to get attached to them. In this last chapter I will tell you about the spiritual as well as the scientific implications of psychic abilities, together with ethical implications of which we should also be aware.

The universe is not only queerer than we suppose,
it is queerer than we can suppose.
— J. B. S. Haldane

Ingo Swann:

The New York Artist Whose Remote Viewing Spanned the Solar System

Why do I believe in ESP? Two of the main reasons come from my opportunities to sit with Ingo Swann in our laboratory in California. The first was when he drew pictures of a secret US cryptographic site in Virginia, and the second was when he gave a stunning description of a Chinese atomic bomb test three days before it happened, with only the geographic coordinates for guidance.

In the fall of 1972, Dr. Hal Puthoff and I started a psychic research program at Stanford Research Institute (SRI). We were both laser physicists born in Chicago in the 1930s, and we had both carried out research for a variety of US government agencies for many years. Our great partner and teacher in the SRI program was Ingo Swann, who was a uniquely creative and inspiring visionary painter from New York. He was also a remarkable psychic, whose wide-ranging investigations into little-traveled perceptual pathways allowed him to make important and astute contributions to our understanding of psychic abilities.

Ingo came to Hal's attention in early 1972 through recently published experiments in which Ingo was reliably able to raise and lower the temperature of thermistors (solid-state heat sensors) in distant thermos bottles. These experiments were conducted at the City College of New York by Professor Gertrude Schmeidler, whose most famous research showed conclusively that people who believe in ESP score slightly positively on ESP tests, while nonbelievers use their ESP to score slightly (but reliably) below chance. She coined the terms "sheep" and "goats" for believers and nonbelievers in this highly significant and often-replicated demonstration.

Ingo Swann's remarkable psychic ability enabled him to sit at his desk with us at SRI and describe distant MX missiles in their silos, a secret NSA listening post in Virginia, a future Chinese atomic bomb test, and the previously unknown rings of Jupiter, which he discovered psychically. It was Swann who introduced Hal and me—and the world—to what has become known as remote viewing. When I went to SRI in the fall of 1972 to start a research program with Hal, he had already carried out a remarkable psychic experiment with Ingo. In this trial, Ingo was psychically able to describe and *perturb* (affect) the operation of an almost perfectly shielded, super-conducting magnetometer buried in a vault in the basement of the Varian Physics Building at Stanford University. Swann was apparently able to increase and decrease the sine-wave decay frequency of a superconducting magnet that had been operating with perfect stability for more than an hour—until Swann focused his laser-like attention on it! No one at Stanford was amused—particularly not the graduate student whose thesis depended on the stability of the system nor the navy, which was paying for it. This incident gave rise to the first of many governmental inquiries into our activities, especially regarding our ability to see or perturb things at a distance—things that were supposed to be secret, hidden or imperturbable—like superconducting gyroscopes on spacecraft such as the one employed in NASA's Gravity Probe B mission.

It is now forty years since that incredible experiment and the other ones alluded to above. I believe the perturbation of the magnetometer was probably Ingo's doing, just as I have described it. However, as a life-long experimental physicist, I have seen all kinds of unexplainable and bizarre things happen, even to the best quality-controlled NASA space-ready systems. This phenomenon is called the *brass hat effect*. It is so well understood that many a general, in my experience, have come to expect failure upon their appearance in the lab! I personally had an ultra-reliable, high-power laser fail right in front of the general on delivery day. That's why my belief in remote viewing and ESP is not based on a single remarkable trial, but rather on hundreds of remarkable trials that we call an *experimental series*, conducted over decades. Our CIA contract monitor, Ken Kress, who was a PhD physicist, wrote up Ingo's activities at Stanford University and concluded his CIA report by saying, "These variations were never seen before or after Swann's visit." Of course, nobody publishes a scientific paper based on a single observation, and not surprisingly Hal and Ingo were not invited back to Stanford to try again.

Ingo and I are now both enjoying our seventy-seventh trip around the sun. This journey brings us together a least once a year when I visit New York City on my way to teach remote viewing at the Omega Institute in Rhinebeck, New York. It gives me great pleasure to get together with him near his home on the Bowery, enjoy a glass of wine, and reminisce about some of the amazing things we have done and seen. When I am sitting at a café with Ingo, I sometimes think of Jesus's assertion about "when two or more have gathered together in my name" as we recall the remarkable things that were accomplished in the SRI program. It was definitely a time of miracles.

And now, perhaps it is time for everyone to expand their awareness as Ingo and I and many others have learned to do. Our physical bodies and brains work excellently. I believe it is finally time for the human species to transcend the common conception of the limitations of space and time. *Nonlocal* or unobstructed awareness is unlimited by these ordinary constraints. We can experience nonlocal awareness when we come to realize that it is who we really are—our true nature. Time for another glass of wine.

In 1972 Hal and I began to investigate remote viewing in the way any physicist would—in controlled experiments. We put a laser in a box and asked Ingo to tell us whether it was on or off. We would ask him to describe pictures hidden in opaque envelopes or in a distant room. Ingo did all these tasks excellently, but he found them to be very boring. He told us many times that, if we didn't give him something more interesting to do, he was going back to New York and resume his life as a painter. (Ingo is a wonderfully talented visionary artist.) He said if he wanted to see what was in an envelope, he would *open* it—and to see into the next room, he would simply open the door. Since he could focus his attention anywhere in the world, he told us more than once, "These experiments are a trivialization of my ability!" So we developed more challenging tests for him. I show a contemporary photo of Ingo in figure 1.1.

Figure 1.1. New York artist and psychic, Ingo Swann, who taught us and the world how to do remote viewing.

In the actual chain of psychic events, Ingo taught us how do remote viewing, we taught the army, and the army taught the world. (In fact, Ingo coined the term *remote viewing*.) There are now more than a dozen ex-army men and women teaching remote viewing in the United States. We meet annually to talk about the latest developments in applied RV—investing in the stock market, looking for lost children, prospecting for treasure, etc.—at the conference of the International Remote Viewing Association (irva.org).

Project SCANATE

In response to Ingo's request for something more challenging than pictures in the next room, Hal asked a friend at the CIA to give him geographical coordinates of something interesting that Ingo might view remotely. The latitude and longitude were duly provided over the telephone to Hal—who, of course, had no idea where the coordinates were or to what they were related. Project SCANATE (Scanning by Coordinates) was based on Ingo's belief that he could describe any distant location, given only its coordinates!

Much of the laboratory procedures and findings that follow were first described in *Mind Reach*, a book that Hal and I coauthored in 1977 to offer a popular description of our early remote viewing research.[1] Margaret Mead wrote the introduction for the book, pointing out that psychic awareness was not exactly a new idea for anthropologists who study and live with "primitive" people.

For the first SCANATE trial Hal and Ingo settled themselves in our clean and quiet workroom, and Hal recited the geographic coordinate numbers to Ingo. To begin the trial, Hal said to Ingo, "We have a target that needs a description." Hal wrote "Project SCANATE, May 29, 1973" on his notepad and started his tape recorder. This was the beginning of our "demonstration of ability" tests and the first scanning by coordinates. Hal writes of this episode:

> Ingo closes his eyes and begins to describe what he is visualizing. Opening his eyes from time to time to sketch a map, Ingo says, "There seems to be some sort of mounds or rolling earth. There is a city to the north. I can see taller buildings and some smog. This seems to be a strange place, somewhat like the lawns you would find around a military base. But I get the feeling that there are some old bunkers around. It may be a covered reservoir. There must be a flag pole, a highway nearby, and a river to the far east. There is something strange about this place. Something underground. But I'm not sure." Ingo then draws a map (see figure 1.2).[2]

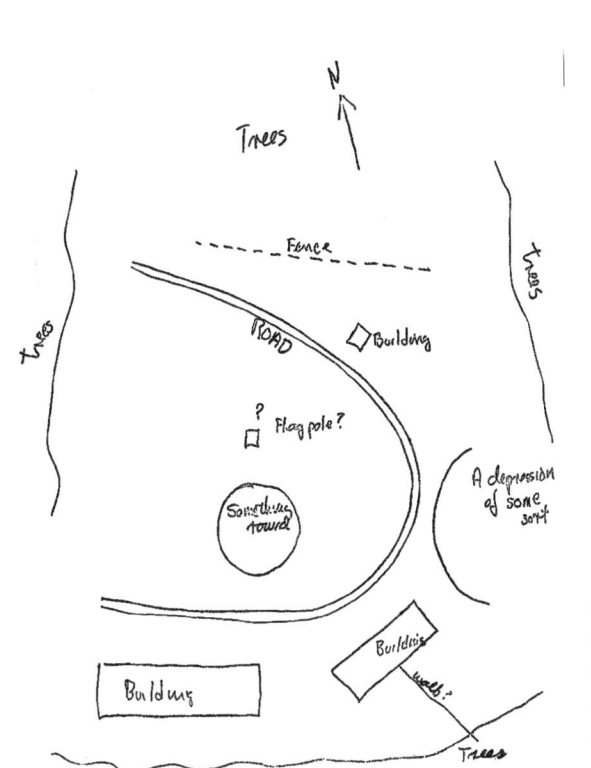

Figure 1.2. Drawing by Ingo Swann of East Coast target site, confirmed in every detail. The reward was our first contract.

Hal goes on to say, "Three weeks later, when we received a phone call from our challenger, we learned that, not only was Swann's description and drawing correct in every detail, but that even the distances, flag pole, underground bunkers, and directions on Ingo's map were correct." The target turned out to be a super-secret National Security Agency (NSA) listening post at the navy's Sugar Grove facility.

In chapter 3, I will describe how Pat Price was able to view the same target a day after Ingo had done so. Interestingly, the coordinates that had been given to Pat and Ingo were *not* for the facility, however, but actually for the CIA agent's vacation cabin a quarter mile over the hill from the NSA site. Yet Pat had not only viewed the facility instead, he had also been able to *read the code words written on the file cabinets* there. When the two CIA agents who came to investigate asked why he had so accurately described the "incorrect" location, Pat said, "The more intent you are on hiding something, the more it shines like a beacon in psychic space." (That should scare plenty of people.)

A decade later, I had an opportunity to describe this work to the USSR Academy of Sciences in Moscow. Tea cups shook in the lecture theatre when I told the assembled dignitaries that from our findings it appears that *it is no longer possible to hide anything.*

SCANATE into the Future

Thus Project SCANATE, created by Ingo Swann, was off to a successful start. During the twenty-year course of our SRI program, Ingo and the intelligence officers he trained described many operational targets for our government sponsors. One of the most striking was his detailed and completely correct 1975 viewing of a future but failed Chinese atomic-bomb test, identified simply from the geographic coordinates of latitude and longitude. All Ingo was told by the two CIA agents one Monday afternoon was, "We would like to know what is going to happen at these geographical coordinates this coming Thursday." I watched Ingo as he sketched his psychic view with colored pencils showing a line of trucks in the distance and a hemispheric pyrotechnic display of the failed bomb test, which he precognized and drew on that Monday—*three days in advance of the actual test.* The conflagration he described was the result of uranium burning in the air, not a mushroom cloud. We received our feedback from our contract monitor the next Friday and had a little celebration.

Teaching Remote Viewing

Ingo taught many army-intelligence officers how to do remote viewing. Having retired from the army, many of them now teach it to the general public, as I do. I teach it for the gratification of teaching something that students are really happy to learn. Because it is a natural ability and easy to learn, it's likely that a number of remote-viewing schools can show you how to do it. However, since none of them carry out double-blind trials or publish any information about their protocols, I contend that it's impossible to determine if any actual *learning* takes place—beyond just learning the *process.* This contention is the subject of an on-going, friendly conversation I have with the International Remote Viewing Association (irva.org).

I believe there is presently no evidence that there is any benefit to paying thousands of dollars to attend any such remote-viewing school—as compared with reading this book or Ingo Swann's wonderful book *Natural ESP.*[3] But I could be wrong. The claims many of these schools make are confusing to the public, as implied by their very names—Controlled Remote Viewing (CRV®), Extended Remote Viewing (ERV®), and Technical Remote Viewing (TRV®), for example. Joe McMoneagle, who was one of the first, and by far the most successful of the army viewers, has also written an excellent book,

Remote Viewing Secrets, in which he unscrambles these acronyms.[4] He also describes a very clear and sensible approach to learning remote viewing, based on his more than thirty years of experience.

Distant Targets

Intrigued by what we had seen at our SRI labs, we set up a pilot project with Ingo. Coordinates were supplied to us by other SRI researchers and also by our CIA colleagues—who were overseeing our investigations. One early result came when Hal read Ingo the numerical coordinates of a location in Mount Hekla, an active volcano in Iceland. As usual, Hal didn't know to what the coordinates pertained. But, within a few seconds of hearing them, Ingo expressed feelings of vertigo, sickness, and being cold, describing a sense of being at great height above a fiery furnace. Ingo said, "I am over the ocean. I think there's a volcano to the southwest." He told us later, with serious displeasure, that we should never again put him into such a dangerous situation.

Our last example of a terrestrial SCANATE target was phoned in by our CIA contact, who was still challenging our work. (In these carefully controlled experiments, no maps were permitted, and Ingo was asked to reply as soon as he heard the coordinates read to him.) The coordinates were for the French Kerguelen Island in the South Indian Ocean. The National Geographic map showing it appears in figure 1.3. At the time of our trial, the island was a French and Soviet meteorological station for radar mapping of upper atmospheric research. Ingo's first words were as follows:

> My initial response is that it's an island . . . maybe [there's] a mountain sticking through the cloud cover. There's something like a radar antenna . . . a round disc. There are some buildings very mathematically laid out. To the southwest there is a little airstrip. It's very cold.

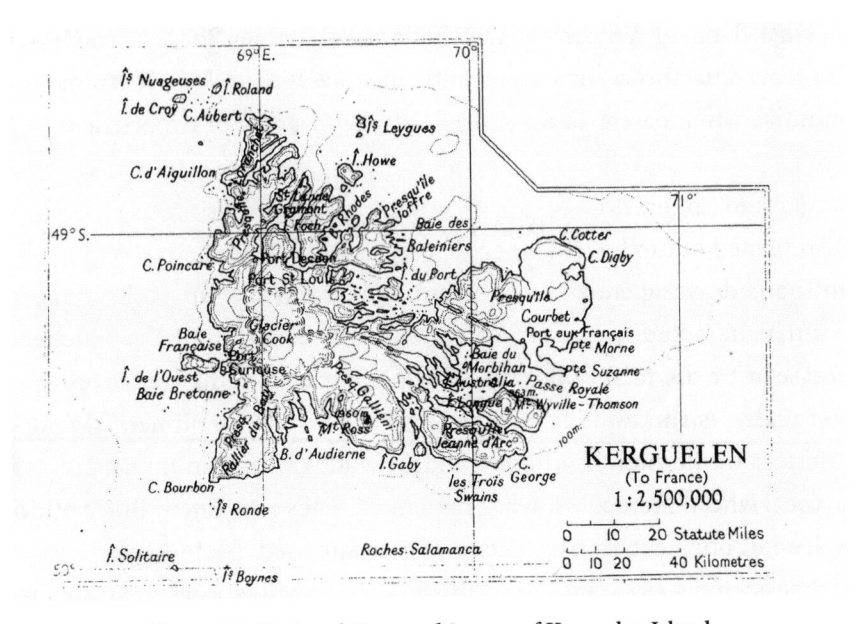

Figure 1.3. National Geographic map of Kerguelen Island.

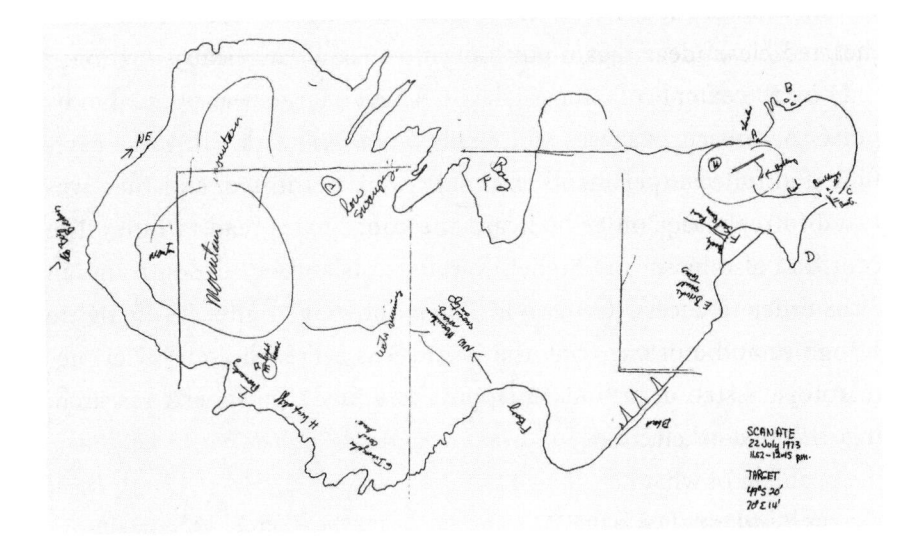

Figure 1.4. Ingo Swann's psychic impressions upon being read the geographic coordinates of Kerguelen Island.

Ingo then started drawing the map shown in figure 1.4. The drawing correctly shows an island with many bays and inlets and a large mountain to the west, just where Ingo drew it. The lines on the drawing are from successive pieces of paper he required as his drawing became larger and larger. It took us two years to confirm the airstrip—which also turned out to be just where Ingo put it. The outstanding accuracy of Ingo's drawing ended our concerns about the hypothesis of doubters that Ingo had "memorized the globe." Based on his description of the secret NSA facility and the small airstrip and radar antennas on Kerguelen Island, we felt we could put this hypothesis to rest. But the real test would be to ask Ingo to describe something that was off the planet, where there are no possible maps to memorize. That was the nature of our next experiment.

By April of 1973 we were carrying out a wide variety of remote viewing trials with both Ingo and our newly discovered psychic police commissioner, Pat Price—whom I feature in chapter 3. Ingo had formulated clear ideas that our remote-viewing capabilities are limited only by the extent to which we can control and eliminate the mental noise that obscures the psychical signal. He felt that we all have the potential for *unobstructed awareness*, and he has devoted a good portion of his subsequent time to helping people experience that awareness, as I also have.

In order to access this awareness, however, we must first learn to recognize and quiet our "mental noise." One of the primary causes of this noise is the desire to name the things that we experience. Ingo was the first to elucidate, in contemporary *signal-to-noise* language, the problem of what he calls *analytic overlay* (AOL), which is his term for the tendency we have to name and try to grasp our initial psychic images. These initial fragmentary images are precious to us, as they are often the most descriptive thing that a new remote viewer is likely to see. But when the desire to name and thus make the images concrete emerges, as it rapidly does, it greatly interferes with our ability to go further into the remote-viewing experience. Naming, along with memory, analysis, and imagination, are the principal inhibitions to psychic functioning first elucidated specifically in 800 CE by the Buddhist dharma master Padmasambhava in his inspiring book *Self-Liberation through Seeing with Naked Awareness,*[5] which I discuss in chapter 12. The concept was later rediscovered in 1943 by the French electrical engineer René Warcollier, as he elaborates in his comprehensive little book *Mind to Mind.*[6]

Swann's Jupiter Probe

During the SCANATE phase of our research, we didn't yet know the physics underlying remote viewing, but we thought that we were beginning to understand its psychology. We wanted to explore the limits of remote viewing, since it appeared that there weren't any terrestrial boundaries. That desire to explore the limits was the inspiration for Ingo's proposal to explore the planet Jupiter. (NASA had just launched the Pioneer 10 spacecraft.) As Ingo put it on his *Supermind* Web site:

> The Jupiter Probe was one of a number of early experiments designed to try to discover the dimensions and extent of human remote sensing faculties. It was felt that radical experiments should be undertaken in the attempt to establish the dimensions of those faculties. One such radical experiment, the "Jupiter Probe," took place in 1973 at Stanford Research Institute in the Radio Physics Laboratory.
>
> The purposes of the experiment were: (1) To try to ascertain if long-distance remote sensing could extend to a very far distance; (2) to record the time it took before impressions began to be given; and (3) to compare the impressions with published scientific feedback.

Feedback expected: Technical data and analyses drawn from information telemetered back to Earthbase from NASA spacecraft and information would be published in scientific media: the Pioneer 10 and 11 "flybys" of 1973 and 1974, and the later Voyager 1 and 2 probes of 1979 which confirmed my [Ingo's] drawing of rings around the planet.

There were two participants in the Jupiter probe who simultaneously took part in the experiment—myself (in California) and Mr. Harold Sherman (in Arkansas). Mr. Sherman was a noted psychic who had earlier (in the late 1930s) taken part in a long-distance viewing between New York City and the Arctic. Those exceedingly successful experiments were undertaken in conjunction with the noted Arctic explorer, Sir Hubert Wilkins (see "Thoughts through Space" by Sir Hubert Wilkins and Harold M. Sherman, Creative Age Press, New York, 1942, re-issued by Hampton Roads Publishers in 2003). The raw data needed to be independently guarded so that it could not be said it was altered after the fact. Thirty copies of the raw data were prepared, including statements regarding the purposes and design of the experiment. Feedback sources: First scientific and technological feedback sources began becoming available in September 1973, four months after the experiment took place. Additional feedback sources continued to accumulate by stages up through 1980.[7]

What follows is a transcription of the official recording made of Swann's Jupiter Probe on April 27, 1973:

6:03:25 (3 seconds fast): "There's a planet with stripes."

6:04:13: "I hope it's Jupiter. I think that it must have an extremely large hydrogen mantle. If a space probe made contact with that, it would be maybe 80,000–120,000 miles out from the planet surface."

6:06: "So I'm approaching it on the tangent where I can see it's a half-moon, in other words, half-lit/half-dark. If I move around to the lit side, it's distinctly yellow toward the right."

(Hal: "Which direction did you have to move?")

6:06:20: "Very high in the atmosphere there are crystals . . . they glitter. Maybe the stripes are like bands of crystals, maybe like rings of Saturn, though not far out like that. Very close within the atmosphere. I bet you they'll reflect radio probes. Is that possible if you had a cloud of crystals that were assaulted by different radio waves?"

(Hal: "That's right.")

6:08:00: "Now I'll go down through. It feels really good there (laughs). I said that before, didn't I? Inside those cloud layers, those crystal layers, they look beautiful from the outside. From the inside they look like rolling gas clouds—eerie yellow light, rainbows."

The data indicate that Ingo had identified a ring around Jupiter, a sketch of which (see figure 1.5) appears in the raw data and is also verbally identified. Conventional scientific wisdom held that Jupiter did not possess any rings. The existence of the ring was discovered and confirmed in early 1979, six years after the Jupiter Probe had taken place. As *Time* magazine wrote:

Coming within 278,000 km (172,400 miles) of the swirling Jovian cloud tops, the [Voyager probe] robot survived intense radiation, peered deep into the planet's storm-tossed cloud cover, provided startling views of the larger Jovian moons—and, most surprising of all, revealed the presence of a thin, flat ring around the great planet. Said University of Arizona astronomer Bradford Smith: "We're standing here with our mouths open, reluctant to tear ourselves away."[8]

Indeed, Jupiter has a series of rings circling it! Unlike Saturn's rings, which are clearly visible from the earth even through small telescopes, Jupiter's rings are very difficult to see. So difficult, in fact, that they weren't discovered until they were first confirmed by the Voyager 1 spacecraft in 1979.[9]

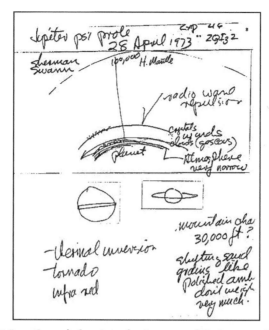

Figure 1.5. Ingo Swann's drawing of a ring around Jupiter, seen in his 1973 psychic probe. The ring was confirmed by NASA six years later.

Figure 1.6. NASA's sketch of the rings of Jupiter.

Chapter 1

Solving the Naming Problem: Memory vs. ESP

Other people have noted "the naming problem" I mentioned earlier as one of the principal inhibitions to psychic functioning. J. B. Rhine was the father of modern parapsychology. In 1927, he founded a department at Duke University to investigate psychic phenomena. In an effort to quantify psychic functioning, he made use of specially designed cards, called Zener cards or ESP cards, shown in figure 1.7. With five different symbols and five of each in a pack of twenty-five cards, one knew mathematically how many were expected for each run through a deck. (This was a more mathematical alternative to a picture-drawing experiment, in which someone looks at a picture and asks a subject to copy the mental image, telepathically.)

Figure 1.7. ESP cards used by J. B. Rhine in card-guessing experiments in the 1930s (but not anymore).

An important fact—known by René Warcollier in the 1940s and by Buddhists twelve hundred years earlier, but apparently not by Rhine in the 1930s—is that *it is much harder to identify a symbol you already know by name than it is to describe something you have never seen.*

In careful testing over more than a decade, Rhine found that students who were visually separated from the cards could nonetheless often correctly name many more cards from a shuffled deck of twenty-five than the five correct ones that would be expected by chance alone. It didn't matter whether the experimenter looked at the cards or not. If no one knew the card to be guessed, the ability being tested was called *clairvoyance.* If the card was known by the experimenter, it was called *mixed clairvoyance* and *telepathy,* or *general ESP.*

The two types worked equally well for Rhine. Students working in a nice, quiet lab, with friendly and encouraging experimenters, would frequently score well above what would be explainable as chance for weeks on end. These highly significant statistical results rightfully encouraged researchers to believe that they had a real phenomenon.

However, in time, the scores of these talented psychic students began to decline to chance levels. This decline did not invalidate their previous highly significant data, but it was very disappointing to the researchers. They called this structural problem "the decline effect." It was as though the researchers found a very creative way to demonstrate ESP in the lab and then extinguish it! We now know that there were two factors leading to the decline effect: The first is the boredom that sets in when people in general—and in this case, the students— become habituated in doing any task over and over again. The second and more subtle factor has to do with mental noise.

From personal experience, Ingo Swann was able to articulate that the sources of noise interfering with psychic functioning include memory along with naming, imagination, and analysis—which together, as I have mentioned, he called *analytic overlay* (AOL). If you already know the cards you will be asked to guess, you can then form a perfect mental image of each of them. That mental image from your memory will in general be more robust and stable than the diaphanous image afforded you by ESP. It would be nice if genuine psychic images carried a tag that said, "This image is brought to you by ESP"; but, alas, that is not the case. One can only learn *by practice* to discern psychically derived images from mental noise (see chapter 11).

The point of this digression is that it is much easier to describe a picture in a magazine, chosen from an *infinitude* of possible images, than it is to describe one of five symbols that already exist in your visual memory. Hence my conclusion that, along with boredom, it was analytical overlay that caused the decline effect during Rhine's card experiments in the 1930s. In our own controlled remote-viewing experiments, conducted over a decade at SRI, we ourselves *never saw any evidence of decline*. That's real progress, if I say so myself.

Another experiment involving Ingo Swann took place in 1987, when he demonstrated that he is in a psychic class by himself. At SRI with physicist Dr. Edwin May, who was part of the SRI program staff, Ingo had the idea that he could learn to overcome the disastrous effects of mental noise on psychic perception, that is, the noise caused by knowing the target pool from which the one correct target will be selected. Choosing the two most boring possible targets, Ingo said that he would try to learn psychically to differentiate two types of graph paper: polar-coordinate paper with circles and rectangular, cross-section paper with squares (figure 1.8). Ingo was at home in New York City, well-separated from Ed at his lab in Menlo Park, California.

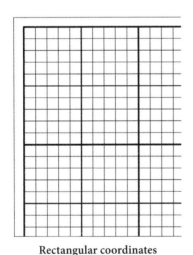
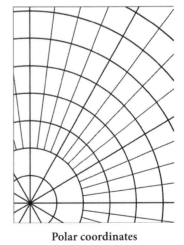

Rectangular coordinates

Polar coordinates

Figure 1.8. The two types of graph paper used in Ingo Swann's experiment attempting to overcome mental noise

As I said, there were only two types of targets. Ed would initiate the experiment with a call to Ingo in New York. Ed's assistant, in another closed room, would operate an electronic random-number generator that generated an odd or even number. If it was odd, she would look at the polar-coordinate paper. If it was even, she would look at the cross-section graph paper. When she had made her choice, she would ring a little desk bell, and Ed would then tell Ingo over the phone that a target had been chosen. In this exceptionally boring experiment, Ingo got 38 correct answers out of 50 trials, corresponding to 76 percent, where only 50 percent was expected by chance. Another way of saying this, which may better communicate the difficulty of the task, is to point out that, in 50 guesses for polar vs. rectangular coordinates, Ingo got only 12 of his calls incorrect. The odds against these results show that, although AOL is a serious problem, it can be overcome with talent and practice. Such an outcome—again, of 38 correct in a binary test of 50 trials—is significant at odds better than 10^{-4}, or more than ten thousand to one better than chance expectation. Obviously ESP works—even with the most difficult possible targets.[10]

*Even scholars of audacious spirit and fine instinct
can be obstructed in their interpretation of facts
by philosophical prejudices.*
—Albert Einstein

2

Convincing NASA and the CIA to Support ESP Research at SRI

The first government support for our ESP research had its origins in May of 1972—on a windswept pier at St. Simons Island off the coast of Georgia. I had just finished speaking to a hundred futurists at the NASA Forum For Speculative Technology. My talk was about Soviet ESP research and experiments I had done with an electronic ESP-teaching machine. After my presentation, I walked down to the pier at the water's edge with astronaut Edgar Mitchell, rocket pioneer Wernher von Braun, NASA director James Fletcher, science-fiction writer Arthur C. Clarke, and NASA's new-projects administrator George Pezdirtz, the organizer of the conference. (I think of them as my "pier group.") I was at this conference because I was looking for a way to leave my job in laser research at GTE Sylvania, where I had worked for the past decade. I wanted to start an ESP program at nearby SRI. The outcome of my conference talk was successful, and NASA promised me support.

But read the following for the strange chain of events that led to the final handshake: In the early spring of 1972, I gave a weekend workshop demonstrating my new ESP-teaching machine at the Esalen Institute in beautiful Big Sur, California. There I met its charismatic founder Mike Murphy—with whom I have been friends ever since.

Chapter 2

A month after my workshop, Mike called me to ask if I could stand in for him and give a talk on psychic research. He was unable to keep the date of the talk for which he had been scheduled at Grace Cathedral in San Francisco. From my Esalen workshop, Mike said that he saw I was quite familiar with the material on which he was supposed to speak. I agreed and gave my version of his talk about American and Soviet psychic research. (This was just after the publication of Ostrander and Schroeder's *Psychic Discoveries Behind the Iron Curtain*.[1]) As fate would have it, NASA deputy administrator Art Reetz, who was in San Francisco on NASA business, stumbled into my talk at the famous church. He liked my presentation and thought it would be of interest to his NASA colleague George Pezdirtz, who was organizing a conference of speculative technology to be held the following week at St. Simons Island. Pezdirtz, who led NASA's new-programs organization, would also become my good friend and one of our greatest supporters in the government research community for the next decade. If Reetz hadn't stumbled into Grace Cathedral on that April evening, there might have been no ESP research program at SRI! And I would certainly not have met all the NASA luminaries in that salubrious seaside setting.

At St. Simon's Island, I was delayed at the lecture hall answering questions about ESP research while most of the group left to grab sweaters to counter the chilly evening breeze before a stroll on the pier. Later, when I arrived at the pier, I was still in my short-sleeved shirt. I stood there trying to remember my kundalini meditation in order to summon up enough warmth to keep from freezing. Struggling not to shiver, I explained the concepts of contemporary psi research—ESP—to the men I knew could determine my entire future as a researcher of psychic phenomena. As I said, I was successful. I had come to this meeting as a member of my "pier group."

That experience in finding support for my ESP research showed me that the top people in such organizations (the NASA administrator, the undersecretary of defense, the CIA director of intelligence, the commanding general of Army Intelligence, etc.) know from their own life experience that psi is real and are willing to admit it—privately. Astronaut Edgar Mitchell had carried out ESP card-guessing experiments from space and had had a transformative spiritual experience viewing the earth while standing on the moon. Wernher Von Braun told us of his beloved psychic grandmother, who always knew in advance when someone was in trouble and needed help back in the old country. Von Braun also did excellently with the ESP teaching machine that I had brought to the meeting. Fletcher was concerned that the Russians were ahead of us in psychic research—a fear based in part on material in Ostrander and Schroeder's *Psychic Discoveries* and also on three reports on Soviet psychotronic research that had recently been published by the Defense Intelligence Agency (DIA). "Psychotronic research" pertains to the Soviet interest in human capability to in-flow information psychically and to out-flow intentionality to affect the behavior or feelings of a distant person. The Soviets were especially interested in focusing attention on Western leaders, either positively or negatively. Counterintuitively, only the science-fiction writer Arthur C. Clarke expressed skepticism, despite his hugely successful book *Childhood's End*—which is all about psi.[2] Finally, with Mitchell's great assistance and continuing help from Dr. Pezdirtz at NASA, physicist Hal Puthoff and I were offered a contract to start a research program—if we could find a home for it.

As I had originally hoped, that home turned out to be Stanford Research Institute in Menlo Park, California, where Hal was already employed. Hal and I, together with Pezdirtz, Mitchell, and Willis Harman—a distinguished former Stanford electrical-engineering professor who now led the Future Technology Division of SRI—descended upon Charles Anderson, SRI's broad-minded president. In his spacious, oak-paneled office, Mitchell and Pezdirtz played the NASA card—arguing that this was just the right moment to start an ESP research program and offering NASA's financial help. Hal and I promised Anderson that we would try very hard to keep a low profile. Anderson said okay. (Sometimes "piling on" has its value.)

The resulting NASA program was partly an investigation of whether people could really improve their ESP scores by practicing with my ESP trainer. The other part of the program was to see if we could replicate earlier work showing that the brain wave measurements of one person could be altered by the thoughts and experiences of another, distant person. Eventually, in our one-year program, we showed that significant learning does take place in some people who had practiced with the ESP teaching machine. And we replicated findings from a decade earlier, showing that the EEGs (brain waves) of some participants could be significantly altered when they attend to a distant friend who is being stimulated with randomly generated, annoying light flashes.[3] Our NASA program was called the Development of Techniques to Enhance Man/Machine Communication.

We were unfortunately not able to keep our promise to Dr. Anderson with regard to publicity. Our first year's program brought in 1 percent of SRI's income and 95 percent of its publicity—largely because of our research with Israeli psychic Uri Geller.

Making Friends with the CIA

Two years later, in 1974, Hal and I were given an opportunity to brief high-level CIA officials about our remote-viewing research with artist Ingo Swann and policeman Pat Price. Day after day, for two years at our lab at SRI, I would ask one of these two great psychics to describe his mental impressions of what it looked like at my partner Hal's hiding place—at one of sixty randomly selected target locations in the San Francisco Bay Area, all within a half-hour's drive of our laboratory. The double-blind, carefully judged experimental results of these trials were highly statistically significant with the odds of a chance occurrence being one in a hundred thousand. I was always the interviewer because I don't drive a car due to my very poor vision. (This is probably one of the reasons I became interested in psychic perception and stage magic at an early age.)

Many of our CIA contacts came from our earlier professional incarnations as laser physicists, during which time we had made various kinds of exotic hardware for them. While I was at GTE Sylvania, the marketing manager introduced me to Dr. Christopher (Kit) Green, who became the branch chief of the Life Science Division (LSD). In 1974, Kit arranged for Hal and me to brief a large audience of intelligence officers in the very room where the ill-fated Bay of Pigs affair had its inauspicious beginning in the late 1950s. In this closed-door briefing—conducted in a heavily draped lecture room—we were surprised by how many CIA men stood up to describe psychic intuitions that had come to them over the years or to their psychic grandmothers. Some had stories of occurrences of ESP in the field that had saved their lives. The consensus among the operations-oriented listeners at the CIA was that we were "wasting our time viewing churches and swimming pools in Palo Alto" when we could be "looking at Soviet sites of operational interest."

This successful briefing led to a formal presentation of our ESP findings by Hal and me with the Deputy Director for Intelligence (DDI) at the CIA. At that time the DDI was John McMahon, a daring and courageous attorney and intelligence officer who was well known for not suffering fools gladly. But Hal and I were ourselves self-confident and energetic only children who were accustomed to briefing tough customers and getting our way. So, John listened to our story and quickly saw the potential importance of our remote-viewing data—if it were true. We wouldn't have gotten this far had we not been known to the agency for our past laser work. After the briefing, McMahon told us that he had one particular site in the Soviet Union at which he would like us to look. It was a kind of "demonstration of ability" task. If we could provide useful information about it, then he would support our research. The deal was that we would spend half our time trying to understand remote viewing and publishing our findings and devote the other half to CIA operational tasks about which we could say nothing. The most classified thing about our program would be the name of the agency who was supporting it. We lived with that bargain for two decades, and everyone kept their agreements.

What Can We Say Today?

In 1995, the Directorate of Science and Technology at the CIA commissioned the American Institutes for Research, together with a statistician and a critic with no security clearance, to review the twenty years of classified research in remote viewing from SRI and the Science Applications International Corporation (SAIC). Jessica Utts, a renowned statistics professor from UC Davis, wrote the following in her contribution to the report to the CIA concerning the remote-viewing work done at SRI:

> Using the standards applied to any other area of science, it is concluded that psychic functioning has been well established. The statistical results of the studies examined are far beyond what is expected by chance. Arguments that these results could be due to methodological

flaws in the experiments are soundly refuted. Effects of similar magnitude have been replicated in a number of laboratories across the world. Such consistency cannot be explained by claims of flaws or fraud. The magnitude of psychic functioning exhibited appears to be in the range between what social scientists call a small and medium effect. This means that it is reliable enough to be replicated in properly conducted experiments with sufficient trials to achieve the long run statistical results needed for replicability.[4]

As Dr. Utts described it to us, "The SRI data is stronger than the FDA experimental evidence showing that aspirin prevents heart attacks."

But in order to tell this ESP research story, it had to be declassified. My problem had been that most of our reports to the CIA were stamped, "EXEMPT FROM AUTOMATIC DOWNGRADE." My heart sank as I saw this rubber stamping, because it meant that the reports would not be declassified in twenty years, as was customary for secret material at that time. Indeed, it would *never* be declassified—they wanted to lock our miracles away forever! So, in May of 1995, after sixteen months of work and with the help of two congressmen, two lawyers (one of whom was my son Nicholas), and Senator Clayborne Pell, I was finally able to have most of my SRI research documents from the CIA declassified and returned to me. I facilitated the declassification through a Freedom of Information Act (FOIA) request to the CIA, in which I asked them to release the information or explain to a judge why they would not. After a long exchange of correspondence, they sent me a formal letter of release. It is only because of this success that I can relate some of our most remarkable adventures with Pat Price and the CIA. In figure 2.1, I show the letter I received from the CIA that allows me to tell you of our CIA adventures without fear of any of us going to prison.

Central Intelligence Agency

Washington, D.C. 20505

Mr. Russell Targ
1010 Harriet Street
Palo Alto, California 94301

Reference: P94-1192

Dear Mr. Targ:

This is in response to your 20 September 1994 letter in
which you presented an appeal of our lack of response to your
10 May 1994 Freedom of Information Act and Privacy Act
request for reports with the approximate titles, "Perception
Augmentation Techniques, Stanford Research Institute, Final
Report, 1973, 1974, 1975." You stated that "[t]he authors
are Harold E. Puthoff and Russell Targ" and "[t]here would be
at least two reports from 1973/4 and 1974/5."

Your appeal has been presented to the appropriate member
of the Agency Release Panel, Mr. Anthony R. Frasketi,
Information Review Officer for the Directorate of Science and
Technology. Pursuant to the authority delegated under
paragraphs 1900.51(a) and 1901.17(c) of Chapter XIX, Title 32
of the Code of Federal Regulations (C.F.R.), Mr. Frasketi has
directed that a thorough search be conducted of those records
systems which could reasonably be expected to contain
documents responsive to your request. As a result of these
searches, three responsive documents were located.
Mr. Frasketi has reviewed the documents and has determined
that the documents, reports dated 31 October 1974, 1 December
1975 and one undated, can be released in their entirety.
Further, in regard to your appeal and in accordance with CIA
regulations appearing at 32 C.F.R. paragraph 1900.51(b), the
Agency Release Panel, meeting as a committee of the whole,
has affirmed this determination.

A copy of the three documents as approved for release
are enclosed. We appreciate your patience while your appeal
was being considered.

Sincerely,

Edmund Cohen
Chairman
Agency Release Panel

Enclosures

Figure 2.1. Letter to Russell Targ from the CIA giving him permission to reveal
previously classified results from the SRI remote-viewing program.

Convincing NASA and the CIA

On the *Nightline* television show of November 28, 1995, Robert Gates—former Director of the CIA and now the Secretary of Defense—told the TV audience that the government's SRI and Fort Meade remote-viewing program was permanently closed, "because the Berlin wall has come down, communism has failed, and the United States no longer has enemies that require such an experimental program." He estimated that "the intelligence community had invested about $20 million over the twenty-three-year period during which the threat was being dealt with." Also on this fateful TV show was my friend and colleague Dr. Edwin May from the SRI program. He presented our impressions from our twenty-three years of research and applications.

In the next chapter I will describe Pat Price's 1973 psychic response to the CIA director John McMahon's request for information about a Soviet site—a response so excellent that it led to a congressional investigation as well as to the funding of our program for a decade!

Every man takes the limits of his own vision for the limits of the world.
—Arthur Schopenhauer

3

Pat Price:

The Incredible Psychic Policeman

With the CIA's funding, we had a chance to start our ESP research in earnest. To meet John McMahon's requirements described in the last chapter, Hal Puthoff and I began Project SCANATE (scanning with geographical coordinates) at SRI with painter Ingo Swann and retired police commissioner Pat Price. These were what the CIA called "demonstration of ability" trials. Using coordinates provided to us, our two psychics were able to look into and describe correctly a NSA secret cryptographic site in Virginia. This was a free test for the CIA to determine whether they would have any further conversations with us about anything. Ingo Swann made a detailed drawing of the distant site, as we described earlier, and Pat was able to name correctly the site and *read code words* from the National Security files, as confirmed by both NSA and the CIA. Reading anything is an exceptional feat in our remote-viewing experiments. In my experience, Price's ability remains unprecedented.

As Price began his narrative that day, he said he was psychically "flying into the site at 1500 feet" and described many elements similar to those of Ingo. But Price went on to say that "it looks like an old missile site—big, roll-up steel doors cut into the hillside, well-concealed with large, 100-foot rooms underground . . . some kind of command center." He even correctly read off several classified "code-word" labels on a folder on a desk and a filing cabinet—"CUEBALL, 8-BALL, RACKUP," etc.—including the NSA name of the facility, which was "HAYFORK or HAYSTACK." We, of course, had no idea if any of this was correct. But it was all confirmed when we had a visit from officers from both the CIA and NSA.

Pat Price, whom we mentioned in chapter 2, was an unexpected gift to our program at SRI. One day in June of 1973, Pat called Hal Puthoff to say that he had been following our research for some time (we are not sure how). Pat felt that he had been doing the same kind of psychic work for years, successfully using remote visualization to catch crooks when he was the police commissioner in Burbank, California. He told us that he would sit with the dispatcher in the police station, and when he heard a crime reported he would scan the city psychically and then immediately send a car to the spot where he saw a frightened man hiding!

We soon brought Price into our lab experiments. After we began working with him we realized that this exceptional man actually lived his life as a completely integrated psychic person. Over the years we have now worked with many other talented individuals, but we never met anyone else who showed the same, continuous psychic awareness of the world around him that Pat did.

Psychic Description of Soviet Weapons Factory

In July, 1974, Price described and drew to scale a Soviet Siberian weapons factory at Semipalatinsk with remarkable detail; it included an enormous, eight-wheeled gantry crane and a concealed sixty-foot steel sphere then under construction. What he drew was all confirmed by satellite photography—the crane at once and the steel sphere three years later.

My witnessing of this miraculous work of Pat's is one of the reasons I believe in ESP. To elaborate from data recorded in my lab notebook: on that July day in 1974 I sat with Pat in our little, copper-screened, electrically shielded room and gave him the slip of paper with the geographical coordinates that I had received from the CIA agent, Ken Kress—who was waiting for us in the vault in the basement of our building. Needless to say, neither Pat nor I had any idea what the test target was. Not even the CIA knew what was going on there at that time.

Pat leaned back in his old oak desk chair, polished his gold rimmed glasses, and closed his eyes. After a few moments he began to describe his mental images. He said, "I am in the sunshine lying on top of a three-story building in some kind of R&D [research and development] complex. The sun feels good." As he was psychically lying there, he said, "Some kind of giant gantry crane just rolled over my body. It's going back and forth. . . . This is the biggest damn crane I've ever seen. . . . It runs on a track, and it has wheels on both sides of the building. It has four wheels on each side of the building. I have to draw this."

With that, Pat asked for a ruler to make the drawing of the whole facility, with gas cylinders, buildings, rails, and pipes. He then made a detailed drawing of the gantry crane, shown on the left in figure 3.1. A tracing of the actual crane from a photograph of the whole site taken in May, 1974 is shown on the right. In comparison, while some parts of Pat's overall sketch were correct, others appeared not to be. Pat disagreed. He felt he had it right. As it turned out, some things he drew in July of 1974 that weren't in the satellite photograph *had indeed been changed in the two months* since the May photo had been taken. The accuracy of Price's drawing is the sort of thing that I, as a physicist, would never have believed had I not seen him draw it myself.

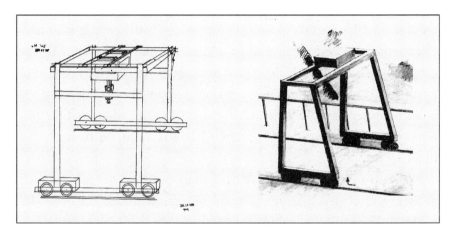

Figure 3.1. Above left is Pat Price's July, 1974 drawing of his psychic impressions of a gantry crane at the secret Soviet R&D site at Semipalatinsk, showing remarkable similarity to the actual crane on the right as enlarged from a CIA tracing of a satellite photograph taken in May, 1974. Note, for example, that both cranes have eight wheels. (For the tracing of the entire site, see figure 3.2.)

Figure 3.2. Here is a tracing by a CIA artist of a May, 1974, satellite photograph of the Semipalatinsk target site. Such tracings were made by the CIA to conceal the accuracy of detail of satellite photography at that time.

Price went on to draw many other items at the site, including the cluster of compressed gas cylinders shown in the satellite photo (see figure 3.2) and at the top of his drawing in figure 3.3. Other things he drew appeared in older satellite photos that we were shown only months later.

After he completed his drawing of the crane, Pat and I went downstairs to meet with the agent in his vault and see what he thought of Pat's work. The agent unrolled the large 1974 satellite photo of the facility as shown above in figure 3.2 and said, "It looks like you're looking at the right place. Now can you tell us what they are doing in the building under the gantry crane? That's what we'd really like to know."

The next day Pat and I went back to our little copper-clad cell. Pat began to focus his attention on the *interior* of the building on the roof of which he had been lying the day before. Thus one of the most interesting things he saw was not in the CIA drawing at all, because it was inside the building and so unknown to anyone in our government at the time of this 1974 experiment. He described a large interior room and said, "There's a lot of activity. They're trying to make a giant steel sphere. It looks like it's going to be about sixty feet in diameter. They are making it out of "gores" and trying to weld them together. But it is not going well, because the metal is so thick." He said that the gores looked like sections of an orange peel (see figure 3.3).

The sphere turned out to be a containment vessel for a particle-beam weapon to shoot down US satellites that were taking pictures. *But its existence was not discovered until three years later*, in 1977, when the United States used just such satellites to probe the site again. Data confirmed that Price had the size of the sphere and the gores correct to within 96 percent of the true value. In his 1974 remote viewing, Price had said that the Soviets were having trouble welding everything together because the hot pieces of metal were warping and that he was aware that they were looking for a lower-temperature

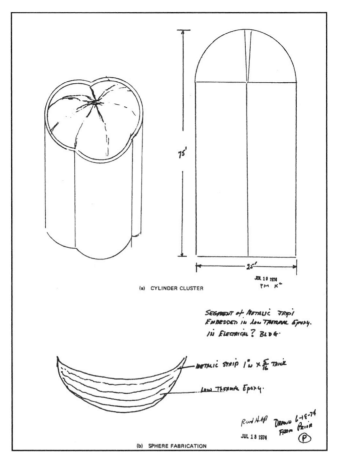

Figure 3.3. Pat Price's drawing of his second July, 1974, remote viewing of the Soviet Semipalatinsk site. Details include a cluster of gas cylinders shown at the top of this figure and in the May, 1974, satellite photo (see figure 3.2). The sixty-foot steel gores for the sphere construction are shown at the bottom of the figure.

welding material. Even this technical detail was confirmed three years later in 1977, when the sphere-fabricating activity at Semipalatinsk was described in *Aviation Week* magazine and we truly discovered how accurate Price's viewings had been:

Pat Price

SOVIETS PUSH FOR BEAM WEAPON . . . The US used high resolution photographic reconnaissance satellites to watch soviet techni-
cians dig through solid granite formations. In a nearby building, huge
extremely thick steel gores [sic] were manufactured. These steel seg-
ments were parts of a large sphere estimated to be about 18 meters
(57.8 feet) in diameter. US officials believe that the spheres are needed
to capture and store energy from nuclear driven explosives or pulse
power generators. Initially, some US physicists believed that there was
no method the Soviets could use to weld together the steel gores of
the spheres to provide a vessel strong enough to withstand pressures
likely to occur in a nuclear explosive fission process, especially when
the steel to be welded was extremely thick.[1]

Although in 1977 we were happy to receive this confirmation, unfortunately Pat Price had died in 1975, just one year after his remote
viewings of the Soviet facility. So, from the point of view of the experiment, he had made his perception of the sixty-foot spheres and
"gores" without any feedback, which is usually an important element
of remote viewing. This shows that Price's remarkable perception was
by virtue of *a direct experience of the site.* He was not reading the
mind of the sponsor, because no one in the United States knew anything about "spheres" or "gores" at that time. Nor could Pat have been
looking precognitively at his feedback from the future, because he
died before the details of the sphere he saw were independently confirmed. And, in fact, no one in the West has ever seen the gores. So, to
the best of my knowledge there is nowhere Price could have obtained
his information, except at the Soviet nuclear test site in Semipalatinsk
(unless, of course, he looked thirty-five years into the future and precognitively read this book.) My experience of sitting with Pat as he
drew the gores, and then later seeing them confirmed, is an additional
reason for my belief in ESP.

Chapter 3

This 1974 experiment was such a stunning success that we were personally invited to undergo a formal congressional investigation by the House Committee on Intelligence Oversight to determine if there had been a breach in national security. Hal and I went to Washington, D.C., for the interrogation. We were supported by our CIA contract monitors—physicist Ken Kress and physician Kit Green, the branch chief for the LSD (Life Science Division) at the CIA. Also there was our steadfast supporter Jack Verona, the deputy director for research at the Defense Intelligence Agency (DIA), together with Senator Claiborne Pell and Representative Charles Rose, who had an on-going interest in our work. Of course, no security breach was found, and our research into psychic functioning was supported by the government for another twenty years. The house committee told us to "press on." To celebrate, we were taken to lunch in the White House dining room in the basement of the residence. Lunch was black-eyed peas, collard greens, and a delicious pork roast from a hog that had just been slaughtered and brought in by a senator.

Price's remote-viewing miracle was described in the 1975 classified final report "Perceptual Augmentation Techniques" that Puthoff and I sent to our government sponsors in Washington. The report was as follows:

> The exceptionally accurate description of the multi-story crane was taken as indicative of probable target acquisition, and therefore the subject (Price) was introduced to sponsor personnel who collected further data for evaluation. The latter contained both additional physical data which were independently verified by other sponsor resources, thus providing additional calibration, and also initially unverifiable data of current operational interest. Several hours of tape transcript, and a notebook full of drawings, were generated over a two week period. A description of the data and an evaluation is contained in a separate report. The results contained noise along with signal,

but were nonetheless clearly differentiated from chance results generated by control subjects in comparison experiments carried out by the COTR (Contracting Office Technical Representative).[2]

(I hope that ultra-conservative summary doesn't make us sound stupid!)

Until the end of the decade when we met Joe McMoneagle, Pat was the most remarkable psychic we ever saw, and he remains the only one who was able to read printed words at a distance psychically. He was a cheerful, even-tempered "man among men." Once during this period, a young secretary who was typing Pat's descriptions of distant sites asked him if he could "psychically follow her into the ladies' room." He said, "If I can focus my mind on any place on the planet, why would I want to follow you into the ladies' room?" That was Pat!

Figure 3.4. A 1974 photo showing, from left to right, myself and retired police commissioner Pat Price as we were getting ready to take off in a glider to investigate Pat's psychic abilities aloft.

The Kidnapping of Patricia Hearst

On the night of Monday, February 4, 1974, a group of American terrorists kidnapped nineteen-year-old newspaper heiress Patricia

Hearst from her apartment near the University of California in Berkeley where she was a student. The kidnappers identified themselves as the Symbionese Liberation Army (SLA).

They were radical anarchists whose oft-repeated slogan was "DEATH TO THE FASCIST INSECT THAT PREYS UPON THE LIFE OF THE PEOPLE." The conservative and wealthy Hearst family was a perfect target for them. While the press was trying to find "Symbia" on the map, the Berkeley police department was trying to locate the daughter of one of the most prominent celebrities in the city of San Francisco—namely, the publisher of the *San Francisco Examiner* and president of the nationwide Hearst syndicate of newspapers

The Berkeley police department called us at SRI to see if we could help with this most troubling of high-profile cases. Hal, Pat, and I drove north to Berkeley to find out what Pat could do to help them. As it turned out, Price identified and *named* the kidnapper of Patricia Hearst from the fat, loose-leaf mug book filled with hundreds of photos. He stood at a large oak table in the station house, turned the pages of the mug book, and then put his finger on the face of a man and announced, "That's the ringleader." The man he fingered was Donald DeFreeze, who was indeed identified as the ringleader within the week.

The detective in charge then asked Pat if he had any idea where they were at the time, in the most famous query of all movie lawmen, "Which way'd they go?" Pat said, "They went that way," pointing north. He said, "I see a white station wagon near a restaurant. It's across the highway from two large, white gas-storage tanks near an overpass."

One of the detectives said, "I know where that is. It's on the way to Vallejo, where I live."

The detectives then dispatched a police cruiser, and within ten minutes it radioed back that they had found the kidnap car fifteen miles north of us. The car still had cartridges rolling around on the floor—the same caliber of shells we saw earlier in the day on the bedroom floor of Hearst's Berkeley apartment. So there was no doubt they had found the right car. This experience in the police station where Price identified the kidnapper and then located the kidnap car right in front of me is one of the strongest reasons that I believe in ESP. How could I not! How about you?

We received a letter of thanks and commendation from the Berkeley police department for our efforts during the several days we worked with them. But because the Berkeley Police Department, the Alameda County Sheriff's Office, and the FBI did not cooperate with one another, all our work was fruitless. Each agency wanted sole credit for finding the heiress. (This was much like the scandalous events preceding 9/11, when the CIA and the NSA refused to share their vital terrorist information with the FBI, who otherwise could have picked up two of the hijackers as they traveled across the country on their way to destroying the World Trade Center in New York.)

Around the same time, for the sake of science we at SRI worked with Price, carrying out nine formal, double-blind remote-viewing trials in which Price was asked each day to describe Hal Puthoff's randomly chosen hiding place. From a pool of sixty possible locations, Price had seven first-place matches in his nine trials. The odds against chance of this result were one in a hundred thousand! It is as though Hal had been kidnapped nine times by terrorists and Pat was able to find him the first place he looked seven out of nine times.

Convincing Statistical Evidence for Psi

I have now described several remarkable psychic perceptions: Swann's view of the NSA listening post in Virginia and his drawing of an island in the Indian Ocean, as well as Price's description of the Soviet weapons factory in Siberia and his locating of the Patricia Hearst kidnap car. I will now describe further experiments we carried out to discover the reliability of Price's descriptions. The highly statistically significant findings from these experiments were published in *Nature*[3] and the *Proceedings of the Institute of Electrical and Electronics Engineers.*[4]

In the experimental protocol that we established at SRI, our laboratory director and SRI vice president Bart Cox oversaw all our early experiments. His staff had put together a box of sixty file cards, each containing a target location somewhere in the San Francisco Bay Area and within a half-hour's drive from SRI. These cards resided in Cox's safe. After the remote-viewing subject had been properly sequestered with me, Cox would use an electronic calculator with a random-number feature to choose one of the target locations. Then he would go to the target location, usually with Hal Puthoff.

Since I do not drive, I would almost always be the one to stay with the remote-viewing subjects in our electrically shielded room and work with them as an interviewer or facilitator to create a description of the location the travelers were visiting. I viewed myself as a kind of psychic travel agent whose job was to help the viewer describe his mental pictures of the place Hal and Cox were visiting. After the viewer had described the target and the travelers had returned, we would all go to the site together for feedback, so that the viewer could learn which parts of his or her mental picture had accurately matched the target.

In one of the early formal studies, I sat with Price in the electrically shielded Faraday cage on the second floor of the SRI Radio Physics Building. Meanwhile, Hal and Bart went to Bart's office on the ground floor and chose a card from a target pool of which I had no knowledge. (The target turned out to be a swimming-pool complex at Rinconada Park in Palo Alto, about five miles south of SRI.)

After the allotted thirty minutes had elapsed, I told Price that the travelers had probably reached their destination. As usual, he polished his glasses on his white linen handkerchief, leaned back in his chair, and closed his eyes. Price then proceeded to describe a circular pool of water about 100 feet in diameter. (The large pool at Rinconada Park is actually 110 feet in diameter). He also saw a smaller, rectangular pool about 60 by 80 feet on a side. (This second pool happens to be 75 by 100 feet.) He went on to describe a concrete block building—which corresponded to the cinder-block locker room at the Rinconada Park swimming-pool complex.

Price's drawing of this site is shown in figure 3.5. Its remarkable accuracy was one of the hallmarks of his work. However, this illustration also shows one of the problems that must sometimes be dealt with in remote viewing. Having described the target site with great physical accuracy, Price then told me he thought the target seemed to be a "water purification plant." He went on to draw some nonexistent water-storage tanks and to put rotating machinery into his drawing of the pools.

Hence, in spite of Pat's technical precision, it appeared that he had mistaken the overall nature of the site, given that it was in fact a public swimming park and not a water plant. That was the way I understood the situation for twenty years. However, on March 16, 1994, I received the Annual Report of the City of Palo Alto, celebrating its centennial year. On page 22 of the report I was stunned to read that "in 1913 a new municipal waterworks was built on the site of the present Rinconada Park." The photograph in figure 3.6 shows those two water tanks exactly where Price had drawn them! Rinconada Park had only replaced the water-treatment plant in 1922.

For years, we had assumed that Price had simply made up an erroneous water purification plant and water tanks. In reality, he had looked sixty years back in time and told us what had been there before

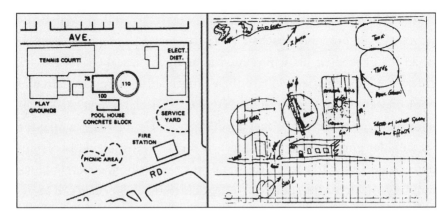

Figure 3.5. Pat Price's psychic impression of Rinconada Park in Palo Alto, 1974.
His drawing (on lined paper) is on the right. The city map is on the left.

Figure 3.6. The water tanks at the top of Pat Price's drawing had indeed been
where he indicated they were, *but not for the past fifty-two years!*

the swimming-pool complex was built! This amazing result demonstrated the ability of the nonlocal mind not only to travel through the
three-dimensional world but also to penetrate the barriers into the

fourth dimension—*time*. It also taught us the lesson that, in remote-viewing targeting, one must specify not only the target location to be observed but the time frame as well.

We carried out nine trials like the one just described. They were then formally evaluated by Dr. Arthur Hastings, an experienced judge of semantic content who was a psychology professor—not part of the SRI team—and is now dean of the Institute of Transpersonal Psychology in Palo Alto. He was given all nine of Price's transcripts, with his drawings if there were any. Hastings then went to each of the target locations and ranked the transcripts from "1" for the best match to the site to "9" for the worst match. For example, if Hastings were standing at a boat dock full of little boats, he would give Price a "1" for the transcript where Price is talking about a boat dock with little boats, etc. Hastings had no information other than Price's narrative in the transcripts that could lead him to match them to the correct targets. But because of Price's very detailed descriptions, Hastings' was not a difficult task. He was thus able to make a correspondence in a blind fashion for all of the transcripts—judging seven of the nine of them as a "1" in terms of matching. Moreover, Price had specifically named the boat dock, the Baylands Nature Preserve, and Hoover Tower on the campus of Stanford University.

I should mention that Pat had actually viewed and described the Redwood City Marina a half hour *before* the travelers were anywhere near that watery destination, which was fifteen miles north of the SRI on San Francisco Bay. In fact, just shortly after Cox and Puthoff had left SRI's radio-physics building and headed for their car, Price had turned to me in the lab and said, "We don't actually have to wait for them to get to their place. I could tell you right now where they will be. Then we can get some coffee!" I said that he could try that if he wanted to. Price said, "They've gone that way" and pointed north, which was correct. "They are standing at some kind of dock or marina

... lots of little boats. Some have their masts stepped and their sails furled. I can smell the sea air. . . ." An hour later, we were all standing on the dock observing just what Price had precognitively described.

The chances of correctly identifying seven out of nine locations with a high degree of accuracy through remote viewing (where each target is used only once) is one in 2.9×10^{-5}, or about three in 100,000. I show the distribution of rankings in table 1. That is, you would have to do an experiment like this a hundred thousand times to obtain as good a match as we did with Pat Price.

Target Location	Distance (km)	Rank of Associated Transcript
Hoover Tower, Stanford University	3.4	1
Baylands Nature Preserve, Palo Alto	6.4	1
Radio telescope, Portola Valley	6.4	1
Marina, Redwood City	6.8	1
Bridge toll plaza, Fremont	14.5	6
Drive-in theater, Palo Alto	5.1	1
Arts and Crafts Plaza, Menlo Park	1.9	1
Catholic church, Portola Valley	8.5	3
Swimming-pool complex, Palo Alto	3.4	1
Total sum of ranks		16 $(p = 2.9 \times 10^{-5})$

Table 1. Distribution of rankings assigned to transcripts associated with each target location for experienced viewer Pat Price.

When Pat Price died in 1975, he was fifty-seven. Two years later Admiral Stansfield Turner, then the director of the CIA, told reporters about his encounter with a remarkably psychic man who sounds suspiciously like Price. As recorded in the *Chicago Tribune*:

Pat Price

WASHINGTON: The CIA financed a program in 1975 to develop a new kind of agent who could truly be called a "spook," Director Stansfield Turner has disclosed.

The CIA chief said that the agency had found a man who could "see" what was going on anywhere in the world through his psychic powers.

Turner said that CIA scientists would show the man a picture of a place and he would then describe any activity going on there at that time.

The tight-lipped CIA chief wouldn't reveal how accurate the spook was, but said that the agency dropped the project in 1975.

"He died," Turner said, "and we haven't heard from him since."[5]

In the next chapter I will describe our adventures with Hella Hammid, whom I brought into the program as a control subject because she promised us that she was an amateur with no previous experience with remote viewing. In an experimental series of remote-viewing trials like the one I have just described, it turned out that she achieved even greater statistical significance than Price had. She also performed a stunning precognitive series.

The world of our sense experience is comprehensible.
That it is comprehensible is a miracle.
—Albert Einstein

No physics was harmed in writing this book.
—Russell Targ

4

Hella Hammid:

The *Life* Photographer Who Became Our Most Reliable Psychic

As a psi researcher, I had the good fortune to have a lovely and wise woman as my psychic accomplice. SRI's great success with Pat Price and Ingo Swann caused our government sponsors to ask us to find someone to work with who was not an experienced psychic. They wanted a "control" subject. "What can an ordinary person do?" they asked.

I chose photographer Hella Hammid, whose passions were cobalt blue glass, beauty in the world, and her famous egg-custard soufflé. She had spent most of her life looking at the world through the view-finder of her Leica, so for her to become an accomplished remote viewer was a completely apropos extension of her life's visual orientation. Hella was a longtime friend from New York, and she promised me that she had no previous psi experience, although she was very excited about the challenge. Thus, in 1974, Hella came to work with us at SRI as a "control." And in spite—or perhaps because—of that, she became our most reliable remote viewer for almost a decade. Hella left the program when I did in 1982, returning to her highly successful photography in Los Angeles.

Hella was born in Frankfurt in 1921 and came to the United States from France in 1938, along with countless other Jews fleeing the Nazis. Since the 1950s, she had been a portrait photographer and a regular contributor to *Life* magazine. And then in the 1970s, she began her career with us as a psychic superstar. It was a label she thought hysterically funny, because she had no more idea than we did, then or now, about how psi worked.

The reason Hella was so appreciated at SRI is that her warmth and grace permeated the entire laboratory. Hella died in Los Angeles, in the evening of the first of May 1992—the fiery third night of the Rodney King riots, which her home overlooked. I miss her, and she is often in my thoughts as I continue the work that we used to do together. She was charming as well as very astute, as you might be able to ascertain from her 1980 photograph with Ingo Swann in figure 4.1.

Figure 4.1. Photographer Hella Hammid (right) and artist Ingo Swann.

As I have said, Pat Price and Ingo Swann had had experience in the psychic world long before they came to SRI, but Hella and I had to figure it all out for ourselves from scratch. Pat and Ingo had been psychic since childhood and didn't require any instructions; they instructed us.

In the initial trial of the first formal series with Hella, I remember sitting on the floor of our laboratory while Hella settled herself on the couch and asked me, "What do I do now?" As usual, my partner Hal Puthoff had already driven off to an undisclosed target location, and our job was to describe where he had gone to hide. Or, more correctly, what it looked like where he had gone to hide. I didn't exactly know what to tell Hella to do at that time, but I can now describe the process.

This was Hella's first remote viewing. I told her to close her eyes and relax. Then I reminded her that "Hal is now at some interesting Bay Area location." I, of course, had no idea where Hal had been sent. I asked Hella, "Tell me what you experience with regard to where Hal is now."

She said, "I see a lot of motion. Something is moving very fast." And she made the little sketch with the number one as shown in figure 4.2 below.

I replied, "That's very good," which is what I always say to a first sketch. A bit of positive feedback is always helpful.

We then took a little break, in order to make room for entirely new images to appear in her awareness. Then I asked her to take another look to see if anything new appeared on her mental screen. Her second psychic look revealed, as she said, "Some kind of trough up in the air. But it's full of holes, so it wouldn't be able to carry water."

I thought that sounded promising. After another little break, I asked Hella, "If you stand where Hal is standing, what do you see?"

She said after a long pause, "I see squares within squares within squares."

I asked her to draw that. The whole session took about fifteen minutes. Later, the judge had no trouble matching Hella's drawing of nested squares to the wire frames of the pedestrian overpass where Hal had been pacing back and forth during our session and watching cars speed by on the eight-lane freeway below.

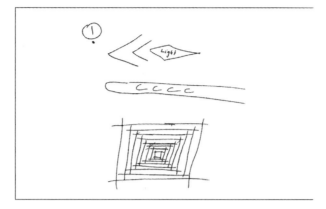

Figure 4.2. Hella Hammid's drawing of her first remote viewing in series of nine. She described "some kind of trough up in the air" and saw "squares within squares within squares."

Figure 4.3. The pedestrian overpass target where Hal Puthoff was actually walking when Hella drew her sketch.

Since I have left the SRI program, I have sat with hundreds of aspiring remote viewers, all of whom have wanted to know, "What do I do now?" But now I know how to answer such questions. A *shibboleth* is a kind of linguistic password, often containing secret information understood only by one's own clan. In the same sense, although there are many ways to initiate a remote-viewing session, some specific words seem to me to work much better than others. For instance, I never ask a person to *name* a target or object. That task is impossible for inexperienced viewers. They cannot correctly analyze or name any-thing in remote viewing. Instead, you want them to tell you what they are *experiencing—what they see on their mental screen.* If you ask inex-perienced viewers to describe or tell you about a distant place where someone is hiding, they will hardly know how to begin. But if you ask them to describe the surprising images that pop into their awareness, they know where to look for the information. I ask viewers to tell me what they are experiencing with regard to where the outbound person is hiding. I will often say, "I have a target location, or object that needs a description." The idea is that the viewer *already knows* the answer. All the interviewer is doing is trying to get the information out of the viewer's subconscious and onto the paper or the tape recorder.

Hella taught me much of what I understand about the process of teaching remote viewing. During her nine trials of viewing distant geographical targets, she achieved statistical significance of almost one in a million (1.8×10^{-6}) that her impressions could have occurred by chance, which was even more successful than Price had been in a similar series. In nine double-blind trials of outdoor locations, Hel-la obtained five first-place matches and four second-place matches. Both her results and Pat's were published in the March, 1976, issue of *Proceedings of the IEEE,* stimulating successful replications at Princ-eton University and universities in Russia, Holland, and Scotland. Altogether, there were a total of fifteen successful replications by 1982 when we tallied them up to be recorded in my book *The Mind Race: Understanding and Using Psychic Abilities.*

Just to put these numbers in perspective, we can recall that Joltin' Joe DiMaggio got a base hit less than one in every three times at bat (lifetime batting average: 0.325). The fact that he failed to get a hit two out of three times at bat didn't detract from his prowess as a star slugger. Even for Joe, we have to look at the stats. Similarly, we could say that Pat Price got a home run seven out of nine times at bat in our experiment. And he made an out the other two times. Hella Hammid hit a homer five of her nine times at bat and got a triple the other four times! That's why her statistical significance is a little greater than Pat's. But I'd be happy to have either of them on my team.

Table 2 shows the distribution of Hella's scores in the nine trial series. Her five first-place matches and four second-place matches gave a total score of thirteen. Price, on the other hand, had seven first-place matches, together with a six and a three, giving a total score of sixteen. In this game, a perfect score would be nine, indicating nine first-place matches.

Target Location	Distance (km)	Rank of Associated Transcript
Methodist church, Palo Alto	1.9	1
Ness Auditorium, Menlo Park	0.2	1
Merry-go-round, Palo Alto	3.4	1
Parking garage, Mountain View	8.1	2
SRI International Courtyard, Menlo Park	0.2	1
Bicycle shed, Menlo Park	0.1	2
Railroad trestle bridge, Palo Alto	1.3	2
Pumpkin patch, Menlo Park	1.3	1
Pedestrian overpass, Palo Alto	5.0	2
Total sum of ranks		13 $(p = 1.8 \times 10^{-6})$

Table 2. Distribution of rankings associated with each target location for Hella Hammid.

We conducted several successive formal studies in which Hella accurately described medium-sized household objects hidden in wooden boxes, small exotic objects hidden in aluminum film cans, and even microscopic targets the size of a microdot, such as those used by spies to conceal messages in letters. All these viewings were carefully judged and found to be statistically significant as well. So in the end, our control subject became our most extensively published SRI psychic viewer.

Hella was a cautious viewer in that she did not elaborate her descriptions beyond what she actually saw psychically. Pat Price, on the other hand, would go to extremes to give highly detailed descriptions of target sites. These were usually correct, but sometimes they were entirely off the mark, which is why Hella achieved a slightly better statistical result than Pat in our formal out-bounder (or "beacon person") experiments. However, we would not say that one viewer was more psychic than the other. Rather, we would say that they had different styles. If a terrorist had planted a bomb somewhere in the city, I would probably call Pat to try and find it. If I had lost my keys somewhere in the house, I would call Hella to describe what piece of furniture they had fallen behind.

Objects in Aluminum Film Cans

In our investigation of the range and scope of remote viewing, we asked Hella to describe the appearance of some concealed small objects. We wanted to know if it was possible to describe the color and shape of an object inside an aluminum 35-mm film can. Since there is no light in such a can, we were interested in the perception of a colored object where the color was not manifest. Again, these were double-blind experiments. I did not know the contents of any of the ten target cans. In our experiment, twice a day for five days Hal would randomly choose a sealed can and take it to the park across the street from our laboratory. Meanwhile, in our second-floor, windowless lab, I would interview Hella regarding her psychic impressions of the

contents of the can at the time—or what *she would see in the future* a
half hour later when she opened the can in the lab. (It's worth noting
that an aluminum film can was a familiar and friendly item for Hella.)

When the target was a spool of thread and a pin with a head, Hella
made the drawing at the top of figure 4.4 and described "a nail with
a head, long and thin and silver." When the object was a curled up

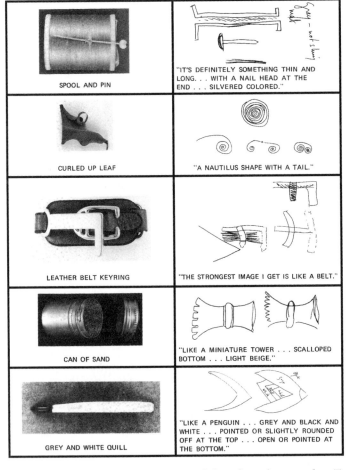

Figure 4.4. Hella's film-cans experiment, with four first-place matches. Target
objects in metal containers are on the left. Captions under her drawings on the
right are her first psychic comments.

leaf, she drew spirals and talked of a "Nautilus shell." When we had a key-ring "belt," she expressed surprise as to how you could get a "belt" into a film can. Several of these trials were filmed live by the BBC television for their documentary *The Case of E.S.P.,* which included a large segment on our research. (In retrospect, I think that a can full of sand—one of the targets—was a poor remote-viewing choice, because it has no shape apart from the can it is in. But, of course, I was not the one choosing targets.) Figure 4.4 shows the first five cans and their contents. In blind judging, Hella received four first-place matches and one second-place. What we learned from this experiment is that a viewer can psychically see an object down to the size of a *pin* from a quarter of a mile away—even when it is inside a light-proof, electrically shielded can.

Precognition Experiments

In physics, we consider phenomena that are not forbidden by known equations and principles to be mandatory in their appearance. That is, we assume that everything not so deemed outside the range of possibility will eventually be found to occur. Consequently, as Hal and I sometimes found our viewers to be describing targets accurately *before* they were chosen, we thought that this precognitive element of remote viewing should be formally investigated. We were well aware that most people's first experience with psychic phenomena is from their precognitive dreams.

Furthermore, I consider precognition to be an important part of psychic phenomena. I frequently have startlingly accurate dreams of this kind. But since the audience for this book is meant to include the skeptic who doesn't believe in ESP, any recitation of my personally exciting dreams will be of no more interest than my last LSD trip. I describe my dreams in my autobiography, *Do You See What I See:*

Memoirs of a Blind Biker. In this present book, though, we will stick to the data.

In the formal precognition experiments we did with Hella at SRI, we instructed her to describe Hal's hiding place a half hour *before* it was randomly chosen. In table 3 below, I show the order in which we carried out each phase of our experiments with her. Hal and I were living in a kind of psychic bubble in those first few years of our SRI program. What I mean is that almost every remote-viewing trial we did yielded a successful outcome. When we first presented our remote-viewing results to the Parapsychological Association (PA) annual meeting at Santa Barbara in 1975, people thought we were lying about our data. No one in academic parapsychology research such as we were doing had ever seen such consistency of highly significant results. There were several reasons for our success: First, we were working with highly gifted viewers rather than with psychology students. Also, we were asking them to do a task that corresponded to the most readily manifested form of psychic functioning, as compared with card guessing. Finally, we had an excellent rapport with our viewers. They felt that they were part of our research team uncovering the secrets of the universe, rather than being treated as psychic rats run through a maze—as ESP subjects frequently feel when the experimenters' clear attitude is, "How are we going to keep these crooks from cheating?" I heard a paper on exactly this topic at the 1992 meeting of the PA.

With regard to our psychic bubble, in 1975 we had just submitted a lengthy paper to the *Proceedings of the Institute of Electrical and Electronics Engineers* (IEEE). After a lot of negotiations, it appeared that they would accept our paper for publication in this highly prestigious scientific journal. To accomplish this goal, all we had to do was show the journal's editor, Dr. Robert Lucky (no kidding!), a senior scientist at Bell Laboratories, how to do a small remote-viewing series with electrical engineers at his Murray Hill lab. Hal and I described our protocol to him in detail and visited his lab to give a pep talk to the engineering staff. To replicate our experiment, he chose a viewer and an interviewer from his research department. Then he went out to hide each of five days at lunchtime, while the viewer/interviewer team tried to describe where he was and what he was doing. At the end of the week, the team carefully randomized their five transcripts and put each into an envelope. (These are electrical engineers, so they are quite capable of randomizing envelopes.) Then, over the weekend, Lucky visited each of his lunchtime locations and tried to match the viewer's transcripts with the locations as he revisited them. After a lot of mental struggle he finished the task and handed in his set of attempted matches. He was pleasantly surprised to discover that he had them *all correctly matched*—at odds better than one in a hundred (8×10^{-3}). This is a truly amazing statistic with only five trials, similar to coin tossing eight heads or tails in a row. We were even more pleased when he called to tell us that we had passed the last obstacle to the publication of our paper. We even overcame a skeptical reviewer who was then research director of Hewlett Packard. He had (now famously) written on the first page of our paper, "This is the kind of thing I wouldn't believe, even if it were true."

Back to Hella's precognition experiment: Hal and I wanted to minimize the amount of time we would have to spend, while still including a statistically significant precognition demonstration series. For an experiment to reach minimum statistical significance, it has to achieve at least one-in-twenty odds against chance occurrence (0.05). Therefore, we calculated that if *all* Hella's transcripts were matched in first place, we would have to carry out only four trials. The simple calculation says that any one of 4 targets, times any one of 3, times any one of 2 represents the 24 possible arrangements. And one divided by 24 (one in four-factorial) equals 0.04, which is less than the 0.05 demarcation line for significance. That is, the probability of four correct without replacement is one in four factorial $(1 / 4!) = 0.04$. What could be simpler than that? Our assumption that *all the trials* would all be correct is what I mean by our being in a psychic bubble. No sensible scientist would do such a series. Table 3 below describes our protocol for the precognition experiment.

Time Schedule	Experimenter/Subject Activity
10:00	Outbound experimenter leaves with ten envelopes (containing target locations) and random number generator; begins half-hour drive.
10:10	Experimenters remaining with subject in the laboratory elicit from subject a description of where outbound experimenter will be from 10:45–11:00.
10:25	Subject response completed, at which time laboratory part of experiment is over.
10:30	Outbound experimenter obtains random number from a random number generator, counts down to associated envelope, and proceeds to target location indicated.
10:45	Outbound experimenter remains at target location for fifteen minutes (10:45–11:00).

Table 3. Experimental Protocol for Precognitive Remote-Viewing Experiments with Hella Hammid.

In our precognitive, remote-viewing experiments, the fun began when the out-bound experimenter Hal returned to the lab to meet with the viewer and interviewer—in this case, Hella and me—who were eagerly awaiting his return. Hella had already given and recorded her description of his hiding place a half hour *before* he chose it. We received the feedback we wanted when Hal returned with us to the day's site.

I won't keep you waiting—all four trials were successfully matched in first place. Again, it was not a difficult task. With this remarkable result, we felt—after a lot of soul searching—that it was only appropriate to include this significant (though small) demonstration in our pitch for publication and respectability with the IEEE. Here are Hella's precognitive comments with regard to Hal's future location:

1. At the long-neglected and shockingly scummy Palo Alto Yacht Club, Hella identified in her recording (which we took with us to the site) "some kind of congealing tar, or maybe an area of condensed lava that has oozed out to fill up some kind of boundary."

2. At Stanford Hospital's enclosed garden, she said, "I see some kind of formal garden. Very well manicured, behind a double colonnade."

3. At a squeaky swing set in a Menlo Park playground, Hella recorded, "I see a black iron triangle that Hal has somehow walked into. I hear a rhythmic squeak, squeak, squeak, once a second like a rusty piston that needs oiling."

4. When the target was Palo Alto City Hall, she described "a very tall structure located among city streets covered with Tiffany-like glass."

I want to emphasize that every word of the above summary was spoken by Hella *half an hour before* Hal had even chosen his target. For reasons we don't understand, these four transcripts show exceptional accuracy and coherence. It's as though Hella made a special effort in these trials, though our interaction was as friendly and lighthearted as always. With the results of this experiment, along with data from the research of Princeton's Robert Jahn[1] and others, Hal and I became convinced that there is no data from any source indicating any more difficulty in describing *future* targets than describing contemporaneous ones. In fact, the future ones appear somewhat easier! That's one reason why we call remote viewing a *nonlocal* ability (independent of space and time). I discuss the physics supporting this hypothesis in chapter 10.

Chapter 4

SCANATE with Binary Coordinates

After almost a decade of work, Hella's descriptions became increasingly spare and accurate. They demonstrated the opposite of a decline effect. One day we did an experiment for which we told her that, rather than stationing a person at the target site, we had its geographical coordinates instead. The interviewer was our longtime physicist colleague Dr. Ed May, who gave her the location of the target in binary form—with each number for latitude and longitude turned into ones and zeros instead of the usual degrees, minutes, and seconds. What Hella got to see was a file card showing something like the following: 10010100110-N and 11001001101-W. Hella commented, "That's an interesting-looking pattern." Then she closed her eyes, gave a great sigh (which was always a sign of good psi for her), and said, "I see some kind of round structure." She laughed and continued, "It looks like a belly-button-shaped energy expander. There are four rays coming out of it." When we listened to the audio tape after the experiment, it was clear that this entire initial exchange took less than five minutes.

Then Hella requested some clay to make a model of what she psychically saw. She felt that the new medium would allow her an additional mode of expression for what she was experiencing. The target was the University of California, Berkeley Bevatron—a hollow, circular particle accelerator that is, indeed, an "energy expander" and has four beam tubes leading to the experimental labs, or target buildings. Figures 4.5 and 4.6 show the remarkable similarity between her drawing and the beam tubes and accelerator fifty miles away. Figure 4.7 shows her clay model of the surprising images appearing in her awareness.

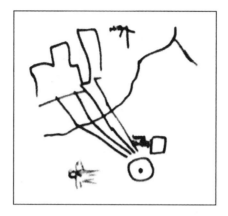

Figure 4.5. Hella's drawing. She described "a belly-button-shaped energy expander, with highly illuminated rays shooting out."

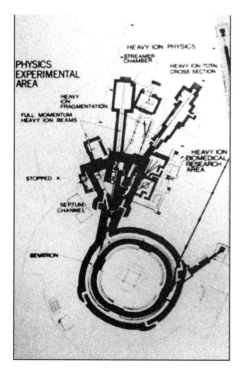

Figure 4.6. The official schematic of the Berkeley Bevatron target showing the circular accelerator and beam tubes.

Figure 4.7. Hella's clay model of Berkeley Bevatron, showing the belly-button energy expander, beam tubes, and target building.

With Hella, we often saw this kind of almost magical connection between the function and the form of the place. As I write this account thirty years after the fact, I am a little concerned about the uncanny functional similarity between her clay model and drawing and the university schematic of the facility. One could conjecture that she was psychically experiencing her feedback of the schematic, rather than remote viewing the huge concrete and steel tangle of pipes that comprise the actual machine—but the ESP is very remarkable nonetheless.

At the end of a decade of this kind of remote viewing, I began to think of Hella as our oracle, who would often say words to which she attached no particular meaning. One day when the target was the Stanford Linear Accelerator, she said she saw "polished metal tubes or cylinders. . . . This has something to do with a trajectory." Such a description is entirely appropriate for an electron accelerator. With English as her third language, I had never heard Hella say the word *trajectory* in our more than fifteen-year friendship.

We now know that an important ingredient of our remote-viewing success derives from the rapport between the remote viewer and the interviewer—acting together as a single information-gathering team. The remote viewer's role is that of perceiver and information channel. The interviewer's role is designed to be that of an analytical control— from my point of view, as I said before, a kind of psychic travel agent. My first job is to help the viewer to silence the ongoing mental chatter—mental noise, or the "monkey mind," as the Buddhists say. This division of labor between viewer and interviewer mirrors the two primary modes of cerebral functioning as we understand them: respectively, the *nonanalytic* thinking style that predominates in spatial pattern recognition and other holistic processing thought to predominate in psi functioning, as contrasted with the *analytical* cognitive style that characterizes verbal and other goal-oriented reasoning processes. Only very experienced remote viewers appear to have the ability to handle both cognitive styles simultaneously. This nonanalytic or artistic functioning is sometimes considered to be indicative of "right-brain" activity. (But not for us left-handers.)

The examples described in this chapter, taken together with the precognition experiments described previously, offer strong evidence that we each stand at the center of a vast personal coordinate system like a spider web, in which we can see in all directions and remember both the past and the future, because the threads of time keep tugging on us to manifest the future we will actually experience. As we learn to participate in this expanded awareness of space and time, past and future, we create the opportunity to experience the transcendence described by the world's mystics.

The Earliest Remote-Viewing Experiment

To the best of my knowledge, the first description of a well-controlled remote-viewing experiment was given by Herodotus, in Book I of his histories. The experiment he describes—probably the first controlled experiment of any sort—was carried out by Croesus, King of Lydia, in 550 BC. Croesus was interested in evaluating the accuracy of the half-dozen oracles that had sprung up in and around Greece as a result of the success of the Oracle at Delphi. Thanks to Herodotus, we have a detailed account of just what happened.

The following bit of scholarship was stimulated by a memorable trip I made to Delphi in 1982, when I was able to visit and experience the Temple of Athena and the Temple of Apollo, which is the site of the oracle, shown in figure 4.8. Incidentally, you can still visit the oracle's inspiring ruins—even the ruined temples at Delphi are a most affecting experience.

Figure 4.8. Site of the Oracle at Delphi, showing the Temple of Athena (standing) and the ruins of the Temple of Apollo on the left. After almost a thousand years of continuous operation, the temple complex was destroyed by Emperor Constantine in the fourth century because it was not Christian.

But back to the threatened king: Croesus wisely considered himself endangered by the warlike attitude of the Persians, who were daily becoming more powerful. Herodotus further tells us:

> With this in mind, Croesus resolved to make instant trial of the several oracles in Greece, and one in Lydia. . . . The messengers who were dispatched to make trial of the oracles were given the following instructions: They were to keep count of the days from the time of their leaving Sardis, and reckoning from that date, on the hundredth day, they were to consult the oracles, and to inquire of them what Croesus, King of Lydia was doing at that moment. The answers given to them were to be taken down in writing, and brought back to him.[2]

It was customary in those days that even the priestess prophesizing at the Oracle at Delphi in ancient Greece had an interviewer. As she sat on her tripod in the Temple of Apollo, the priest would ask her questions relating to the information sought by the customer, whether it were a merchant or a king seeking to know the future, as described by Oxford historian C. W. Parke.[3] Her ramblings would then be unscrambled and put into hexameter verse, which was the form expected by the customer, much as we at SRI would write a remote-viewing report for the CIA.

Hence, as soon as King Croesus's messengers entered the sanctuary at Delphi and put their questions to the priest, they were answered by the priestess through the priest in hexameter verse as follows:

> *I can count the sands and measure the oceans* [which the messengers had just crossed];
> *I have ears for the silent, and know what the dumb man nameth* [the messengers had not said anything to the priestess].
> *Lo! On my sense there striketh the smell of a shell-covered tortoise,*

Boiling now on a fire with the flesh of a lamb in a caldron—
Brass is the vessel below, and brass is the cover above.[4]

The Lydian messengers wrote down these words as she recited the description of her vision. Then they set off to return to Sardus. Herodotus continues:

> When the messengers had come back with the answers which they had received, Croesus undid the rolls and read what was written on each. This he had no sooner done, than he had declared that Delphi was the only true oracle. For on the departure of the messengers, he had set himself to think of what was the most impossible thing for anyone to conceive of the king doing, and then waiting for the appointed day he did what he had determined. He took a tortoise and a lamb, and then cutting them into pieces with his own hands, boiled them together in a brazen caldron covered with a lid that was also brass.
>
> Croesus was enormously impressed with this result. He gave thanks to the Gods and the Oracle with an enormous sacrifice of 117 large gold ingots, surmounted by a lion of gold.[5]

According to Oxford historian Parke, those 117 gold ingots would have weighed 570 pounds, and he assures us that Herodotus did indeed witness these gifts. I estimate their worth to be more than $10 million in 2010 US dollars. Parke says that "Modern scholars have been tempted at times to be skeptical of these treasures. But the truth and accuracy of them by Herodotus cannot be seriously questioned."[6]

Croesus then returned to the oracle to enquire about his country's forthcoming war with Persia. He received the famously ambiguous reply that "A great kingdom will be lost." Croesus did not realize that the kingdom would be his own.

There is no place for dogma in science. The scientist is free to ask any question, to seek any evidence, to correct any error. Where science has been used in the past to erect a new dogmatism, that dogmatism has found itself incompatible with the progress of science, and in the end, the dogma has yielded, or science and freedom have perished together.

—J. Robert Oppenheimer

5

NASA's Program for an ESP-Teaching Machine and Distant Brain Wave Communication

We finally received a NASA contract called "Development of Techniques to Enhance Man/Machine Communication" in the spring of 1974, and not a moment too soon.[1] The CIA had been giving us intermittent funding to do tasks, but they hadn't amounted to anything SRI considered a real program. We had also had important but small funding from private foundations such as Werner Erhard's EST Foundation and the Institute of Noetic Sciences, as well as a gift from Richard Bach—after he did a very successful remote viewing of a large complicated church, while sitting in our lab at SRI. But NASA's was the first program that felt to SRI management like real support.

This two-part program was primarily based on the four-choice ESP-teaching machine that I had developed and that offered feedback, reinforcement, and the option to decline to answer, or PASS. It was similar to the machine I had demonstrated to Wernher von Braun and the NASA administrators two years previously at St. Simons Island. The other research proposal I had described then was based on a 1965 paper in *Science*. It presented an extraordinary EEG experiment showing that when lights were flashed in the eyes of one identical twin, his brother in a distant, shielded room showed a synchronized change in his brainwaves. The paper had the exciting title, "Extrasensory Electro-encephalographic Induction between Identical Twins."[2]

In our NASA program with the ESP-teaching machine, our participants learned to recognize a "unique psychic feeling" when they obtained a *correct* answer, which was indicated by the ringing of a cheerful bell and the illumination of the button under their finger. If they pushed the *wrong* button, some other *correct* button would light up, and no bell would ring. Working with 147 subjects for a year at SRI, we found that eight of the people demonstrated statistically significant learning. Six of these eight were *each* significant at odds of a hundred to one. The chance of finding this high level of improvement from 147 learners is three in a thousand. (We would only expect one or two at the 0.01 level of significance, by chance.) We concluded that *ESP abilities could be enhanced by feedback and reinforcement*, just as we had expected and proposed.

The ESP trainer offered multi-sensory feedback, reinforcement, and an opportunity to PASS, meeting all the requirements needed for learning this skill. Thus, through practice, our ESP-teaching machine improved participants' ability to recognize their intuitive impressions. Let me explain: The user is presented with four colored squares. For each trial, one square (a push button) has been selected at random by the ESP trainer. The task is to choose the correct square. The trainer allows a person to become aware of what it feels like when they psychically choose the correct square by providing visual and audio feedback and reinforcement. When one doesn't have that special feeling, we encourage the user to press the PASS button. *So this is not a "forced-choice" test*, in spite of the fact that the ESP-teaching machine offered only four possible targets.

One encouraging finding was that *none* of the 147 volunteers showed a systematic decrease in their scoring. That is, no one showed a significant decline, as one often finds in card-guessing experiments.

One would expect four up and four down by chance, whereas we found eight up significantly and none down significantly. That's why we claim learning. We attributed this to the inclusion of the PASS button, which relieved participants from being forced to guess when they didn't have that special feeling. We think that the simple inclusion of the PASS button is a major advance in ESP testing, and it is still used today.

All of the participants worked by themselves with the ESP trainer. There was an electrically connected data recorder in an adjacent room that kept a printed paper-tape record of every button push for every participant. The ESP-teaching machine and its printer are shown in figure 5.1. They were designed and built for the NASA program by our good friend and fellow investigator Tim Scully at his company, Mendocino MicroComputers.

Figure 5.1. The ESP-teaching machine used in our one-year NASA program. Two of the five encouragement lights are illuminated at the top of the machine. The printer to the right (usually in another room) records all data on fanfold paper tape.

Ingo Swann spent some time in the 1970s with the machine, though he was not part of the official learning protocol because we wanted to work with inexperienced subjects. Nonetheless, Ingo carried out a series of 500 trials, scoring 167 hits, where only 125 would be expected by chance. This score had a significant departure from chance expectation with a probability of 1.6×10^{-5} (one in a hundred thousand). This is very good, even for a master psychic.

My daughter Elisabeth, who had participated in many ESP studies with me since childhood, was an early participant in an ESP-teaching machine experiment using an earlier embodiment of the machine. When you pressed any button, the *correct* one of four colored lights would then be illuminated. (That is, if you pushed, say, the button associated with the green light, and the correct answer was yellow, the yellow and not the green light would light up.) A score of six out of twenty-four was expected by chance. Encouragement messages were: *A Good Beginning* for six out of twenty-four; *ESP Ability Present* for eight; *Outstanding* for ten; *Useful at Las Vegas* for twelve and *Psychic, Medium, Oracle!* for fourteen. Some people could learn to increase their score by practice, even though the machine was making its choices randomly. Elisabeth, at age ten, was one of the most successful from the outset, often scoring in the highest category.

In 1971, before the NASA program, I decided to take my ESP teaching machine to the general public. I designed a stand-up, coin-operated version and had it manufactured by a young engineer named Nolan Bushnell, who two years later started the $2 billion Atari Corporation to make his own electronic games. Figure 5.2 shows ten-year-old Elisabeth with the ESP game in a Palo Alto Round Table pizza parlor. (The *San Francisco Chronicle* ran a story on us in 1971 and captioned this photo, "ESP IN A PIZZA PARLOR.")[3] The three installations in Palo Alto were very successful; however, I couldn't get national distribution for the machine. I was told that the distributors in Chicago "didn't know what an 'esp' was."

Figure 5.2. Photographed by the *San Francisco Chronicle* in 1971,
Elisabeth Targ is operating the first commercial ESP-testing machine.

You can now have an ESP machine for yourself at no cost on your iPhone. I have made this four-choice game available as a free application for the iPhone. It is called ESP Trainer. After a year, we have had more than ten thousand downloads from Apple's iTunes store. And I have received many e-mails from people describing their very high scores with the ESP Trainer for the iPhone.

Distant Mental Influence

Can the thoughts of one person affect the brainwaves or other physiology of a distant person? This was the question I posed in the second part of our NASA program—the part dealing with EEG measurements of brain activity. In the course of my life, I have occasionally felt pretty certain that I was in telepathic contact with another person. One of my current favorite books is Robert Burton's *On Being Certain: Believing You Are Right Even When You Are Not.*[4] It addresses the wide variety of ways in which we delude ourselves, from biased and self-serving misperceptions to false or distorted memories. Bearing all that in mind, my impression from my magician days in college is still that I could cause a person across the room to feel fear, or show embarrassment or laughter, as the result of my unspoken thoughts. But, as a scientist, I have always wanted to determine if that were really true. I was responding to this longtime interest in the Svengali mode of hypnosis, in which the magician says to his subject, "Relax and close your eyes. My mind has complete control of your every thought!"

At a meeting of the Bay Area Parapsychology Research Group in the 1960s, I witnessed a famous Czech parapsychologist, Milan Ryzl, give just such a hypnotic command to a lady volunteer in a telepathy experiment. (Modern hypnotists no longer use this master-slave approach.) Nonetheless, the experiment was very successful. She perfectly described the picture he had drawn before coming to the meeting, which he proceeded to show us.

Dr. Ryzl, who had been a chemical engineer, achieved fame in parapsychological circles for his amazingly successful clairvoyance experiments in the 1960s, in which he psychically communicated fifteen numbers (decimal digits) to a gifted psychic.[5] His research goal was to achieve *perfect* accuracy in sending a message. To accomplish this objective, Ryzl had an assistant randomly select five groups of numbers of three digits each. The fifteen digits were then encoded into binary form (1s and 0s) and translated into a sequence of fifty green and white cards, which were placed into opaque sealed envelopes. Ryzl was working with an exceptional hypnotic subject named Pavel Stepanek in this experiment—which is one of the most striking in the annals of psi research. Through use of a redundant coding technique requiring almost twenty thousand psychic calls for green or white cards (1 or 0), all fifteen digits of the number were transmitted *without error* (odds of 10^{-15}).

As a result of my daylong briefing in 1972, I convinced NASA to allow me to carry out a mental-influence experiment—patterned after the successful light-flash trials with identical twins reported in *Science* several few years earlier. There is extensive literature dealing with surprising psychic connections between identical twins. An excellent reference is *Twin Telepathy* by the English investigator Guy Playfair.[6] At that time NASA and I both knew that the Russians were interested in a variety of "thought control" experiments. So it was not too hard to stimulate NASA's interest in the significance of my proposed experiment. In the following section, I will set the stage with some remarkable Soviet experiments that were on our minds around that time.

The basic question is that, while thoughts are certainly efficacious, are they material? In a telepathy demonstration, I might tell you that I am visualizing something and ask you to tell me what comes to mind. (You already have a mental picture, right?) If I have an ice-cream cone in mind, you might come to have a visual impression of something conical. You might even have the "feeling" of ice cream. One way of describing this event would be to say that my thoughts (mental images) triggered the thought of ice cream in your awareness. The Buddhist answer, which I find convincing, is that thoughts are neither material nor nonmaterial. That is, the question about the materiality of thoughts is incorrectly posed. But there is no doubt (in my mind) that the thoughts of one person can cause pictures and sensations to occur in the awareness of another person. My research has shown that this telepathic causality is just as real as that described by the equation for "force equaling mass times acceleration" in Newtonian physics. (The force appears to be the cause of the acceleration.)

In physics we know that light cannot be described as merely a wave or a particle. A Buddhist would say that it is neither a wave nor not a wave. Physicist Niels Bohr famously declared that light is both a wave and a particle, as described in his theory of complementarity, which is a basic idea of quantum theory. Similarly, I would say that mind and matter enjoy a complementary relationship, just as particles and waves do. There is no end of materialism because the whole mind-body split is ill conceived. We should speak of the complementarity of consciousness.

Soviet Thought Experiments

Hypnosis is generally practiced in a face-to-face encounter with the hypnotist talking directly to the patient or subject. However, hypnosis research indicates that almost any person can learn to cause another to become entranced and that this effect can apparently be induced from a distance. Hypnosis at a distance has been studied in the laboratory in Russia since the early part of the twentieth century. During the 1920s and '30s, Russian physiologist and professor at the University of Leningrad Leonid L. Vasiliev conducted hundreds of hypnosis experiments with the direct support of Joseph Stalin. Vasiliev researched hypnotic inductions achieved without words and often carried out at a great distance from the hypnotized individual. These subjects were often sequestered in an electrically shielded room that he had constructed of lead and sealed with mercury (which today, we would not consider a very good idea). His careful research over decades, along with some telepathy experiments carried out by J. B. Rhine at Duke University in the 1930s, are among the best laboratory data we have for *pure mind-to-mind connections* that do not involve precognition or clairvoyance.[7] Vasiliev's fascinating book *Experiments in Mental Suggestion,* first published in England in 1963 and republished by Hampton Roads in 2002, summarizes his and his colleagues' forty years of hypnosis studies at the Leningrad Institute for Brain Research.[8]

Official Soviet psi research in this century has prominently featured pain induction and behavioral manipulation from a distance. One of Vasiliev's most famous experiments was conducted between Leningrad and Sevastopol—with a distance of *more than a thousand miles* between the experimenter Vasiliev and his highly hypnotizable female subject, whom he could reliably put to sleep and awaken telepathically.

Vasiliev's research gave Western parapsychologists their earliest evidence that neither distance nor electromagnetic shielding reduced the accuracy or reliability of psychic functioning. Research in ESP and "biological imposition" from a distance funded by the government in the Soviet Union began again in earnest in 1965 and frequently involved two experienced psychics who were able to communicate with each other telepathically over long distances quite well.

Strangulation from a Distance

The Russian actor Karl Nikolaev and his biophysicist friend Yuri Kamensky were well known for their apparent ability to transmit visual images to each other telepathically, frequently in stage performances in Moscow. My good friend the Russian parapsychologist and writer Larissa Vilenskaya had discussed with Kamensky the remarkable long-distance experiments he did with Nikolaev involving the transmission of feelings between Moscow and Leningrad—five hundred miles apart. Larissa describes her experience with many Russian researchers in my 1983 book, *The Mind Race*.[9] Kamensky was wired up in a Moscow EEG lab and given randomly timed instructions to send emotional feelings to his friend Nikolaev, who was similarly wired up on the receiving end in Leningrad. Larissa was a member of the Popov Parapsychology club with her good friend Edward Naumov, who was with Kamensky in Moscow during these experiments. Unfortunately, Naumov was imprisoned for several years in the 1970s because of his friendship with Western parapsychologists. When I met him in Moscow in 1983, he looked very gaunt and pale, although he was still wearing his trademark black suit and white shirt. Larissa told me that, in one study, Kamensky transmitted feelings of severe pain; and in another, he even imagined that he was strangling his friend! He was so successful in his effort to suffocate Nicolaev distantly that the physicians monitoring the changes in Nicholaev's EEG and heart rate in Leningrad became concerned that he might actually die—so they terminated the experiment!

Interviews with Nikolaev in the 1970 book, *Psychic Discoveries Behind the Iron Curtain,* revealed how he had spent many years teaching himself Raja Yoga methods of breathing and relaxation so that he would be more receptive to telepathic communication.[10] He was proud of his psychic capabilities and welcomed his many scientific opportunities to demonstrate his ESP connection with Kamensky. However, he was greatly surprised when his friend and partner sent him intense negative feelings instead of the images he was used to perceiving. When Vilenskaya asked Kamensky why he would want to transmit feelings of pain and strangulation and physical blows in his research, he answered that he believed that negative emotions were transmitted more reliably and more strongly than happy or positive feelings.[11] As Tolstoy said on the first page of *Anna Karenina*, and as every Russian knows, "Happy families are all alike; every unhappy family is unhappy in its own way." Perhaps that's why sending punches and strangulation is more likely to get someone's attention than radiating your happy and blissful feelings.

Flashing Lights at a Distance

Shortly after T. D. Duane's 1965 *Science* magazine article about his EEG experiment in which light flashes seen by one twin systematically altered the EEG result of the other distant twin, Kamensky organized a similar experiment in Leningrad with his friend Nikholaev. As described in *Psychic Discoveries behind the Iron Curtain*, Kimensky was seated at a binocular device that would flash bright lights in his eyes on a random schedule. He would sit there trying to visualize the face of his telepathic partner Nikhaelov, who was located in a separate building. The psychic connection between the two was so strong that the difference between the flash case and the no-flash case was often clearly apparent on the EEG chart of a single epoch, rather than having to average over many, many trials as is usually the case in this kind of brain wave study.

Hal Puthoff and I decided to replicate this experiment with the professional and technical help of the electro-physiology group at SRI. They also allowed us to use their shielded EEG monitoring room and their state-of-the-art detection and analysis equipment.

It is well known in EEG circles that a person resting with eyes closed will have a dominant brain wave output in the frequency range of 10 to 12 Hz (cycles per second). This is the so-called "alpha" production—a coherent brain wave pattern that many people in the 1970s and 80s were training themselves to develop for relaxation purposes using biofeedback. It is similarly well known that if you deliberately flash lights in the eyes of such a resting or meditating person, you will "knock them out of alpha" and usually into a higher frequency and more chaotic EEG regime.

All of that has been well understood since the time of Hans Berger's pioneering EEG research in Germany in the 1930s. The variation on this experiment that we wanted to do consisted of having a person rest in an alpha state with her eyes closed, while her good friend in a distant room was stimulated from time to time with annoying light flashes occurring on a random schedule. The result we hoped to see would be a decrease in the amount of electrical energy in the 10–12 alpha band of the resting person when the remote person was stimulated. In our case, the question was, would Hella be knocked out of alpha when lights were flashed in Russell's eyes thirty feet away? In figure 5.3, I show the double-walled opaque and electrically shielded room we used for our EEG experiments.

Figure 5.3. A research assistant (not Hella Hammid) in the electrically shielded room used for EEG experiments at SRI.

As Hella rested in her light-tight shielded room, I was in a similarly light-tight room down the hall in SRI's EEG laboratory. We had constructed a very simple electro-mechanical light-flash apparatus, comprising a rotating disk with holes around the periphery spinning in front of an automobile headlight in an opaque wooden box. The whole thing was battery operated and always rotated during the experiment, so that there would be no electrical transients, spikes, or interference caused by switching a typical strobe lamp on or off. During light-flash periods, an electrical solenoid would open a shutter and expose the light for ten seconds to the person sitting in a chair in front of it. The flash rate would be controlled by choosing which ring of circles in the perforated disk was exposed to the sender seeing the flashes. All sessions were entirely computer controlled and consisted of twelve episodes each using either no flash, 6-Hz flashes, or 16-Hz flashes. Hella was thought of as the receiver in her shielded room. She had no way of determining what was happening to the sender down the hall.

Using this protocol, seven sessions of data were collected for Hella over a period of seven days. The peak EEG power under each of the three conditions was calculated and found to be significantly diminished in the 12-Hz band on *each* of the seven trial days. The decrease for the 16-Hz flashes was statistically significant at $P = 0.04$, with a 24 percent decrease for peak power and a decrease of 28 percent for average power, which was significant at $P = 0.03$. The 6-Hz case

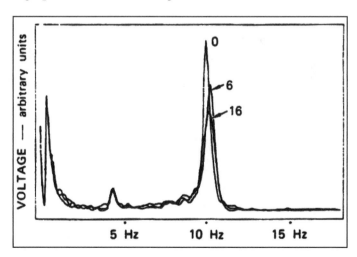

Figure 5.4. Occipital EEG spectra, 0–20 Hz for one subject (Hella Hammid) acting as a receiver, showing amplitude changes in the 9–12 Hz band as a function of strobe frequency. Three cases: 0 Hz, 6-Hz flashes, and 16-Hz flashes ($P < 0.03$); (twelve trial averages).

showed decreases of -12 percent and -21 percent but did not quite reach statistical significance. We published this significant data in the *Proceedings of the IEEE*; I show it here in figure 5.4.

We took this result as strong direct evidence that Hella was subconsciously aware of the light flash when it occurred in the distant room. It is very encouraging for EEG researchers to be able to see the evidence so clearly on a chart. We replicated this entire experiment the following year, with support from the US Navy, which was interested in communicating with submerged submarines, just as NASA was interested in communicating with spacecraft. The replication was at the Langley Porter Neuropsychiatry Institute in San Francisco, with a completely different team of neurophysiologists working with us. Using their facilities for every phase of the experiment, we again saw a significant deviation in Hella's EEG output when the remote 16-Hz flash occurred. In both cases the decrease of EEG power resulted (as expected) from a shift in the frequency of Hella's dominant EEG output. But in the Langley-Porter case, her systematic frequency shift was to a lower frequency, rather than to a higher frequency as seen at SRI. This does not, of course, diminish our confidence in the significance of the *demonstration of her subconscious activation as a result of the remote light flash stimulus.*

In the next chapter I will describe very exciting work in which we rounded up half a dozen Army Intelligence officers to see if we could help to organize an Army Psychic Corps. It turned out that some of our volunteer remote viewers became the most psychic people we ever encountered.

In order to be a perfect member of a flock of sheep,
one has to be, first and foremost, a sheep.
—Albert Einstein

6

Taking ESP to the Army

"As I walked away from the dusty old Lockheed C-130 turboprop that brought me to Vietnam, I had a clear flash of a bight yellow jet transport right in front of me. At that moment, even with the sound of gunfire in the distance, I knew I would leave Nam safely. A year later I was evacuated on a yellow Air America jet." That's what Joe McMoneagle told me in response to my question about any psychic experiences he might have had during his service as an intelligence officer in the army.

In 1978, Hal Puthoff and I were asked by Dr. Walter LaBerge, the undersecretary of defense for R&D, to help organize a remote-viewing center under army command on the East Coast. Our direction came from Commanding General Albert Stubblebine of Army Intelligence and Security Command (INSCOM), whose task it was to collect intelligence in all intelligence disciplines for use by worldwide unit commanders. General Stubblebine was an enthusiastic supporter of all aspects of our program and its operational expansion. But he unfortunately gave up his command and retired from the army in 1984, after a thirty-two-year distinguished career. I hope we weren't responsible for his early retirement.

In the late 1970s, the army was finding it embarrassing to have to go to California for their psychic intelligence. To solve this problem we were asked to select six Army Intelligence officers from a group of thirty who had been chosen for us. These six were to learn remote viewing and set up an operational Army Intelligence program at Fort Meade, Maryland, similar to the more research-oriented one we had at SRI.

Hal and I spent a day in the basement of the training center at the sprawling Fort Meade base and interviewed each of the thirty prescreened and self-selected men and women who were waiting for us. These adventurous officers had volunteered for one of the most bizarre-seeming assignments that had ever come down from the Pentagon. We talked to these interesting people, one by one, to try to judge their potential for the "Psychic Army Corps" that we were asked to initiate. We were looking for individuals who were intelligent, outgoing, and self-confident. In all the history of ESP testing—and our experience as well—cheerful, bright, extraverts do much better than dour or depressed introverts. Colonel Scotty Watt was to have operational command of the new organization. He was a large, amiable man and, like many military officers, proved to be much smarter than he let on in our early meetings with him. And his delightful wife Judy made us an extraordinary chocolate angel-food cake that I remember vividly, even though it was more than thirty years ago.

As our six new trainees came to SRI one at a time, I instructed them on our protocols for remote viewing. I would sit in our dimly lit viewing room with each of these rather bemused army officers. I had the challenging job of trying to make them feel comfortable about closing their eyes, quieting their minds, and describing the surprising images that would appear in their awareness—without feeling weird about it. They were trying to visualize where Hal and their commanding officer had gone to hide in the San Francisco Bay Area, within a half-hour's drive from SRI. As usual, I asked them to make drawings of the images that came to them with regard to the distant target. Later, the drawings and transcripts would be compared in a double-blind fashion with the six places that had been visited during the week of their individual series. Dr. Ed May was the judge.

Working with these six officers—five men and one woman—we carried out thirty-six outdoor remote-viewing trials at our SRI lab with six trials, matched as a group, for each viewer. We obtained a remarkable result of nineteen first-place matches (while just six, comprising one from each viewer, would be expected by chance). Four of these inexperienced viewers obtained four first-place matches each. This would happen only three times in a thousand of such experiments (P = 0.003 each). And the probability for the whole experiment was significant at odds better than three in a hundred thousand (P = 3×10^{-5}), which is most remarkable from a mere thirty-six formal, double-blind trials with inexperienced viewers! The "effect size" for the series (a measure of individual strength) was a whopping 0.66, (4 standard deviations from chance divided by 6, the square root of the number of trials). We would expect one first-place match from each series. But, on average, we got three. We were now seven years into the program, and we had not seen the slightest indication of a decline of degradation of anyone's performance. This gave us our first clue that there might be a lot more psychic ability in the population than is generally suspected, even though our parapsychological colleagues still found it hard to believe. In figure 6.1, I show the distribution of hits for the six viewers.

When I describe these or other SRI experiments as "formal studies," I am indicating that they had predetermined starting times and a fixed number of trials, just as any academic study. But, in addition, we had continuing scrutiny from our SRI Scientific Oversight Board comprising top-level SRI scientists and managers. We also had army oversight from US Army Intelligence Command Colonel Scotty Watt and civilian statisticians or scientists he brought along with him.

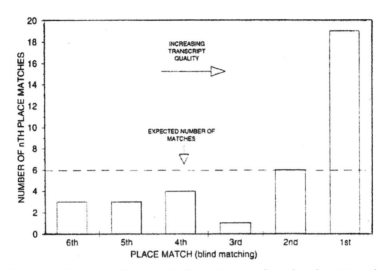

Figure 6.1. Highly significant results from thirty-six formal trials at SRI with six inexperienced viewers from the US military. The illustration shows that more than half (nineteen) of the results were matched in first place, where by chance one would expect only six (1/6 of the thirty-six trials).

We found that these remote-viewing abilities appear when they are encouraged and disappear or are repressed when they are forbidden or ridiculed. They are like a plant: if you water it, it will grow. It is my impression that Iceland, Holland, and Brazil—which never had any witch burning—are intensely psychic countries, while the United States, France, and England are not. In the West, the Catholic Church has historically strongly discouraged any kind of psychic ability, which is seen as a kind of *freelance spirituality*. The Crusades to the East, the Albigensian massacre of fifty thousand spiritually minded Cathars in France, the Inquisition terrifying all the thoughtful people of Europe, and witch burning throughout the world (including the United States) have had a very chilling influence on people's interest in exploring their psychic abilities. It's okay for one to talk to God in a prayerful manner. But problems apparently occur when one thinks God is returning the call. This was a serious problem in the seventeenth century among the deeply orthodox American Puritans, who banished spontaneously arising prophets. Their religious leaders sometimes sent them and their children out of the village to be murdered by the Indians. Anne Hutchinson is a famous example of such a woman who was too spiritual for her own good—banished to the wilderness and her death with all her children. It was not until Victorian times in the West that we have seen a new interest in spiritualism, the occult, and other psychic matters. In spite of the skepticism of Descartes and the so-called Enlightenment, which cast out the alchemists, it was the British and the French who led this resurgence, with a number of Nobelists in physics actively participating.

At SRI we carried out a one-year program for the optimization of remote viewing with our six courageous army volunteers. The objective of this program was to familiarize these friendly folks with the SRI remote-viewing protocols, to produce enhanced levels of ability, and to establish screening tests and procedures for enlarging the military population from which such individuals could be selected by the army in the future. So, this was indeed the first step in the forming of what became a sizable psychic corps—with perhaps a total of fifty people. That program continued at Fort Meade until 1995, when the government claims to have lost all interest in remote viewing. To the best of my knowledge, there is no longer any governmental activity concerning RV, although it is always possible that there is a new, secret program in the basement of the Pentagon of which I have no information. The 2010 movie *The Men Who Stared at Goats* is a humorous and mainly fictional representation of such a secret psychic government corps. As I mentioned earlier, no animals were killed or injured in our program, except for a rat who died as a result of a psychic healer trying to reduce its excessively high blood pressure. The movie *Suspect Zero*, with Ben Kingsley, gives a much better screen representation of what applied remote viewing might look like. But, as usual, the psychic is killed in the end: In Hollywood films, people with psychic ability are almost always marginalized or come to a bad end. The fine films *Phenomenon*, with John Travolta, and *Resurrection*, with Ellen Burstein, are recent examples of "no good deed going unpunished."

By 1979, at SRI we had been systematically investigating RV, which, in army terms, "utilizes the acquisition and description by mental means of information blocked from ordinary perception by distance or shielding and generally considered to be secure from such access by any known physical means." A variety of training protocols were examined with the goal of helping the participants familiarize themselves with a wide range of SRI remote-viewing techniques. In addition to outdoor targets, we used 35-mm slides, alphabet letters, small hidden objects, specially selected secure distant locations, and target locations demarcated only by geographic coordinates of latitude and longitude. I have said that when our six participants had been selected they were inexperienced with regard to paranormal perception in general and RV in particular. There is, though, one exception, that being a man who had taken part in an ESP card-guessing study many years earlier with J. B. Rhine. Interestingly, that one man, who was an ESP enthusiast, was the least successful by far.

Joe McMoneagle: Super-psychic from Army Intelligence

One illustrative example of an RV trial for a real-time San Francisco Bay Area outdoor target was with the aforementioned Army Intelligence viewer, Joe McMoneagle, who was one of our six volunteers. He produced a mixture of responses, some excellent and some noncorresponding, in his series at SRI. Several of his descriptions were among the best obtained in the program, and his overall consistency in performance resulted in *each of his individual series* reaching statistical significance—that is, with an outbound target person as well as with geographic coordinates. Programs conducted in 1980 were directed at training participants to bring their RV ability under more conscious control and to learn to recognize and overcome the factors that limit that reliability. These limiting factors center around the generation of erroneous data by the viewer from memory, analysis, and imagination, all of which together comprise analytical overlay (AOL).

An example of the successful resolution of such noise is the following: Joe was closeted with me as interviewer in the laboratory at SRI to await the target team's arrival at their destination. I did all the interviewing for this program, as I did for most of my decade at SRI. In this, Joe's very first trial, the target—as always, unknown to me—was the Art Museum on the Stanford campus. Joe made quite a number of tentative outline sketches of different shapes around the edge of the paper. He said that these were "associated with the face of a building." Finally, he made a careful perspective drawing of the building he was visualizing (see figure 6.2). A photograph of the target is shown for comparison in figure 6.3.

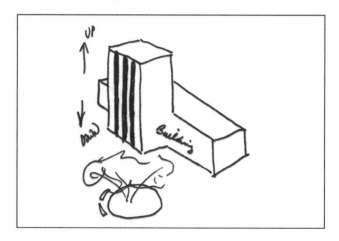

Figure 6.2. Joe McMoneagle's remote-viewing sketch. Note the groups of windows that Joe aptly described as looking like "piano keys."

Figure 6.3. Photograph of the Stanford University Art Museum.

Joe's narrative described the face of the building as follows: "There is a white-and-black pattern, a white-and-black striped pattern like piano keys. . . . It's like an inverted rectangle, with a square fastened to the back, or a rectangle laid down behind it. Like two buildings in one. One building. I have the sense that there is dirt by the walls." He went on to talk about trees, flowers, and bicycles, all of which can be found directly in front of the target building. The result was obviously remarkable.

In this program we also extensively trained all the viewers to focus on remote targets using only pure geographical coordinates (that is, only latitude and longitude). We found this practice to be equally successful and of great interest to our customer, the US Army. Our report to this customer said the following:

- Remote viewing was researched in response to the fact that the Soviet Union was engaged in large-scale research into psychotronic applications phenomena. The national security implications of failure to match a technological breakthrough by the Soviets is obvious. In this respect, the remote-viewing research was a product of the Cold War and is analogous to myriad other projects.

- Initial research was carried out at Stanford Research Institute (SRI). Certain psychically gifted individuals were able to describe distant locations, often with amazing accuracy.

- With this fact established, the military intelligence community approved further funding. Research continued, but the main effort soon switched to development (applications), based on two key findings: First, remote-viewing ability is latent in nearly all humans. Second, it is possible to teach ordinary people to perform remote viewing.

- Groups of students recruited from the ranks of the funding client agencies were trained at SRI. Their mission was to gather data, using remote viewing, regarding targets of special interest to the client agencies. Usually, these were targets inside the Soviet Union that had resisted the standard intelligence-gathering techniques.

- The minimum accuracy needed by the clients was 65 percent. In the later stages of the development (training) part of the effort, this accuracy level was achieved and often consistently exceeded [meaning that two out of three targets were correctly described].

- The data indicating that a viewer can describe an individual slide as it is shown on a screen indicates that targeting on high-resolution transient targets (charts, maps, etc.) is not out of the question. This indication, coupled with our findings that a viewer may be able to describe and identify alphabet letters, is a most encouraging development and one deserving of further work. Extension of the RV process to include high-resolution material, especially with a reading ability, would constitute a significant breakthrough for operational applications.

Over many years, we have learned to look for intelligent, successful, and outgoing viewers. Of the six we chose from Army Intelligence, Joe McMoneagle was the star—though one of the others, Mel Riley, was excellent as well. And all six continued with the program on the East Coast. Joe was also a photo interpreter, as well as an excellent remote viewer and an artist. Thirty years later, he remains probably the premier viewer in the Western world. A year before I left the program in 1982, Joe drew a cartoon illustrating his impression of me looking at one of his remarkable psychic hits. I show his drawing in figure 6.4.

Figure 6.4. Joe McMoneagle's cartoon of Russell.

A case in point: In 1979 Air Force Intelligence had satellite photos showing a lot of activity at a very large building in a Soviet port city near the Baltic Sea. Could they be building a huge battleship, or perhaps their first aircraft carrier? This was a perfect job for a remote viewer. Joe had outstanding success because he could sometimes describe what was going on *inside* a building that was represented only by a speck on the film. What he described in a series of RV drawings was a massive submarine—more than five hundred feet long, three times the size of any subs then in existence. Not only that, he said the missile-firing tubes were in front of the sail, or raised control center, which was unlike any sub at that time. If true, this placement would allow the sub to fire a missile while moving forward. Also, the large building in question was seen on the film to be a quarter of a mile from the sea. This detail seemed to discredit the accuracy of Joe's remote viewing, inasmuch as one would naturally expect a submarine to be on or at least by the water.

I know for a fact that many intelligence analysts at the CIA laughed at Joe's drawings. However, as the months wore on and satellite pictures started to come in, it became clear to everyone concerned that Joe McMoneagle had indeed psychically described the construction of an astonishing, five-hundred-foot Soviet Typhoon-class submarine—a full year before it was known to anyone in the West. Moreover, the pictures showed that the building's quarter-mile gap from the water had been quickly dredged and bulldozed by the Soviets to make a channel for the launch. This caper is described in more detail by Paul Smith in his comprehensive history of the remote-viewing project at Fort Meade in Maryland, where he was a trainer and security officer for seven years. His excellent book is called *Reading the Enemy's Mind.*[1]

In the same year, a Russian TU-22 Backfire bomber crashed in northern Africa, and after a week of fruitless searching one of our contract monitors, Dale Graff from Air Force Intelligence, asked the Intel psychic group at Fort Meade to help find it. There was great interest in locating the bomber before the Russians did, because the plane, which was fitted out for reconnaissance, was full of crypto-code books, in addition to possible nuclear weapons. If we could find the bomber first, we then would have the keys that would allow us to read the Russians' mail—always an exciting prospect for the intelligence community.

Joe was given a large map of Africa on which he could try to match and record his mental pictures as they emerged. The first thing he saw on his mental screen was a river flowing to the north. Working with his eyes alternately open and closed, he followed the river until it flowed between some rolling hills. After a half-hour's work, he drew a circle on the map and said the plane was between the river and a little village shown by a dot. Within two days, the TU-22 was found by our ground forces within the circle that Joe had drawn.

With regard to admission by the government of its use of remote viewers under operational conditions, government officials have on occasion been relatively forthcoming. President Jimmy Carter, in a speech to Emory College students in Atlanta in September 1995, is quoted by Reuters as saying that during his administration a Russian plane went down in Zaire, and a "meticulous sweep of the African terrain by American spy satellites failed to locate any sign of the wreckage." The former president said, "It was then without my knowledge that the head of the CIA [Admiral Stansfield Turner] turned to a woman [sic] reputed to have psychic powers." As told by Carter, "she gave some latitude and longitude figures. We focused our satellite cameras on that point and the plane was there." He must have been referring to Joe's fine remote viewing.

Remote Viewing after SRI

I left the SRI program in the fall of 1982—ten years after I had helped to start it. The program had become increasingly classified and operational, and I was no longer allowed to publish anything in the open literature. Also, I felt that I had not gone to graduate school to become a psychic spy for the CIA. In particular, I wanted to publish the very significant study we had just concluded with the six army volunteers. I also wanted to give a paper on this highly significant experiment at the centenary meeting of the Society of Psychical Research that was to take place at Cambridge University. I attended the conference, having left the SRI program the previous month. I then coauthored *The Mind Race* with Keith Harary, in which we could describe most of the research that I couldn't publish while working at SRI.[2] That book, published in 1984, was one of the more popular books I have written. Of course, I still couldn't talk about any of the operational tasks we had done. With the program under new government operational scrutiny, Hal Puthoff left SRI in 1985 to pursue his original research on zero-point energy fluctuations and the possibility (hope) of extracting energy from the vacuum of "empty" space. No free energy has been seen thus far, though reasonable men still cannot agree as to whether this feat will eventually prove possible. It may turn out to be related to the "dark energy" that comprises seventy-five percent of the universe. Hal is now at the Institute for Advanced Studies in Austin, Texas.

With Hal's departure, the program's guidance was taken on by our colleague Dr. Edwin May, another physicist, who had been with us since 1975. And five years after taking charge, Ed and all our SRI research moved to a nearby research conglomerate called SAIC—a Fortune-500 research and engineering company. Ed managed the program and greatly expanded its scope to include many other research organizations, until it was all closed down in 1995.

In May of 1987, the air force asked Ed to carry out a series of four experimental trials dealing with a variety of directed energy systems, microwaves, and particle-beam weapons. The viewer in these trials was Joe McMoneagle, who regularly came to California to work with Ed. In the two trials I describe here, an air force representative came to Ed's offices, introduced himself only to Ed, and announced that he was going to visit two sites that day, one at 10 a.m. and another at noon. Ed as usual had no idea where the agent was going, and Joe didn't know anything about the purpose of the experiment. By this time, Joe no longer worked with an interviewer—he had no need of one.

At ten o'clock, closeted in a quiet office, Joe produced a single drawing, which I show in figure 6.5. He said that the target was some sort of very large R&D facility with a row of trees to the east. He went on to say that that the agent was walking around in "an unusual T-shaped, six-story building covered with glass," which he drew at the upper left of his sketch. The facility was Lawrence Livermore Laboratory, a US nuclear research laboratory fifty miles east of SRI. And the T-shaped building he drew is the administration building of the site, where the agent was walking about.

Although remote viewers always like to have feedback from a trial (to experience closure) before attempting another similar trial, none was forthcoming in this case. At noon, Joe again headed for his little office and began to quiet his mind and expand his awareness. He saw some rolling hills with poles scattered on them. He drew these, as I show in figure 6.7. Joe said that this site was part of an energy grid and that there was something rotating on the top of the poles he had drawn. The site in this case was the Altamont Pass Wind Farm (figure 6.8), about a hundred miles to the east of SRI in the foothills of the Sierra Nevada mountain range.

Later in the afternoon, the agent returned to the lab and offered photos and feedback to Joe and Ed regarding the two sites he had visited. Both the air force and the CIA were very impressed with the accuracy and detail in Joe's responses to these two targets (incidentally, Joe had never previously seen either site.) Over time in the research program, Ed was particularly gratified to see that, as with Hella, there was not the slightest evidence of decline in Joe's psychic abilities.

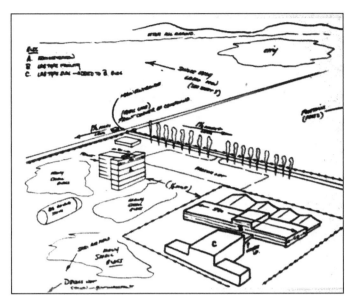

Figure 6.5. Joe McMoneagle's remote-viewing sketch shows what he described as a "six-story, T-shaped building, covered with glass."

Figure 6.6. The Lawrence Livermore R&D facility. Note the line of trees in the photo and in Joe's drawing.

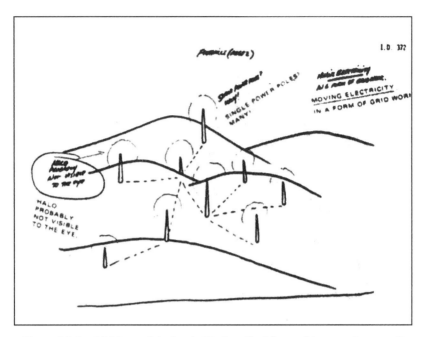

Figure 6.7. Joe McMoneagle's sketch. He described "something rotating on tall poles . . . part of an electrical grid."

Figure 6.8. The Altamont Pass Wind Farm.

An Interviewer Isn't Always Necessary

For beginning remote viewers it is important to know that it is not essential to have an interviewer. I know that I have emphasized how helpful it is to have an interviewer working with you to perform the analytic part of the remote-viewing task, but you can learn do it by yourself. Experienced viewers can ask themselves the various searching question as they go along. I will describe this in chapter 11, in which I write about learning remote viewing.

One of our brightest and most engaging contract monitors from the CIA was a young female PhD who had great curiosity about the possibility of ESP. She was a mechanical engineer whom I'll call Dr. P. She told me that she joined the CIA immediately after getting her degree from Cal Tech and reading *Psychic Discoveries Behind the Iron Curtain*,[3] because she felt sure that the CIA must have a program similar to what Ostrander and Schroeder described in Russia—and she was right.

In the course of our research, we already had a physician and a physicist as contract monitors. But when Dr. P. showed up in 1976 we were in for something different. She brought a more hands-on approach. She said, "I sent two guys out to California, and after a week they come back and they think they're psychic! I want to go over the whole protocol." We were happy to oblige her. Hal and I found Dr. P. very entertaining. She was an attractive woman, with long dark hair, and, for some reason that we never discovered, she frequently arrived at our laboratory at 9 a.m. in what we considered very stylish party dresses—quite different from what we were accustomed to at SRI. Dr. P. wanted to be treated just like one of the remote viewers in the program, in order to see where we had slipped up—or, perhaps, had fooled her envoys. She did two remote-viewing trials in which she turned in excellent drawings and descriptions of the randomly chosen target locations where Hal had gone to hide. (In both of these trials, I was the interviewer.)

The next morning, Dr. P. had a new plan. She wanted to do the remote viewing by herself—with no interviewer. After all, she proposed, I might have known the answer all along and encouraged her in the correct direction. That made sense. So we gave her the tape recorder and some paper and left her in our laboratory suite. We thoroughly taped the door closed after we left, because we didn't necessarily trust *her*, either.

Hal and I were sent by our random-number generator to go and visit the merry-go-round at Rinconada Park, five miles from SRI. We went to the park, took pictures, and made a tape recording of the little children on the merry-go-round calling out "push me, push me." When we returned to SRI thirty minutes later, the door was still taped shut, and Dr. P. was hunched over in the corner of the room. She had spent most of the time with her hands over her ears because she was concerned that there might be subliminal clues coming from hidden speakers in the walls. (She obviously was with the CIA after all.)

When we came back we found that Dr. P. had drawn a circular object divided into six wedges like the merry-go-round, situated on a central rod, and there were arches on the main circular platform. She said she thought the whole thing was called a "cupola," although she wasn't sure what a cupola was. (Neither were we, but we now know that a cupola is the circular, open-work decorative structure on top of some Russian and Victorian buildings.) Her excellent and unassisted remote-viewing drawings are shown below, in figure 6.9, after which our contract with the CIA was renewed for another year. And I should add that this trial is also high on my list of reasons for my belief in ESP.

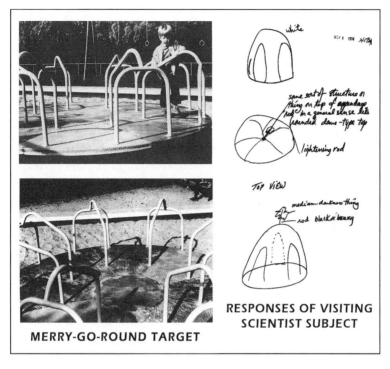

MERRY-GO-ROUND TARGET

RESPONSES OF VISITING
SCIENTIST SUBJECT

Figure 6.9. CIA viewer's drawing of a merry-go-round target. The viewer
worked alone, with no interviewer.

We have now reached the end of my account of the army remote
viewers and CIA contract monitors. However, there *is* life after SRI.
In recent years the evidence for precognition and retrocausality has
become stronger and more widely accepted. We even held a recent
Retrocausal Conference sponsored by the American Association for
the Advancement of Science, and the proceedings were published
by the American Institute of Physics. We are absolutely becoming
mainstream.

For us believing physicists, the distinction between past, present, and future is only an illusion, even if a stubborn one.
—Albert Einstein, March 21, 1955
(To the children of his good friend Michele Besso, after Besso's death)

7

It's about Time:
Forecasting December Silver and Other Precognitive Matters

Einstein wrote numerous articles and essays about our misunderstanding of the nature of time. Physicists have no meter with which to measure the passage of time, like the flow of a river as it passes and turns a paddle wheel. A clock simply counts the clicks and ticks of its mechanical escapement; it doesn't have anything to say about the passage of time. However, as we float down our imaginary river of time, we can sometimes see turbulence up ahead; perhaps it is caused by boulders out of sight just beyond the bend in the river. Thus, the white water we can see in front of us gives us a premonitory glimpse of future trouble hidden up ahead. The evidence is very strong that we can learn to become aware of these glimpses brought to us by our *nonlocal awareness* beyond space and time.

Precognition or premonitions refer to this awareness, either conscious or unconscious, of future events that cannot be inferred from the normal course of events. Another way of understanding this idea is to think of the *future* event as retroactively affecting our awareness at an earlier time—the future affecting the past. In what follows, I will present some very compelling evidence for this ability, both from the laboratory and from what we like to think of as real life. It's important to remember that psychic abilities were not invented in the lab. They were found occurring naturally in the field and have been with us for millennia.

Ludwig Wittgenstein wrote, "Whereof one cannot speak, thereof one must remain silent."[1] This was an early statement of the logical positivist view that scientists and philosophers cannot meaningfully write about things that cannot be verified or falsified, such as the idea that chocolate is better than vanilla. Questions that are inherently unfalsifiable or verifiable like "Did God create the universe?" or "Is consciousness material or nonmaterial?" can create a lot of strong feelings. But there is no experiment or measurement that will answer them, not even in principle. Up to this point, I have hewed to the general principle that verification is essential, especially concerning remote viewing. But I am now going to describe data and experiences that challenge our ordinary understanding of time and causality. And the evidence indicates that there is something seriously wrong with our understanding of causality (*causality* meaning the originating entity that results in an action). This is an important problem because, from a physicist's point of view, if you don't understand causality, you don't understand anything!

A physicist might accept that we can experience something that is occurring hundreds of miles away because it seems a little like "mental radio." Seeing something in the distance by ESP seems causal, like ordinary vision—only more so. Whereas seeing something in the future appears to the physicist (or philosopher) as frighteningly *acausal*. In fact, Einstein even expressed an interest in psychic perception in his preface to Upton Sinclair's book *Mental Radio*.[2] But when we explore our experiences of events *before* they occur, it can create great epistemological resistance. Physicists are firmly committed to Newton's First Law, which states that force equals mass times acceleration

(F = ma). That is, when you push a wagon its acceleration is proportional to the force of your push. The unspoken assumption is that the movement of the wagon comes *after* your push, not before it. That's what we usually mean by *causality*. The event comes *after* the cause; it's all a function of time. However, the data from decades of precognition research show that Thursday's plane crash can cause one to have a frightening dream on the previous night and thereby affect the behavior of the next day's travelers—even before the crash occurs.

In this regard, it is interesting to note that all four of the aircraft that flew into the Twin Towers, the Pentagon, and the farm field in Pennsylvania on September 11 of 2001 were unusually empty of passengers. I was at a conference in Assisi, Italy, at the time, having flown in the previous day, and I kept the *International Herald Tribune* of September 12, 2001 that surprisingly indicated that on that fateful day *each of the four* hijacked planes were carrying *less than half* of the usual number of morning commute passengers. (The load factor for the four planes that day was only 31 percent.) Perhaps one unusually empty plane could be explained away—but not all four. There were lots of unclaimed tickets. And apparently many people just had a gut feeling that this was not a good morning to get on a plane. Similarly, William E. Cox (at J. B. Rhine's Duke University laboratory) investigated train wrecks and found in the 1950s that trains that crashed or derailed on the East Coast had significantly fewer passengers on the day they crashed than the same trains on other days—even taking weather into account.[3] These data provide strong evidence that people can and do use their intuition of the future to save their lives.

In table 4 below, I show the seating capacities and numbers of passengers aboard each flight. Since the published passenger lists do not include the alleged hijackers, I show percentage occupancy numbers and percentages both including and excluding the alleged hijackers. All flights had occupancies of less than 52 percent, and the aggregate occupancy was only 31 percent. Although flights less than half full were not uncommon that year, the fact that all four flights had low occupancy on September 11 suggests something remarkable about the targeted flights.

Flight	Capacity	Manifest	Percent	#With hijackers	Percent
AA Flight 11	158	76	48.1	81	51.3
UA Flight 175	166	46	27.7	52	31.3
AA Flight 77	188	50	26.6	55	29.3
UA Flight 93	182	26	14.3	30	16.5
aggregate	694	198	28.5	218	31.4

Table 4. Occupancy rates of hijacked planes on September 11, 2001.

Precognitive dreams are probably the most common psychic event to appear in the life of the average person. These dreams give us a glimpse of events that we will experience the next day or in the near future. In fact, I believe that the precognitive dream is often caused by the experience that we actually will have at a later time. If you have a dream of an elephant passing in front of your window and wake up the next morning to find a circus parade led by an elephant going down your street (for the first time ever), we would say that the previous night's dream of an elephant was caused by your experience of seeing the elephant the next morning. This is an example of the future affecting the past. There is an enormous body of evidence for this kind of occurrence.

However, what cannot happen is a future event that *changes* the past. It is certain that nothing in the future can cause something that has already happened to *not* have happened. That would be a physical (or logical) contradiction. This is what philosophers call *the intervention paradox*, illustrated by the thought experiment in which you kill your grandmother when she was a child, and you therefore cannot exist—or worse, cease to exist. Such a phenomenon is interesting to think about, but there is not a drop of evidence to indicate that this type of contradiction can occur. The Persian poet-astronomer Omar Khayyam described the immutability of past events beautifully in the famous lines of his timeless epic, *The Rubaiyat*, around 1100 CE.

> *The moving Finger writes; and, having writ,*
> *Moves on: nor all your Piety nor Wit,*
> *Shall lure it back to cancel half a Line,*
> *Nor all your Tears wash out a Word of it.*

We find that precognitive dreams tend to have an unusual clarity and often contain bizarre and unfamiliar material. Dream experts like to speak of the *preternatural* clarity of such dreams. To know that a dream is precognitive, you must learn to recognize that it is not caused by (a) the previous day's mental residue, (b) your wishes, or (c) your anxieties. For example, if you are unprepared for a coming exam and dream about failing it, we would not consider that to be precognition. On the other hand, if you have had hundreds of plane flights and then have suddenly have a frightening dream about a crash, you might like to rethink your travel plans.

One of our CIA government-contract monitors was in Detroit with his colleague overseeing another project for which he was responsible. Although they had gone to bed very late on their last night there, my friend had a hard time getting to sleep. When he finally did fall asleep, he had a frightening dream in which he was in a fiery airplane crash. All through the next day he was concerned about the dream, since he was scheduled to fly out of Detroit that evening. Because the dream had been so horrifyingly realistic, he ultimately decided to try to avoid having that experience in real life. He told his partner that he was going to stay over in Detroit for another day. Of course, he thought that it was very unlikely that his plane would actually crash; but, on the other hand, he had seen enough psychic events in our SRI laboratory to give him pause—and he had an adorable little daughter at home whom he wanted to see again. Since he, like most of us, did not want to appear to be silly or superstitious, he didn't tell his buddy why he was delaying his departure. (And in certain branches of the government, you are taught not to ask too many questions.)

Later that day, after delivering his partner to the airport, our friend was driving away along the frontage road and heard a muffled explosion. It was the crash of his airplane killing all but one passenger, including his partner. Our friend was in shock for a week. (Coincidentally, I spent a lot of time studying this particular crash when I later went to work for Lockheed, developing a laser system to predict and prevent crashes such as this one, which was largely due to wind shear.) I am sorry to say it seems that this plane crash was *karmically* destined to happen because of many, many factors, including temperature, wind, a runway change, and major pilot error. (*Karma* in the Buddhist tradition pertains to the inevitable workings of cause and effect.)

What can we conclude from this true story? First of all, everyone is probably a little anxious about flying. But I, for one, have never had a dream of being in a crash, and neither had my friend. In his business, he was a very frequent flyer—thousands of flights. So, we can postulate, without conducting a survey, that to dream of being in a plane crash is a somewhat unusual event. "But," I hear you saying, "he wasn't in a plane crash. He just witnessed one." This point deals with one of the most interesting questions in all of psychic research; that is, can you use precognitive information to change a future that you perceive but do not like? The problem comes, of course, from the idea that if you change the future so that the unpleasant thing doesn't happen to you, where did the dream come from? There are two fairly sensible answers to that question, both of which might be correct.

First of all, a precognitive dream is not a prophecy; it is a forecast, based on all presently available data, or "world lines." If you view the world as a huge, four-dimensional space-time cube, then we can be thought of as moving through the three-dimensional part like Hansel and Gretel trailing bread crumbs. Similarly, we move along the line of time at a rate of one second per second. Thus, our lives *trace a path* through the three spatial dimensions and one time dimension of this great cube comprising all of space and time. (That path is known as our individual world line.) If I wish to make use of my newly received precognitively derived information, I can change the future. For example, if I am looking forward to having a dinner date with someone and have a very clear dream about meeting her in a colorful and unusual restaurant, I will have a certain level of confidence that the event will come to pass—even though it might also be a wish-fulfillment dream. However, if I tell my perspective dinner companion about my dream, she may well say, "I was planning to meet you at that new and interesting restaurant, but I don't want you to get the idea that I am the slave of your dreams, so I'll see you next week instead." This is the vicious-circle type of paradox about self-referential statements that Bertrand Russell describes in his *Theory of Types*—falsifying the future by using information from the future. The dream is a forecast of events to come about in the future *unless* you do something to change them, based upon this new information. *Such an action does not falsify the forecast.* There is no paradox. To make this clear, since it is a cause of a lot of confusion, we can discuss another hypothetical example.

A messenger has information from a spy who has learned that the enemy is going to attack us at a certain later time. That's the message. Armed with this new data, we launch a surprise attack on the enemy and chase him away. He then, of course, cannot and does not attack us. However, we do not as a result of this eventuality fire the messenger or the spy because their information didn't come to pass. Their message described the probable future, which would have come to pass without the intervention made possible by the message.

A second related question asks, "How can I dream about being in a plane crash if I don't actually get to experience it?" The answer here is quite different. You dream about the real crash and then dramatize the events to include yourself in it. Our friend got to see a plane crash at quite close range, and, since he was supposed to be on the plane, he had no trouble putting himself there in his dream. We would say that the frightening crash he experienced the following afternoon was the *cause* of his dream the previous night. This phenomenon is called *retrocausality*, and it may be the basis of most precognition. But it is important to understand that a future event does not have to be *directly* perceived or experienced in order to have a retrocausal effect or to give rise to precognitive awareness at an earlier time. Studies by Gertrude Schmeidler at City College of New York showed significant precognition in forced-choice trials (in which one knows the range of possible targets) using computer-generated targets *in which the viewers did not receive any feedback.*[4] (That is, they never experienced the target directly.)

In all of this, we are arguing against the existence of any implacable arrow of time. Rather, we would say that there are certain time-irreversible phenomena, such as heat conduction, diffusion, chemical reactions, breaking eggs, and, alas, aging. In all of these cases, a movie of the effect under consideration will quickly reveal whether it is being run forward or backward. On the other hand, there are a wide variety of reversible effects that can be run either way. These include all the laws of mechanics when there is no friction. Paradoxically, there is no discernable passage of time for a swinging pendulum, or for the random Brownian motion of particles floating in a solution in a jar.

So, it appears that the irreversibility of time is more *fact-like* than *law-like*. It all depends on the type of event being observed. There is obviously *no law against precognition*, and, under the right conditions, it is a common occurrence at the atomic and subatomic levels.

Forecasting December Silver

When I left SRI in 1982, I organized Delphi Associates with two other partners, Keith (Blue) Harary and Anthony White. Tony White was a successful businessman and investor. Our other partner, Keith, was a very gifted psychic and psychologist who had been with the SRI program for several years as a researcher and remote viewer. Delphi, a company made entirely out of our imagination, had two large psi projects and a number of small ones during its three-year life. For our first project, our team of psychics and investors wanted to investigate the possibility of using psychic abilities to make money in the marketplace. The second big project was the design of psychic video games for Atari—the Silicon Valley game company. (By the way, we were one of the few consultants to actually get paid, as Atari imploded from $2 billion to zero in the fall of 1985.)

For our market-forecasting project, we were very fortunate to add to our merry band a spiritually minded and enthusiastic big-time investor, Paul Temple, and a highly creative and adventurous stockbroker, John Rende. It is well understood that reading numbers or letters psychically is an exceptionally difficult task, so we knew we couldn't forecast silver commodity prices by asking our psychic to read the symbols on the big board at the Commodity Exchange and forecast future prices a week ahead. Instead, we used a symbolic protocol first described by Stephan Schwartz of the Mobius Society and presented in his book *Opening to the Infinite*.[5] In this scheme, we associate a different object with each of the possible states (prices) the market could produce the following week. We wanted to know a week in advance if the commodity called "December Silver" (which can be purchased any time before December) would be "up a little" (less than a quarter); "up a lot" (more than a quarter); "down a little or unchanged"; or "down a lot." These are four discrete conditions that could be represented by or associated with four objects—for example, a light bulb, a flower, a book, and a stuffed animal. For each week's trial, we would ask our businessman, Tony White—who actually ran the project because of secrecy requirements from Keith and me as viewer and interviewer—to choose four such strongly differing objects (orthogonal targets) and associate one of them with each of our four possible market conditions.

Only Tony knew the objects. And, of course, no one knew the correct object. I would then interview the remote viewer, Keith, over the telephone on Monday and ask him to describe his impressions of the object we would show him the *next Friday*. The broker would then buy or sell silver futures contracts based entirely on what the viewer saw, whether it be a flower, a teddy bear, or whatever. That would be the object associated with what the market did in the next four days, which is why this protocol is called "associative" remote viewing (ARV). At the end of the week, when silver finally closed, we would show the viewer the object corresponding to what the market *actually did*, which was the feedback for the trial.

Our nine forecasts in the fall of 1982 were all correct, and we earned $120,000, which we divided evenly between Delphi and our investor. (And in 1982, $120,000 was a lot of money.) In fact, our enterprise was on the front page of *The Wall Street Journal*. Erik Larson wrote an article about it entitled "Did Psychic Powers Give Firm a Killing in the Silver Market?"[6] And in 1983, television producer Tony Edwards made a film about us for BBC *Horizon*. It later became a PBS *NOVA* program called "The Case of ESP." This was first aired in England as a ninety-minute program on BBC and later as a fifty-five-minute program in the United States. (WGBH Boston explained to me that they had to cut the seven-minute live and very successful remote-viewing session out of the BBC version because American audiences have a much shorter attention span than do English audiences.)

"The Case of ESP" was frequently shown on PBS from 1984 until 1995, at which time for some unknown reason it disappeared from *NOVA*'s files. It is now gone also from the files of WGBH, Boston, which produced the film, and from Time-Life Books, which distributed it for sale. This is not a fantasy, since I have a master BBC tape and several DVD copies of the original program on my desk. (Interestingly, 1995 was also the year in which the remote-viewing program was officially declassified and terminated by the CIA.) The disappearance of the film has never been explained. My guess is that the CIA put pressure on *NOVA* to pull the film, since *NOVA* alone was the US copyright holder, and only they could have accomplished such a complete disappearance.

For full disclosure, I should add that in the following year we were not successful in our silver forecasting, possibly because our investor wanted to accelerate the trial rate to twice a week; therefore, the viewer did not receive timely feedback from the previous trial. My personal belief is that we lost our spiritual and scientific focus and become overwrought with the thought of limitless wealth (although different people have different opinions on the reasons for our failure to replicate the success. But we are all becoming very tired of people telling us that it must just have been our lucky year—you try it).

The good news, though, is that silver forecasting was once again successful in 1996. I worked with my friend and writing partner Jane Katra, a spiritual healer and Ph.D. in health education, and with two other good friends who were mathematicians—Dean and Wendy Brown. In a very friendly and open emotional environment, we used a redundancy-coding protocol and obtained eleven hits of twelve trials for silver futures with six passes, a result not to be seen more than three times in a thousand trials. Each week, Jane and I had our own unique target pool. The idea of redundancy coding is that we must have *agreement* on forecast direction of the market by Jane and me (for silver to go up or down) for the trial to go forward, even though the objects in our individual target pools were entirely different. This highly significant result shows the efficacy of redundancy coding even when the psychics are amateurs. We published our results, even though no money was involved.[7]

The main application of ARV today is betting on sporting events at Las Vegas. Several people in the International Remote Viewing Association have claimed that they are supporting themselves with this activity. One IRVA member sent me photocopies of a hundred thousand dollars in casino checks. At the most recent (2010) IRVA meeting in Las Vegas, I attended a workshop in which we were instructed on the use of a pendulum for forecasting future events. With the pendulum I was given I dowsed two different times for red or black regarding playing cards that would be cut, twice for odd or even regarding dice that would be thrown, and, finally, once for heads or tails in a coin toss. I was correct in five out of five trials and left the room. I like to quit on a win—which is what Ingo always recommends—so this was a case of optional stopping, with a probability of three times in a hundred by chance alone. My ESP told me that I would not be successful on trial six.

The following very useful confidence scale was used in all of our remote-viewing financial forecasting. In order for us to make a move into the market, in an individual trial it was necessary for a viewer's transcript to be ranked four or greater with regard to one of the targets. That is, any trial judged below four would be counted as a pass, even before we knew the market answer.

Confidence Ranking System

7. Excellent correspondence, including good analytical detail (e.g., naming the target), with essentially no incorrect information.
6. Good correspondence, with good analytical information (e.g., naming the function of the target) and relatively little incorrect information.
5. Good correspondence with unambiguous unique matchable elements, but some incorrect information.
4. Good correspondence with some matchable elements intermixed with some incorrect information.
3. Mixture of correct and incorrect information, but enough of the former to indicate that the viewer has made contact with the target.
2. Some correct elements, but not sufficient to suggest results beyond chance expectation.
1. Little correspondence.
0. No correspondence.

Precognition in the Lab

In an exhaustive summary of research data for what we call paranormal foreknowledge of the future, from 1935 to 1989 Charles Honorton and Diane Ferrari found that 309 precognition experiments had been carried out by 62 investigators.[8] And that more than fifty thousand participants were involved in more than two million trials. They report that 30 percent of these studies were statistically significant in showing that people can describe future events, whereas only 5 percent would be expected by chance. The overall significance is greater than 10^{20} to one (more than a billion billion), which is akin to throwing seventy pennies in the air and having *every one* come down heads. This body of data offers very strong evidence for confirming the existence of foreknowledge of the future that cannot be ascribed to somebody's lucky day. There is no doubt that we have contact with the future in a way that shows unequivocally that we misunderstand our relationship to the dimension of time we take so much for granted.

For years, parapsychologists have been trying to find ways to encourage their subjects to demonstrate psychic glimpses of the future. The 309 experiments collected by Honorton and Ferrari were forced-choice experiments in which subjects had to choose which of four colored buttons would be illuminated right after their choice, or which one of five cards they would be shown at a later time. In all these cases, a random-number generator of some sort selected the targets, to which the researchers were blind. Participants had to try to guess what they would be shown in the future from among known alternatives. In some cases they had to choose which target would be randomly chosen in the future, where they *never received any feedback at all* as to which was the correct target actually selected.

There are two kinds of important information for us in this study: First, we see that there is overwhelming evidence for the existence of precognition. Second and more importantly, we learn that there are more and less successful ways to do experiments. Success or failure in these trials was found to vary significantly depending on four different factors. It is important to keep these factors in mind if you want your own experiments to succeed:

- To begin with, experiments are much more successful when they are carried out with subjects who are experienced and interested in the outcome, rather than with people who are inexperienced and uninterested. For example, running ESP experiments in a classroom of moderately bored students will rarely show any kind of success (but people keep doing it, nonetheless). Furthermore, participants who are enthusiastic about the experiment are the most successful in the precognition studies I have been describing, independent of whether or not they have any experience. The difference in scoring rate between experienced and inexperienced subjects was significant at 1000 to 1 against chance.

- Another factor is that tests with *individual* participants were much more successful than experiments with groups. Making the trials meaningful to each participant is important to success. The success level of individuals compared to groups was statistically significant at 30 to 1 against chance.

- I have always found that feedback is one of the very helpful channels in all psi functioning. In precognition, I feel that it is the *experience* the viewer has when shown the feedback at a later time that is often (but not always) the source of the precognitive experience. This view is strongly supported in the forced-choice studies.

- Finally, the data show that the sooner the participants get their feedback, the greater the hit rate. That is, it appears that for forced-choice targets, it is easier to foretell the immediate future than the distant future. In laboratory experiments, people did very well in predicting events seconds or minutes in advance, but they did less well looking hours or days in advance. This seems to be the case for naturally occurring precognition as well. On the other hand, it is also possible that people tend to forget dreams of far future events before they have a chance to be corroborated.

Thus, the four factors that are important in these studies are:

1. Experienced (talented) vs. inexperienced subjects,
2. Individual vs. group testing,
3. Feedback vs. no feedback, and
4. Short time interval between subject response and target generation.

Moreover, I would add a *fifth* point: forced-choice experiments vs. free-response experiments, the latter being much more successful for all the reasons we have been discussing. And I strongly favor individual testing. All the highly successful SRI research was carried out one subject trial at a time.

In the whole data base of the Honorton-Ferrari analysis, there were some experiments that had all four favorable factors and some that had all four unfavorable factors. After all is said and done, 87.5 percent of the psi-conducive studies were successful and significant, while *none* of the totally unfavorable studies were statistically significant. That is, if you do everything wrong, your experiment will fail. Since we now routinely carry out experiments under the most favorable conditions, I think we can say that we have learned something about psi in the past fifty years. Actually, we have learned quite a lot.

We know, for example, that forced-choice ESP tests are a very inefficient way to elicit psi functioning. In the above studies, the experimenters, on the average, had to carry out 3600 trials to achieve a statistically significant result. With the free-response type of experiment, such as remote viewing, we typically have to conduct only six to nine trials. And in the case of our precognition experiments with Hella—which we published in the *Proceedings of the IEEE*—we had a total of four trials.

Presentiment

We are all familiar with the idea of a *premonition*, in which one has inner knowledge of something that is going to happen in the distant future—usually something bad, like a plane crash! There is also an experience called *presentiment*, where one has an inner sensation, a gut feeling, that something strange is just about to occur. An example would be for you to stop suddenly on your walk down the street because you felt uneasy, only to have a flower pot then fall off a window ledge and land at your feet—instead of on your head. That would be a useful presentiment.

I recently had a useful presentiment: One Friday evening, I was quietly paying bills at my desk when I began to worry obsessively about what would happen if I lost my credit card. (I had never previously lost a credit card.) So strong was this fear that I stopped what I was doing, went to the next room to get my credit card from my wallet, and compulsively wrote its numbers in my personal telephone book. The next day I went to a craft fair covering many blocks of University Avenue, the main street of Palo Alto. While there I bought some beautiful blue ceramic bowls. It was a very hot day, and a concessionaire was selling cold beer together with celebratory beer mugs. But, alas, I had spent all my cash. So, I went to an ATM machine in the wall of a nearby bank building, with my credit card in hand, and obtained some beer money. Now, with cash in one hand and a long, colorful bank receipt in the other, I set off to get my treat to deal with the heat. Two days later, while trying to pay for my groceries, I discovered with a shock that my credit card was missing from my wallet. After some thought, I was able to deduce that I had probably left it in the ATM machine at the street fair. But, because of my presentiment, I had the card numbers written down, allowing me to call the card company and ask them to send me a new card. That's the reward for paying attention to your presentiments! Since then I have memorized my card numbers.

Presentiment in the Laboratory

In the laboratory, we know that if we show a frightening picture to a person, there will be a significant change in his or her physiology. Their blood pressure, heart rate, and skin resistance will all change.

This so-called fight-or-flight reaction is called an "orienting response." Researcher Dean Radin has shown at the University of Nevada and at the Institute of Noetic Sciences that this orienting response is also observed in a person's physiology a few seconds *before* they see the scary picture.[9] In balanced, double-blind experiments, Radin has demonstrated that if you are about to see scenes of sexuality, violence, or mayhem, your body will steel itself against the shock or insult. But if you are about to see a picture of a flower garden, then there is no such strong anticipatory reaction (unless you are a gardener). Fear is much easier to measure physiologically than bliss. ("All happy families are alike. . . .")

The pictures that Radin uses in his experiments are from a standardized and quantified set of emotional stimuli used in psychology research. These range from nudes on the beach and men skiing downhill on the positive side, to car crashes and abdominal surgery—generally considered to have a strong negative affect. Pictures of paper cups and fountain pens are found in the neutral range. The exciting result he reports is that the more emotional the picture shown to the subject at a *later* time, the greater in magnitude is the subject's response *before* he or she sees the picture. Radin reports this "dose dependent" correlation with regard to the published intensity of the card's impact to be significant at odds greater than 100 to one. Professor Dick Bierman at Utrecht University in Holland has successfully replicated Radin's findings. But he had to assemble a much more "extreme" set of pictures in order to excite his rather more blasé Amsterdam college students psychically.

We would say that this is a case in which your direct physical perception of the picture, when it occurs, causes you to have a unique physical response at an earlier time. Your future is affecting your past. William Braud, in his excellent book *Distant Mental Influence*, describes these experiments as follows.

Although this presentiment effect is usually taken to reflect precognition (future-knowing) operating at an unconscious body level, these interesting findings can just as well be interpreted as instances in which objective events (the presentation of the slide itself, or the person's future reaction to the slide) may be acting backward in time to influence the person's physiology.[10]

Even stronger results have been obtained by physicists Edwin May and James Spottiswoode, who measure galvanic skin response of subjects who are about to hear a loud noise from time to time in earphones. Again, measurements show that one's nervous system seems to know in advance when it will be assaulted with a disagreeable stimulus.

But the most significant evidence for this so-called pre-stimulus response comes from the Hungarian researcher Zoltán Vassy. In his experiments, he administered painful electric shocks as the psychic stimulus to be precognized. His results are by far the strongest of all, because the human body does not ever habituate to electric shocks. They are always experienced as a new and alarming stimulus, even though the shock resides in your future.[11] Whereas, after I heard a few loud-noise stimuli in May's experiment, my body quickly habituated and realized that the noise was not actually going to hurt me, so I become much more meditative than vigilant—causing a decline in the pre-stimulus response. This reaction may be unique to me, because I am both a researcher and an experienced meditator. But nobody snoozes through an electric shock.

Feeling the Future

Daryl Bem is a brilliant, imaginative and humorous psychology professor at Cornell University. He is also an accomplished practitioner of magic. I am happy to consider him a good friend over the decades I have enjoyed his company. After several years of comfortable tenure investigating perceptual psychology at Cornell University, Professor Bem has recently been devoting himself to a detailed study of precognition and premonition in the laboratory. He is deeply inquisitive and has an almost unlimited supply of undergraduate students to act as subjects for his experiments. Over a period of several years, Bem carried out nine formal experiments to examine how our present feelings and choices can be affected by things that happen to us *at a later time.* For example, a man deciding which of two sisters to marry might have the feeling that although one potential bride, Sue, is much prettier than her sister, in his gut he can already feel that the other, Sarah, will make him happier in the future. We might chalk this up to good judgment. Or we could say that it is the future calling to him. Bem shows us how to find out which is the case.[12]

All nine of Bem's experiments involve one hundred to two hundred college students, each of whom have to make a choice of which of two video screens to select based on something they will see at a later time. But the students are not aware of this future component. Sometimes they will be subliminally precognitive about getting what they *want* in the future. And sometimes the images require them to be psychic about avoiding what they *don't want* to happen.

In Bem's first experiment, secretly called "Detect Erotic," students are asked to volunteer for an ESP experiment for which they will either be paid or receive a unit of college credit. The students think this is a familiar type of ESP experiment in which you have to guess which one of two screens will show you a picture after you press a button. One screen will offer an interesting colored picture, while the other screen will open the digital curtains to show a blank screen. That's what the students expect, and that's what the experimental setup looks like. In reality, there are three types of pictures available—erotic, neutral, or negative. We all know what erotic pictures are. The neutral pictures are flowers and coffee cups. And negative pictures can comprise car crashes or abdominal surgery, etc. But what the students don't know is that the location of the picture will be randomly chosen *after* they make their selection. *And* that the choice of which of the three types of photo will also be randomly chosen after their button press. Thus, at the time of their button press, neither the picture nor its location has been determined. The not-too-surprising result shows that undergraduate college students are much more successful at finding the location of the erotic stimuli than they are at finding coffee cups or car crashes. In fact, the random erotic stimuli were correctly located significantly more often than either of the other types of pictures—statistically significant at odds of one hundred to one. And the students who were rated as "extraverted" found the erotic picture 57 percent of the time, at odds of almost ten thousand to one. As I mentioned earlier, extroverts always do better in ESP tests.

I will describe one other of Bem's experiments, this one about *avoidance*. In this case there were also a hundred students. But the task didn't even look like an ESP test. Each subject had thirty-two trials in which he or she briefly (for 32 milliseconds) saw a pair of neutral pictures, each being the mirror image of the other. The student's task was simply to press a key indicating , as it was put, "the picture you like better." After the student's choice, the "correct" target picture was then determined by a random-number generator. If the student preferred the "incorrect" picture, they were shown "a highly arousing *negative* picture." This was flashed three times for 33 milliseconds. The students were highly successful in avoiding the negative pictures, at odds of 7 in 1000. And again the extraverts were more than twice as successful—avoiding the nasty pictures at odds of 2 in 1000 ($P = 0.002$).

Perhaps the most interesting of Bem's nine experiments is one that shows the importance of studying for an exam after you have taken it. That is, after you take a test, make sure to find the answers to all your unanswered questions. Bem showed each of his students a list of forty-eight words for three seconds for each word. Then they were asked to write down all the words they could remember. That's the test. After the test the students were shown half the words again, and told to write them down and sort them into animal, vegetable, and mineral. You will be interested to know that in the first phase of the test the words studied *after* the test were recalled at odds of 500 to 1 better than the words that were seen only once. This is Bem's "Retro Recall II." It seems to me that good students know this intuitively. And feel drawn to find out the correct answers.

Ben carried out seven other variations on this theme. Two trials involved what he calls *retroactive priming*. That is, he gives his subject a clue to the right answer, subliminally, *after* they have made a choice. We know that subliminal information or pictures in the movie theater can interest you in buying popcorn or Coke. In these experiments Bem asked the subjects to express their feelings about two very similar pictures that they briefly viewed—expressing their opinion as to whether a picture was pleasant or unpleasant. *After* the students had made their choice, in one experiment they saw subliminally the word *beautiful* and in the other the word *ugly*. In both experiments, the students' opinions were significantly colored by the words flashed *after* they had made their choices.

The simple description of all these experiments is that they are demonstrations of how the future affects the past. Bem's overall significance for this series of experiments is more than *a billion to one*. (In other words, the odds that the results were due to chance were only one in a billion.) I show the meta-analysis summary results of his experimental series in table 5.

Experiment	Number of trials	Probability
Detect Erotic	100	.01
Avoid Negative	150	.009
Retro Priming I	97	.007
Retro Priming II	99	.014
Retro Habituation I	100	.014
Retro Habituation II	150	.009
Retro Boredom	200	.096
Retro Recall I	100	.029
Retro Recall II	50	.002

Table 5. Summary of Daryl Bem's nine precognition experiments. Statistical significance for the nine experimental series is 6.6 standard deviation from chance; $P = 1.34 \times 10^{-11}$. And the odds against chance are 74,370,383,777 to 1 (74 billion to one)!

Bem's sixty-page paper documents his hugely significant accomplishment and shows that not only can the future be known and felt, which is why he calls his paper "Feeling the Future," but, more than that, in the right hands these experiments can be replicated with great success over a long period of time. This paper is one in a family of research approaches that show that psi is neither weak nor illusive—a very important finding, indeed.

MX Missile Detection with Associative Remote Viewing

One might ask whether in the information generated in the SRI program of remote viewing there was ever sufficient significance to influence decisions at a policy level. This is of course impossible to determine unless policymakers were to come forward with a statement in the affirmative. One example of a possible candidate is a study we performed at SRI during the Carter administration debates concerning proposed deployment of the mobile MX Missile System. In that scenario, to avoid detection missiles were to be randomly shuffled from silo to silo in a silo field, in a form of a high-tech shell game.

In a computer simulation of a twenty-silo field with randomly assigned (hidden) missile locations, we were able to show rather forcefully that the application of a sophisticated statistical-averaging technique could in principle permit an adversary to defeat the system. In this experiment we used information generated by associative remote viewing as well as sequential sampling, just as we had in the silver-futures forecasting described earlier. Hal Puthoff briefed the results to the appropriate offices at their request, and a written report with the technical details was widely circulated among groups responsible for threat analysis—and with some impact. What role, if any, our contribution played in the mix of factors behind the enormously complex decision to cancel the multi-billion dollar program will probably never be known and must of course be considered *a priori* negligible. Nonetheless, this is a prototypical example of the kind of tasking we did at SRI, which by its nature had potential policy implications.[13] In plain English, it is my understanding that our demonstration of an ability to locate their simulated hidden MX missiles psychically scared the hell out of the Office of Technology Assessment. Ingo Swann was the remote viewer, and three months later the silo shell-game program was killed.

Thus far I have been writing about *transcendent knowing*—the inflow of psychically derived information. But there is another important part of our nonlocal capabilities that I call *transcendent doing*. This is the out-flow of your healing intention. In the next chapter I will describe some of the best and most convincing research supporting both the idea and practice of distant healing and distant mental influence of any sort, whether it be by energy healing, spiritual healing, or just affecting the physiology of a distant person.

Our ignorance about healing vastly exceeds our understanding.
Some people see this mystery as a good thing.

—Larry Dossey, MD

8

Mental Influence and Healing from a Distance

Why do I believe in ESP? Why would you come to believe in ESP? How do we become certain of anything? Beyond my lab experience I have had two very compelling experiences to bolster my belief, neither of which has a probability number associated with it. Would you be more convinced that something "psychic" had happened if (a) you were at a party holding a foot-long, three-eighths thick aluminum rod that you couldn't possibly bend, and, after a little chanting and meditating, it melted like a noodle in your hand; or (b) you were sick in bed with a month-long debilitating mystery ailment diagnosed by CAT scans as cancer, and a compassionate healer came to your bedside and said some comforting words like, "Those are just spots on the film. They don't actually mean you're sick!"—and suddenly all your symptoms disappeared! Which of these experiences would make you a believer? Both happened to me, and I continue to find it a tough decision. I still have that bent aluminum rod on my desk, and I am alive twenty years after the hospital was ready to start chemotherapy on my ailment.

In this chapter I will explore some questions regarding healing and the nature of distant mental influence in the laboratory, in which the thoughts of one person have a measurable effect on the physiology (heart rate, skin resistance, etc.) of another person. And I will relate that phenomenon to the evidence we have for distant healing. To do so, two critical questions must be answered: First, what is the best evidence that the thoughts of one person can actually affect or heal the physical body of a distant person? The second and equally important question pertains to the expectations of the healee or patient. If we are convinced that we are equal measures of *body*, *mind*, and *spirit*, then which of these elements do we hope the healer will affect? The answer we find most congenial will probably depend upon whether we are working with a known psychic healer, an energy healer, a spiritual healer, or someone entirely different.

The charismatic German physician Franz Mesmer marked the first appearance of a healer to be scientifically studied in the Western world. He was, in 1779, the first person systematically to investigate hypnosis and the healing of a person purely through the *intentions* of another. Although this sort of healing had been going on since the dawn of humankind, it appears that Mesmer was the first doctor to recognize and describe the importance of strong rapport and a mind-to-mind connection with his patients. He achieved this connection through the use of rhythmic "magnetic" passes over their bodies until they became entranced—often for more than an hour. Mesmer also was the first to conjecture that psychological trauma might be related to, or be the cause of, physical illness. His methodology, and hence the word *mesmerism*, was the origination of hypnosis for medical applications.

Of course, people have always recognized that certain individuals in their midst possessed a special gift for healing. The founders of the world's great religions—Buddha, Jesus, and Muhammad—were all reported to have been gifted healers. Jesus was the best known of all spiritual healers, and under his inspiration the first generations of Christians practiced healing in community.[1]

What Can We Do with Our Minds?

When I think of what we call *mindfulness* as an activity, I am aware of three distinctly different opportunities. First, there is the *in-flow* of information that we have been describing thus far in this book. This in-flow is what we call *nonlocal awareness, remote viewing*, or, more accurately, *remote sensing*. When we investigate this activity scientifically, over the past forty years we have become increasingly skillful in assisting people to have accurate and reliable psychic experiences—perceptions of distant and future objects, events, and people.

Secondly, there is the possibility of experiencing the *out-flow* of healing intention, or other interactions with the outside physical world—often called *psychokinesis* (PK). This latter can also be associated with affecting the fall of dice, moving a small object on the table top, or even affecting the behavior of a computer. In scientific investigations, the data for remote sensing or perception is very strong, similar to the typical results from ordinary experiments in perceptual psychology as Daryl Bem's experiments show (see chapter 7). The results in distant healing can also be very strong if the experiment is well conceived and executed—that is, if one does everything as well as possible. (My daughter Elisabeth Targ's highly successful healing experiment with AIDS patients described later would be an example of such an experiment.) But taken as a group, laboratory or hospital experiments are quite variable. Consequently, most researchers agree that there is strong evidence for various kinds of distant and spiritual healing, but the results depend strongly on who is doing it. On the other hand, the evidence for laboratory psychokinesis—moving objects—is quite weak. To obtain a given level of statistical significance in a PK experiment requires approximately a hundred times the number of trials that a typical remote viewing experiment does, my rod bending notwithstanding. We would say that the *effect size* for general ESP is ten times the *effect size* for PK.

The third element of mindfulness is not about doing *anything*. It is the opportunity to move awareness from our ordinary conditioned state centered in the ego and judgment to a state of spacious and joyful naked or timeless awareness, often described as being in the now, where we experience the world as it is—free of our conditioning. I describe this at some length in chapter 12.

Hypnosis from a Thousand Miles Away

Leonid Leonidovich Vasiliev was a pioneering Soviet psychology and physiology researcher in the early part of the twentieth century. He specialized in treatment of hysterical symptoms by means of hypnosis. However, he was alternately in and out of favor with the ruling Stalinist regime. When he was supported by Stalin, he was director of the Leningrad Institute for Brain Research, founded by his teacher V. M. Bekhterev to investigate hypnosis for the treatment of hysterical illnesses. Then for a time in the early 1930s his research was considered too spiritual, and he was out of work. But by 1933 Vasiliev was back at his old institute with a proper materialist program to investigate the effects of electromagnetic shielding on the induction of hypnosis.

Vasiliev's principle interest had always been the use of hypnosis for the induction of sleep. The signature of the typical stage hypnotist is the performer who starts his induction with the famous words, "You are feeling sleepy. . . . Your eyelids are getting very heavy." As reported in his book, Vasiliev was surprised to find that his best hypnotic subjects would sometimes drop off into a hypnotic sleep when he only *thought* these words.[2] His most famous later experiments involved the induction of sleep and wakefulness at greater and greater distances, up to many miles from his hypnotic subject. After a number of initial experiments in distant sleep with blindfolded subjects in the laboratory and home-bound patients watched by their landladies, he began formal experiments with subjects under tight laboratory controls such as we might use today.

Vasiliev constructed a steel test chamber about six feet on a side, lined with lead, and sealed with a trough filled with mercury to examine the effects of strict electromagnetic shielding. The wakefulness of a subject inside the chamber was determined by Vasiliev asking her to squeeze a rubber bulb each time she took a breath. The pressurized air blown out of the bulb was conveyed by a copper tube through the chamber wall to a pneumatic recording device that would mark a chart each time the woman squeezed the bulb. (The pneumatic tube was used because wires to the outside would destroy the electrical integrity of the chamber.) Vasiliev describes as "exceptional hypnotic subjects" two of his hysterical medical patients, Ivanova and Fedorova. While under hypnosis, they could accurately draw what he was drawing and even taste substances that he was tasting. He describes these women as "particularly suitable for our purposes."

He then climbed into a second shielded enclosure in a distant room. On a preset schedule, he would visualize and powerfully will his patient either to fall asleep or to wake up from sleeping. He observed that within a few seconds to a minute after his mental induction began, the marking of the chart would cease; and then at the appropriate time he would attempt to awaken the sleeping subject and the marks on the moving chart would begin again—indicating that she had indeed awakened and had resumed squeezing the bulb. Vasiliev repeated these experiments in many variations and demonstrated them to the USSR Academy of Sciences. His great excitement over these results stemmed from the fact that the onset of sleep or awakening did not differ at all, with or without electrical shielding. This showed conclusively that the medium of telepathic transmission could *not* be any known form of electromagnetic waves, because the shielding did not affect the reliability of the psychic connection. If there had been an electromagnetic component, then putting the subject in a cage would have decreased the appearance of psi functioning.

Vasiliev's lasting fame rests on his long-distance hypnosis trials, in which he ruled out any possibility of sensory leakage to his subjects. In these experiments, his research partner Professor Tomashevsky was sent to Sevastopol, a thousand miles from Leningrad, to be the telepathic sender. While there, during prearranged, two-hour experimental periods, he would exert his will as an experienced hypnotist to create a controlling influence on the subject back in the laboratory. The actual times of sleep and awakening were blind (unknown) to any of the Leningrad observers. Their watches were synchronized with Radio Moscow, and the observed times of sleep and awakening for these well-trained hypnotic subjects *were again within one minute* of the onset of the sender's mental influence. An accidental control trial was inserted, as the sender was ill one day. Thus there was no hypnotic intention in Sevastopol, and no appearance of hypnotic induction was observed during the entire two-hour experimental period in Leningrad.

As a scientist reading Vasiliev's remarkable book in the 1960s, I have often reflected on the haunting image of his patients, sick female subjects, some partially paralyzed, huddled in his dark steel cubical, obediently squeezing their little rubber bulbs, waking and falling asleep like little birds, as the walls of the chamber exuded a toxic miasma of mercury vapor from their seams. (Some day there will be a movie.) But there is no doubt that his three decades of careful research provide convincing evidence that the thoughts of one person can indeed affect the behavior of another person at a distance—showing that thoughts are efficacious, nonlocal, and existentially as real as anything else. I believe that the rather disturbing and complex domination of the will described here occurs only between an experienced hypnotist and his completely cooperative, experienced, and submissive subject. But I could be wrong.

These experiments coming to us from early in the last century may appear voodoo-like, or even shocking, by modern research standards. However, to this physicist, the observation that the efficacy of the mind-to-mind connection is independent of both distance and electromagnetic shielding sounds remarkably contemporary and simply like another nonlocal connection. Presenting the most modern view on this subject, the eminent physicist Henry Stapp of the University of California, Berkeley, writes:

> The new physics presents *prima facie* evidence that our human thoughts are linked to nature by nonlocal connections: What a person chooses to do in one region seems immediately to affect what is true elsewhere in the universe. This nonlocal aspect can be understood by conceiving the universe to be not a collection of tiny bits of matter, but rather a growing compendium of "bits of information." . . . And, I believe that most quantum physicists will also agree that our conscious thoughts ought eventually to be understood within science and that when properly understood, our thoughts will be seen to DO something: They will be efficacious [emphasis in original].[3]

Direct Recording of ESP at a Distance

In more modern times many investigators have sought for a more reliable and sensitive way to demonstrate that the thoughts of one person can directly affect the autonomic physiology of a distant person. Observing a correlated change in a distant person's heart rate or skin resistance is a much more objective and convincing indication of thought transference than a telepathic response, which has to be

mediated through the receiver's conscious awareness and then verbally reported or drawn.

Two years after the publication of Vasiliev's book in English, chem-
ist Douglas Dean, at the Newark College of Engineering, showed
conclusively that the autonomic nervous systems of subjects in his
laboratory directly responded to the thoughts of a distant person.[4]
Douglas was a charming and open-hearted Englishman who worked
tirelessly to achieve recognition for parapsychology research. He was
the person most responsible (along with Margaret Mead) for getting
the Parapsychological Association, of which he was the president, accepted with full standing into the prestigious American Association
for the Advancement of Science (AAAS) in 1969. It is also a little-
known fact, discovered by Stephan Schwartz, that Dean and his English Quaker group were awarded a Nobel Peace Prize for their tireless
work with displaced persons and refugees in the aftermath of World
War II.

In Dean's 1965 telepathy experiments, participants lay quietly on a
cot in a darkened room in his lab at the Newark College of Engineering, while an optical plethysmograph—a small light bulb and a photo
cell—recorded changes in the blood volume of one of their fingers,
which is a measure of autonomic nervous system activity. In these
highly repeatable experiments, the "sender" was seated in another
room at a wooden class-room table. At a signal from a light flash, he
would look at randomly ordered cards with names on them, at the
rate of one card each minute. The autonomic activity of the distant
"receiver" person connected to the plethysmograph was observed to
increase markedly when the sender focused attention on cards with
names the percipient had contributed as having personal or emotional significance for him (mother, wife, sweetheart, stockbroker, etc.)
as compared with random, phone-book names contributed by Dean.
While the receiver's heartbeats were registered one by one, he was

unaware of when, during the course of a twenty-minute session, the significant names were being observed for a minute by the sender. The receiver person is totally passive in this experiment. In the late 1960s I visited Dean, and he showed me data from some of his best subjects, where the difference between the two conditions was often so strong that the changes in pulse shape on the recording chart—due to an exciting stimulus card—could be often directly and easily observed, without any sophisticated analysis or averaging required.

The Best Evidence for Distant Mental Influence

Dr. William Braud at the Institute of Transpersonal Psychology (ITP) in Palo Alto, California, has worked for more than three decades to achieve an understanding of what we can loosely call "distant mental influence." Braud, often collaborating with Dr. Marilyn Schlitz—now president and CEO of the Institute of Noetic Science (IONS) in Petaluma, California—carried out dozens of experiments investigating the ability of a person to directly influence the subtle psychological behavior of people in distant rooms, using mental means alone. These experiments included efforts to remotely influence a person's blood pressure as well as his or her state of relaxation, as measured by the electrical resistance changes of the skin (*galvanic skin response*, or GSR). Other studies involved trying to increase the rate of activity of gerbils running on a wheel and influencing the spontaneous swimming direction of small electric knife fish (a kind of carp). All these experiments examining mental influence at a distance were successful, and, most importantly, they were repeatable.[5]

Braud believed that living or *labile* systems or creatures that already exhibit some level of activity are easier to move or affect than systems at rest, which exhibit a high degree of *inertia*. This idea is a kind of psychological statement of Newton's third law, which says that objects in motion tend to stay in motion, while objects at rest tend to remain at rest. Dr. J. B. Rhine, in his efforts to demonstrate mental influence in the 1940s, had also recognized that it is easier to affect the trajectory of falling dice than it is to levitate dice that are resting on the table.

Braud believed that if the creatures were not labile enough, or too sluggish, it might be too difficult to get them started. If an animal's normal behavior is very near the activity ceiling, then the animal may be showing nearly all the action you can expect from it. For instance, a gerbil would be a better target than a snail or a slug, or a hummingbird or a bee. It would be very hard to get the snail's attention and similarly difficult to increase the activity level of the hummingbird.

Braud's highly successful work generally involved increasing and decreasing the degree of relaxation of people at a distant location. But one of his most important experiments involved trying to aid threatened red blood cells psychically. In all his other experiments with living systems, the creature (even a goldfish) had a level of consciousness that could, in principle, be affected by a distant person.[6] In the blood cell experiments, subjects in the laboratory were asked to influence the behavior of red cells, which to the best of our knowledge have not shown any independent consciousness. In these studies, the cells were put into test tubes of distilled water, which is a toxic environment for them. If the salt content of the solution deviates too much from that of blood plasma, the cell wall weakens and the contents of the cell spills into the solution. This unfortunate situation is dispassionately called *hemolysis*. The degree of hemolysis is easily measured, since the transmission of light through a solution containing intact blood cells is much less than through a solution of dissolved cells. A spectrophotometer is used to measure the light transmission as a function of time during the experiment.

The hemolysis experiments were a series with thirty-two different subjects; twenty tubes of blood were compared for each person. The subjects, situated in a distant room, had the task of attempting to save from aqueous destruction the little sanguineous corpuscles in ten of the target tubes. The blood cells in the ten control tubes had to fend for themselves. Braud found that the people working as remote healers were significantly able to retard the hemolysis of the blood in the tubes they were trying to protect.[7] These important experiments demonstrated a case in which the mind of the subject/healer was able to interact with a living system directly and in which one could not reasonably say that the result was due to the placebo effect or a charming bedside manner. Another striking finding in these experiments was that the participants who produced the most statistically significant results were even more successful in protecting their *own* blood cells than they were at preserving the life of cells that came from another person.

This result is open to interpretation. It may be that if psychic functioning is viewed as a kind of resonance, it is as though one is more in resonance with a part of himself than with a part of someone else. In his book *Distant Mental Influence*, Braud summarizes this idea by writing:

Concisely stated, the evidence compiled . . . indicates that, under certain conditions, it is possible to *know and to influence* the thoughts, images, feelings, behaviors, and physiological and physical activities of other persons and living organisms—even when the influencer and the influenced are separated by great distances in space and time, beyond the reach of the conventional senses.[8]

Is It Mind to Mind, or Mind to Body?

Additional studies by Braud and Schlitz showed that if a person simply *attended fully* to a distant person whose physiological activity was being monitored, he or she could influence that person's autonomic galvanic skin responses (electrical skin resistance). In four separate experimental series comprising seventy-eight sessions, the active participant sat in her own little office cubicle and stared intently—now and then according to a set of randomized instructions—at a closed-circuit TV monitor image of the distant person. This intermittent staring was enough to influence significantly the remote person's electrodermal (GSR) responses. The staree simply sat quietly under the TV lights, resting or meditating with her eyes closed. No intentional focusing or mental imaging techniques were used by the influencer, other than staring at the staree's image on the video screen during randomly interspersed staring and nonstaring control periods. Those being stared at were totally unaware of when these actions were taking place.

In these studies, Braud and Schlitz also discovered that the most anxious and introverted people being stared at had the greatest magnitudes of unconscious electrodermal responses. In other words, the more shy and introverted people reacted with significantly more stress to being stared at than did the sociable and extroverted people. Much of Braud's most successful work was centered on his trying to further relax the distant resting subjects. This experiment gives scientific validation to the common human experience of feeling stared at and turning around to find that someone is, indeed, staring at you.[9]

Under the direction of physicist Edwin May at the US government-funded laboratory of Science Applications International Corporation (SAIC) in Menlo Park, California, Marilyn Schlitz and Stephen La-Berge successfully replicated Braud's and colleagues' experiments, making some interesting changes in the protocol. In 1993, they again measured the extent to which people unconsciously sense the telepathic influence of a distant person who is looking at their video image. That is to say, there is a systematic change in their skin resistance or heart rate. As before, the two participants were only briefly acquainted. However, Schlitz's and LaBerge's work differed from the previous work by Schlitz and Braud in significant ways: For one thing, in these new studies the observer was instructed to *try to excite or startle* the person at whose video image they were staring, whereas before the influencers had been instructed simply to stare at the video image without trying to influence the staree directly. And secondly, in the Schlitz and LaBerge experiment the influencers were specifically trying to increase the stress response of the recipient.[10] It is worth noting that, by this time, Dr. May had brought in $14 million in government funds to support the ongoing psychical research. Our government continued to be really interested in the research. I think it is likely that men have known about this phenomenon since the time of the ancient Greeks; namely, that if a man stares at the back of a woman's head in a theater, she will usually turn around and look at him.

Dr. May has another explanation for many of these apparent distant mental-influence phenomena. Since we have often seen evidence of robust precognition in the laboratory, isn't it possible that we have the ability to make decisions based on data we obtain precognitively—decisions such as when to start an experiment, or whom to put in which group? Ed May calls this approach the Decision Augmentation Technique (DAT). Other researchers have called it Intuitive Data Selection. For example, if you are trying to show that your new medicine is effective, you could psychically choose the people who are going to get sick and put them in your control group, and then choose the people who are going to get better and put them in the therapeutic group. And voila, your medicine is proven effective. This kind of intuitive data selection is not cheating. It is a way of psychically enhancing your experimental outcome, whether in medicine or in ESP research. The presence of DAT doesn't show that there isn't any ESP at work. Rather, it shows that one can mistakenly claim causality or healing, when the real answer is precognition. This is an increasingly important concern as it becomes harder and harder to demonstrate the efficacy of psychotropic medications for depression and the like.

What Can We Say about Spoon Bending?

Uri Geller, the Israeli magician and psychic, visited our laboratory at SRI in the winter of 1972. Geller was a delightful guest and was unusually kind and patient with my little children who clamored for his attention. Many people think that Geller is a total fraud and that he fooled us with his tricks. But that is not true. We had more SRI technical and management oversight of our experiments with Uri than in any other phase of our research. Hal Puthoff and I found that in carefully controlled experiments Uri could psychically perceive and copy pictures that an artist and I would randomly select and draw in an opaque and electrically shielded room. Geller's excellent drawings appear in our technical paper in *Nature* and in our book *Mind Reach*.[11] If we consider Geller's picture drawing experiments to be a kind of remote viewing, we could say that Geller was an excellent remote viewer—but by no means the best we saw at SRI.

We have widely reported that Uri did not bend any metal at SRI. And for two decades I denigrated the whole spoon-bending craze as a kind of silliness. However, a few years ago I saw some metal bending that has changed my mind. Our friend Jack Hauk is an aeronautical engineer at McDonnell Douglas. He conducts spoon-bending parties that he calls "PK (psychokinesis) parties." At these events he guides and cheers partygoers on to summon up their supposed psychic abilities and cause spoons to bend. I have seen lots of bent spoons but never anything that appeared either significant or paranormal at these parties—at least, not until 1999.

In our continuing search for large-scale psychokinesis, Jack Hauk and I got together at a Palo Alto ballroom where we were attempting to videotape paranormal metal bending: an effort that almost always ends in failure. As we were cleaning up after another disappointing event, we heard a shriek from the corner of the ballroom. It was my friend Jane Katra, the spiritual healer. She had been sitting quietly meditating with a stainless-steel teaspoon thrust into her fist, when suddenly the spoon came alive in her hand and shocked her out of her reverie. She described the experience as suddenly feeling that there was a cricket wiggling against the palm of her hand: that's what made her scream. As several of us rushed over to see what had happened, we saw her staring at a very strange-looking spoon. While in her hand, *the bowl of the spoon* had curled or rolled up 180 degrees toward the handle. We photographed the spoon and put it into a plastic bag. By the time we reached home, the spoon had rolled up to 270 degrees and now looked like a little Nautilus or snail shell. That is, the actual *bowl* of the spoon, not the handle, is what had rolled up. I can think of no way, by manual force or laboratory technology, that anyone could have accomplished this—certainly not Jane, who has small-boned little hands that have been bruised just by cutting roses.

A month later Jane and I had an opportunity to attend a second PK party. This time I was successful in rising to the occasion and bending a 3/8 inch, foot-long aluminum rod by about thirty degrees, as I mentioned in the chapter opening. As I sat with my eyes closed, meditating and holding the bar at its ends in my finger tips (to avoid accidental unconscious force being applied) the bar just became springy in my hands and bent! I brought an identical bar home for my two athletic sons to try and bend. Neither of those tall, strong oarsmen could bend it at all.

I am not relating these stories to indicate any special psychic prowess on Jane's or my part. Rather, I think it is important finally to report that there *is* such a thing as paranormal metal bending, and that it doesn't require Uri Geller to do it. The corollary to this truth is that if we can bend metal at a PK party, then it is quite likely that Geller, who started this craze, can do it also. The fact that a stage magician can do mental magic or phony spoon bending on the Johnny Carson show does not mean that these things do not actually exist.

Distant Healing in Clinical Settings

Medical researcher Dr. Daniel Benor examined over 150 controlled studies from around the world and described them in his 1992 book, *Healing Research*. He reviewed psychic, mental, and spiritual healing experiments done on a variety of living organisms, including enzymes, cell cultures, bacteria, yeasts, plants, animals, and humans. More than half of the studies demonstrate significant healing.[12]

In December 1998, the *Western Journal of Medicine* published a landmark distant healing study by Fred Sicher and my daughter, psychiatrist Elisabeth Targ. In this mainstream medical journal, they described healing research carried out at the California Pacific Medical Center (CPMC) that details and describes the positive therapeutic effects of distant healing, or *healing intentionality*, on men with advanced AIDS. The writers defined nonlocal or distant healing as "a conscious dedicated act of mentation intended to benefit another person's physical and/or emotional well-being at a distance," adding that "it has been found in some form in nearly every culture since prehistoric time."[13] Their research hypothesized that an intensive, ten-week distant healing intervention by experienced healers located around the United States would benefit the medical outcomes for a population of advanced AIDS patients in the San Francisco area.

To test this hypothesis, the researchers performed two separate, randomized, double-blind studies: a pilot study involving twenty male subjects—ten were prayed for and ten were controls—all stratified by number of AIDS-defining illnesses (cancer, pneumonia, etc.); and a replication study of forty men carefully matched into pairs by age, T-cell count, and number of AIDS-defining illnesses. The participants' conditions were assessed by psychometric testing and blood testing at three points in time: at their enrollment; after the distant healing intervention; and six months later, when physicians reviewed their medical charts. In this pilot study, four of the ten control subjects *died*, while all ten subjects in the treatment group survived. This result, however, was possibly confounded by unequal age distributions in the two groups (a possible instance of DAT).

A replication study was carried out six months later. In it, forty men with AIDS were again recruited from the San Francisco Bay Area. They were told that they had a fifty-fifty chance of being in the treatment group or the control group. All subjects were carefully pair-matched for age, CD4 count, and AIDS-defining diseases. Forty distant healers from all parts of the country took part in the study. Each of them had more than ten years experience in their particular form of healing. They were from Christian, Jewish, Buddhist, Native American, and shamanic traditions—in addition to secular "bio-energetic" schools. Each patient in the healing group was treated by a total of ten different healers on a rotating healing schedule. Healers were asked to work on their assigned subject for approximately one hour per day for six consecutive days, with instructions to "direct an intention of health and well-being" to the subject to which they were attending. None of the forty subjects in the study ever met the healers, nor did they or the experimenters know into which group anyone had been randomized.

By the midpoint of the study, neither group of subjects was able to guess significantly whether or not they were in the healing group. However, by the end of the study, there were many fewer opportunistic illnesses in the healing group, allowing it to be able to identify itself, with significant odds against what one would expect by chance! Since all subjects were being treated with triple-drug therapy, there were no deaths in either group. The treatment group experienced significantly better medical and quality-of-life outcomes (at odds of 100 to 1 against chance) on many quantitative measures, including fewer outpatient doctor visits (185 vs. 260); fewer days of hospitalization (10 vs. 68); less severe illnesses acquired during the study, as measured by illness-severity scores (16 vs. 43); and significantly less emotional distress. In her summary, Elisabeth Targ concludes, "Decreased hospital visits, fewer severe new diseases, and greatly improved subjective health support the hypothesis of positive therapeutic effects of distant healing."[14] The editor of the journal introduced the paper thus:

> The paper published below is meant to advance science and debate. It has been reviewed, revised, and re-reviewed by nationally known experts in biostatistics, and complementary medicine. . . . We have chosen to publish this provocative paper to stimulate other studies of distant healing, and other complementary practices and agents. It is time for more light, less dark, less heat.[15]

Two other significant papers dealing with distant healing were published in prestigious medical journals at about the same time. In 1988 physician Randolph Byrd published in the *Southern Medical Journal* a successful double-blind demonstration of distant healing. The study involved 393 cardiac patients at San Francisco General Hospital.[16] And in 1999, cardiologist William Harris of the University of Missouri in Kansas City published a similar successful study with 990 heart patients.[17]

The outcomes of all three clinical experiments departed significantly from chance expectation. However, it is very important to note that the work of Sicher and Targ required fewer than *one tenth* the number of patients to achieve this significance. One possible explanation for this greater *effect size* $(Z/N^{1/2})$ is that Sicher and Targ worked with healers who each had more than ten years of healing experience, whereas the others worked with well-intentioned but much less experienced people.[18]

Another important paper is a detailed analysis of twenty-three clinical studies of intercessory prayer and distant healing has recently been published by John Astin et al. in the *Annals of Internal Medicine*.[19] They found sixteen studies to have adequate double-blind designs. Their examination of them showed a relatively sizable effect size of 0.4, with an overall significance of one in ten thousand for 2139 patients. In addition, two excellent analyses of the mechanisms for distant intentionality and distant healing studies have been published in *Alternative Therapies*, one by Marilyn Schlitz and William Braud and the other by Elisabeth Targ.[20]

I have to end this chapter with a cautionary note. In the past few years there have been two multimillion-dollar studies of the efficacy of prayer for recovering cardiac patients carried out at major university hospitals. One was the so-called MANTRA (Monitoring and Actualization of Noetic TRAinings) study at Duke University led by Dr. Mitchell Krucoff. The other, known as the Harvard Prayer Study, was under the direction of Drs. Krucoff and Herbert Benson, who popularized "The Relaxation Response." Both of these large studies received significant publicity from national media (especially the *New York Times*), which cited with ridicule and sarcasm the programs' failure to show that intercessory prayer had any benefit to surgical patients.

Before the MANTRA program began, I heard Dr. Krucoff give a talk to about fifty researchers at the Institute of Noetic Sciences, where he described his forthcoming study. He told us that all the healers were to be self-selected members of his own church, not at all chosen for their healing experience or potential. He called this "congregational prayer." I argued from the floor that the most successful studies in healing research had worked with very experienced healers—in Elisabeth's case, for instance, the healers had had decades of experience. Dr. Krucoff replied perplexingly that "the medical model required universality of application."

Dr. Larry Dossey, renowned expert and author of many books on nonlocal intercessory prayer, wrote a journal article dealing with this issue. He says concerning healing prayer experiments: "*Democratizing healing abilities is a noble effort, but the evidence so far suggests that this often results in marginal, or non-significant results* [emphasis added]."[21] Thus my final word on this subject is that, if you are sick and need a healer, find one who has done it before.

Alternative Therapies

In the healing literature, I have found many different holistic and imaginative paths offering promising treatments for cancer. Some researchers described remarkable cures from the use of Laetrile from peach pits. There were opportunities for coffee enemas in Mexico and a healing retreat in the Alps run by the followers of Rudolf Steiner, where the doctors played string quartets for the patients after dinner. A highly regarded healing center in Texas was operated by Dr. Carl Simonton, who reported many remarkable cures of patients who took an active part in their healing through the use of self-healing visualizations.[22]

In California, the Commonweal Foundation offered a variety of supportive and nurturing therapies.[23] There was also the healing-imagery approach of Jean Achterberg.[24] One that seemed the most appealing to me had the patient picture in his mind the bad cancer cells being consumed by the good white blood cells. From the patient's point of view, the good news was that each of these approaches offered a few examples of people with very advanced cancer who followed these procedures and were cured. From the scientists' point of view, the bad news was that not a single one of these healing modalities came with any statistics describing what fraction of the very sick people who were treated actually survived. It looked as though coffee enemas, string quartets, and visualization could each claim *a few astonishing cures*, but the odds didn't look very good. Given the choice, if I had cancer again, I would probably go with the string quartets.

The only researcher who offered encouraging data was H. J. Eysenck in England, who was a pioneer in supportive therapy for cancer.[25] His treatment was similar to Dr. David Spiegel's Expressive-Supportive Therapy that appeared to be successful in helping women with breast cancer in research carried out at Stanford University.[26] Eysenck convincingly showed that people who were socially isolated, or who rarely expressed their emotions—especially the so-called negative ones of fear, anger, grief, or sadness—were significantly more likely to get cancer than emotionally expressive people. He found that repressed feelings were even more hazardous to your health than alcohol or cigarettes. To deal with these negative emotions, he created an approach that he called Creative Novation Therapy, in which he helped the patient to remake himself and change his attitudes and outlook on the world.

Surgeon William Nolan wrote a book entitled *Healing: Doctor in Search of a Miracle,* in which he describes one of his patients who had metastatic abdominal cancer that was so advanced and invasive that it was inoperable.[27] Nolan sewed the man up and sent him home, without telling him that he expected him to die shortly. A year later he saw the man shoveling snow outside his home in Buffalo where they both lived. Nolan was shocked to see the man alive. When the doctor asked the man about his health, the man thanked Nolan for taking such good care of him. He reported that he had been feeling fine ever since the operation. This miraculous cure stimulated Nolan to travel all over the world in search of other instances of spontaneous, nontraditional healing. He visited many famous healers and healing centers, but always came away disappointed. His book chronicles his unsuccessful search for nonmedical cures, although he still believed that his personal miracle had occurred because he had witnessed it himself.

The Institute of Noetic Sciences published a fascinating encyclopedic volume called *Spontaneous Remission*, which catalogues several hundred well-documented cases in which people recovered from metastatic cancer, despite having truly been at death's door. The following comment by Dr. Lewis Thomas is from the introduction of that book and summarizes this situation, which I consider to be the *outstanding research opportunity in medicine today.*

The rare but spectacular phenomenon of spontaneous remission of cancer persists in the annals of medicine, totally inexplicable but real, a hypothetical straw to clutch in the search for a cure. From time to time, patients turn up with far advanced cancer beyond the possibility of cure. They undergo exploratory surgery, the surgeon observes metastases throughout the peritoneal cavity and liver, and the patient is sent home to die, only to turn up again ten years later, free of disease and in good health. There are now several hundred such cases in world scientific literature, and no one doubts the validity of the observations.... But no one has the ghost of an idea how it happens.[28]

We now have, for the first time in the history of our species, compelling empirical evidence for belief in some form of personal survival after death.
—Robert Almeder, Professor of Philosophy,
Georgia State University

9

Evidence that Something Survives Bodily Death

In the introduction to this book I mentioned that with regard to ESP I am writing for both believers and skeptics. One of my recent guides has been the 2008 book *On Being Certain: Believing You Are Right Even When You Are Wrong,* by University of California neurologist, Robert Burton.[1] He writes in scary fashion about how we all delude ourselves from time to time with false memories, incorrect premises, faulty perception, or erroneous logic. In the first eight chapters of this book, I have limited my writing to cases of ESP in which I am as scientifically certain of the truth as it is possible to be. For example, I have no doubt whatsoever that we made $120,000 in the silver commodity markets using only psychic predictions and that our success wasn't due to a lucky nine weeks of guessing. As one skeptical broker said in a film on our exploits, "It's very hard to do anything in life successfully—nine times in a row."

In this chapter I will be writing about reincarnation and the survival of identity after bodily death. One of the many reasons that ESP researchers are interested in survival research is that it is evident that the discarnate entities—whatever they might be—communicate with us and with mediums through some kind of mental telepathy. The evidence that "something" survives is very strong. And it is clear that there is something seriously the matter with our understanding of the phenomenology of survival, because it seems that the surviving entities, or consciousnesses, must reside *outside* of conventional space-time. Nonetheless, the evidence for some kind of survival is compelling. I will describe several quite recent cases in which I have a personal connection, in addition to the historical people who set the stage for us.

For example, in his lifetime of research, psychiatrist Ian Stevenson at the University of Virginia has described many cases in which a child claims to remember an earlier life in another village or city. Indeed, the child is able to identify and *name* his "former" classmates from an old photo in the home of his "former" parents. And sometimes the child can demonstrate skills he had learned in his previous life. In a similar instance, witnessed by renowned psychologist and philosopher William James, a deceased New York lawyer appeared to a Boston medium and was able to identify and describe twenty-nine out of thirty of his old friends. At the end of this investigation, James wrote in Fredrick Myers' book *Human Personality and the Survival of Bodily Death*:

> My own conviction is not evidence, but it seems fitting to record it. I am persuaded of the medium's [Mrs. Piper's] honesty, and of the genuineness of her trance; and although at first disposed to think that the "hits" she made were either lucky coincidences, or the result of knowledge on her part as to who the sitter was and of his family affairs, I now believe her to be in the possession of a power yet to be explained.[2]

The Founding of the Society for Psychical Research

In 1882 a group of English scientists and philosophers at Cambridge University were forming the Society for Psychical Research (SPR).

One of the ringleaders of this distinguished group was the classicist, poet, and superintendent of English public schools, Frederic W. H. Myers. In the introduction to his monumental (1300-page) book, Myers writes:

> In the long story of man's endeavors to understand his own environment . . . there is one gap or omission, so singular that its simple statement has the air of a paradox. Yet it is strictly true to say that man has never yet applied the methods of modern science to the problem which most profoundly concerns him—whether or not his personality involves any elements which survive bodily death.[3]

In the hundred-plus years since Myers wrote those words, modern science has answered his plea and applied itself to the meticulous compilation of thousands of mediumistic communications, apparitions of the recently dead, near-death experiences, out-of-body experiences, and children's accurate memories of previous lives. These data, when taken together, provide the answer that Myers was seeking. And the answer is that it appears much more reasonable to believe that some aspect of our personality survives than it is to assert that nothing survives.

More recently, my friend and indefatigable psychical researcher Scott Rogo related a case that he describes in the 1990 anthology *What Survives*, by Gary Dore.[4] Rogo tells of the 1921 death of James L. Chaffin in North Carolina. Chaffin had written his will in 1905 and left all his money and property to his youngest son, James P. Chaffin, and nothing to his wife or his two older boys. However, four years after the death of Chaffin, Sr., the lucky youngest son who got the inheritance was sleeping fitfully when the spirit of his father came to him in the night. The apparition said, "You will find my will in my overcoat pocket."

The younger Chaffin found the overcoat, which was in the possession of one of his disinherited brothers. They felt a paper sewn inside the lining of the coat. After ripping out the lining, they found a note that said, "Read the 27th Chapter of Genesis in my Daddy's old Bible."

The family Bible was still in the possession of their mother. When the Bible was opened, it cracked and fell into three pieces, and a will dated 1919 was found—dividing the property equally. Since the handwriting was clearly that of Chaffin Sr., the later will was never contested.

The case is unlikely to be either telepathic or fraudulent, because no living person knew the location of the will. The concern among researchers of the day was whether it was the younger son's own *clairvoyant* ability that had enabled him to find the will, even though it had never been spoken of and he had no conscious motivation to find it. This is called the *super-psi* hypothesis, and it has been one of the most contentious topics of psi research for the past hundred years. Super-psi is the alleged psychic ability to know all information in the universe and therefore nullify the evidence for survival of consciousness. That is why demonstration of *skills* of a deceased person (as I describe later) is much prized among survival researchers. I shall describe another, more contemporary example of a case that presents the super-psi possibility concerning the last woman to be jailed for witchcraft in Britain—in 1944.

Churchill Tries to Save an English Witch

In the midst of World War II in 1944, an English medium was imprisoned for witchcraft as a result of her conversation with a drowned English sailor. The medium, Helen Duncan, was conducting a séance for a group of English women one morning in Birmingham when she was contacted by the spirit of a very recently deceased man. The man claimed to be a sailor from the H.M.S. *Barham,* which he said had just been sunk by the Germans. He came forward at this moment because he wanted to talk with his mother, who happened to be in the audience. He told her through the medium that everyone aboard was drowned, including himself—which proved to be true.

The story of the séance and the *Barham* quickly reached British Naval Intelligence, which immediately seized the woman and *arrested* her, since they very much wanted to conceal such sinkings to bolster war-time morale. The medium Duncan was taken to the dreaded Old Bailey prison, at London Bridge, where she was convicted of practicing witchcraft. Winston Churchill, the prime minister of England, was sympathetic to psychic phenomena and interceded on her behalf, but without success. The government argued that the woman was a witch, a menace to national security, and a threat to the government's code-breaking activities. *Mrs. Duncan remained in prison for the entire duration of the war.* But Churchill was so outraged by this ill-conceived action that he personally saw to the repeal of England's 1735 witch-craft act. Churchill's efforts also enabled witchcraft to become recognized as a *bona fide* religion, with the same acknowledged privileges of ministers and clergy. A posthumous pardon for Mrs. Duncan was in the works forty years after her death, according to a 1998 Reuters news account on NPR.[5]

This case is also obviously unlikely to be fraud. It shows that we don't have to go back to the nineteenth century to find high-quality spirit mediums. The super-psi hypothesis would claim that it was Mrs. Duncan's own clairvoyant ability, without the help of any discarnate spirit, that allowed her to access the secret information. However, the super-psi explanation does not adequately deal with the issue here of the meaningful circumstances of the message. The dead son's loving connection with his mother is an important constituent of this—and similar—cases, creating an ostensible need for him to communicate "from the other side." What this well-documented and rather contemporary incident does demonstrate is the unequivocal ability of our minds to function in nonlocal realms, accessing information unavailable through any ordinary channel.

Why We Trust Leonora Piper

Among the best cases from the famous Boston medium Mrs. Leonora Piper is that of George Pellew, a young Yale-educated philosopher and New York attorney. He died in 1892 in an accident in New York City, shortly after a single anonymous visit to Mrs. Piper, who emerged unscathed from two decades of investigation by psychical researchers and skeptics. Professor William James, a professor of psychology at Harvard University, personally organized séances with Mrs. Piper over a year-and-a-half period after Pellew's reappearance in the séance room. Then Professor Richard Hodgson, a professor of law and the greatest and most notorious debunker in the world, took over. And finally Professor James Hyslop, a professor of logic and ethics from Columbia University, took control of the investigations of Pellew's documented appearances.

Although Mrs. Piper, the wife of a Boston physician, didn't know the living Pellew at all, he reappeared to her as a "control" five years after his death in New York City. A control is an apparently independent entity or spirit guide who speaks through an entranced medium. Some researchers believe that controls are not actually external spirits but rather secondary aspects of the medium's own personality. But that doesn't seem to me to fit the Pellew case.

According to Alan Gauld, in his comprehensive 1983 book *Mediumship and Survival*,[6] the control Pellew, speaking through Mrs. Piper, was confronted with 150 different anonymous sitters—brought by James and others—over a period of many weeks; and she (or he) was successful in identifying twenty-nine of the thirty who had been acquainted with the adult Pellew when he was alive. The thirtieth person confused Pellew. It turned out that he had been a childhood friend many years previously who had grown up and changed considerably since Pellew had last seen him. Pellew carried on conversations with each of these people, dealing with intimate matters of their lives and past relationships.

The important issue here is that Mrs. Piper had not known the living George Pellew and therefore would have no way, psychically or otherwise, to identify his friends and the details of their past relationships. Her dramatization of Pellew's character and his idiosyncratic modes of expression seemed so authentic that the thirty friends were convinced they had each spoken with their deceased friend. They were each willing to testify that they had indeed communicated with a disembodied surviving intelligence who appeared to be George Pellew. What more could the poor philosopher do to prove the survival of the human spirit?

Stevenson's Strong Case for Reincarnation

Do we have any evidence to encourage us to believe that we mortals may be able to *"lay it down, and take it up again,"* as Jesus said in John 10:18? The answer appears to be in the affirmative. It is provided by the monumental work at the University of Virginia School of Medicine by physician/psychiatrist Ian Stevenson, who was only recently deceased in 2007. Since 1960, Stevenson had investigated cases in which children, usually three to five years old, began telling their parents about their memories of an earlier life they had lived. His first book, *Twenty Cases Suggestive of Reincarnation*, records that these children often have detailed memories of their "previous" wives, husbands, children, and houses. Frequently, they have graphic memories of how they died and, when relevant, who killed them.[7] In the most valuable of Stevenson's cases, the children's previous families live in a distant city or village and are unknown to the children's present parents. An important subclass of cases describes these young children as showing surprising skills and having information they could hardly have acquired in their present life, such as relating memories in a language different from that spoken by their parents. In one case a young person speaks Bengali in a family that speaks only Tamil. In another, a child skillfully plays a musical instrument he had never seen before. Although the majority of these children with memories and abilities from a previous life live in Asian countries where the belief in reincarnation is common, Stevenson published over eighty papers in recent years concerning such memories in children from European and North American families as well.

In order to verify these remarkable claims, both the child's family members and the distant family are interviewed, ideally before the two families are brought together. When the families are united, often a profoundly emotional scene occurs. Such an occurrence happened when a five-year-old boy greeted his ostensible former wife and children, showing the emotions appropriate for an adult in this situation—emotions that seem amazing from a little boy. In situations such as these, a child is able to name many of the former family members and friends. Surprisingly often, the child is able to tell where money has been hidden in the house, frequently to the embarrassment of a surviving family member.

Dr. Stevenson's most recent investigations of cases suggestive of reincarnation are even more bizarre than the ones involving having the memories of someone who lived before. He had been studying cases in which a child with memories of a past life also has birth marks or physical deformities that correspond to the location of scars on the body from accidents or injuries received in the remembered previous lives. In his stunning book *Where Reincarnation and Biology Intersect*,[8] Stevenson shows graphic photos of children and adults who have physical deformities corresponding to medical reports and X-rays of the person whom the child remembers as a previous incarnation. Sometimes such a child is even able to identify and name the person who killed their former self! In all his studied cases, however, Stevenson found that the children eventually forget about their ostensible previous lives by the time they reach the ages of eight to ten.[9]

What Could Possibly Survive?

Having said this much about the possibility of reincarnation, there remains the significant logical question about *what* of the human being could possibly be reincarnating. In one case the Indian child says, "I am really a wealthy Brahman with a home in Bombay." Yet he seems to be a clerk's son living in Calcutta. The child appears to have vivid and veridical memories of an earlier life that did, in fact, occur to somebody—and is verified. The remembered life experiences obviously did not occur to the present body who is claiming the memories. The child knows that he is a child, but at the feeling level he wants to drink cognac and be with his mistress, as he was in the old days.

Before we are overwhelmed with the idea of born-again souls haunting us, it would be wise to try and define reincarnation in terms of what we observe and separate it from all the different belief systems that lay claim to it. Philosopher Robert Almeder has defined the term in a lengthy essay in the 1997 *Journal of Scientific Exploration*. He considers the following description to be a minimalist definition of reincarnation:

> There is something essential to some human personalities . . . which we cannot possibly construe solely in terms of either brain states . . .

or biological properties caused by the brain. . . . [F]urther, after biological death, this non-reducible biological trait sometimes persists for some time, in some way, in some place, existing independently of the person's former brain and body. Moreover, after some time, some of these irreducible essential traits of human personality . . . come to reside in other human bodies, either some time during the gestation period, at birth, or shortly after birth.[10]

Even though I am not primarily a survival researcher, I have had a peripheral connection with two recent cases convincing me of the strong likelihood that something does indeed survive—sometimes for quite a while. I am happy to include two relevant stories in this chapter. One is of a friendly ghost of a murdered child who saves the life of a lost little girl. The other is the story of a deceased chess player who plays a match with a living chess master and lasts almost fifty moves at the grandmaster level of play. Both are very well documented.

The Lost and Found Child

The following remarkable story of five-year-old Haley and her incredibly helpful spirit friend was told to me at a book-signing event by the grandmother of the lost and found little girl. Grandma was the mother of one of my laser colleagues in Boulder, Colorado, where the event was held. The following is the story as she related it to me in 2008:

> For years I had no reason to believe in a spirit world, but I had no reason not to, either. My granddaughter Haley had just turned six years old. She was a bright, only child with a reserved personality. [On Sunday, April 29, 2001] her grandfather and I thought she would enjoy a spring wildflower walk, and so we joined forces with three other adults for an outing.

Evidence that Something Survives Bodily Death

We decided to take a side trip to the Ozark Mountain Wilderness, one of our state's most photogenic places, on the way to our wild flower walk. Haley managed the easy downhill trail but resisted leaving because she wanted to go to a small waterfall partly down the cliff and high above the river below. In typical pouty child fashion she insisted on being carried back up the hill when we hurried her to stay on our schedule. Three of the adults went ahead while a friend stayed with me to move slowly forward at a pace Haley could easily overtake. A couple of glances back indicated she was coming our way; but, not wanting to start the pout again, we stayed out of her view. However, when I looked back a third time, she was not visible, nor did she come along after a short wait.

I decided she must have gone back to the falls, so I quickly returned, though I could not see her. A previously unnoticed side trail looked like a possible choice she might have taken, but soon I saw forking paths and dense foliage, which made it clear that she was dangerously separated from us. At this point the situation took on a life of its own.

Soon a massive search of the wilderness area began, including its many cliffs, tangled brush, and waterfalls. Eventually, it involved dogs, helicopters, and hundreds of people who were organized by the search-and-rescue officials in authority. Prayers were offered, and help of every conceivable nature was put into play. It was hard to believe that all this effort produced nothing, leaving us distraught and drained by the third day. I went to a meeting of the American Society of Dowsers in nearby Fayetteville. There, one of America's great dowsers, Harold McCoy, considered our desperate situation. He said that the little girl was "being taken care of by a kind woman" and that she would be "found by two men on horseback within the day." [All these details were confirmed to me, Russell Targ, at a recent national dowsers' conference, by Gladys McCoy, the wife of Harold. I am sorry to report that Harold McCoy died in 2010.]

Chapter 9

In the afternoon of the third day, two local residents who knew the country well and owned mules had a hunch as to where Haley might have gone, and they decided to make their own search rather than be part of the large organized effort. After much effort, just as they were about to give up, they found her lying exhausted on a boulder at the edge of the river at the bottom of the cliff. After a very difficult trip out, they brought her to the hospital and safety.

As one might imagine, this story brought Haley and her family a great deal of attention, so they decided to take a little vacation to escape the glare of publicity. It was not until this time that Haley started talking about the friend she had made while lost. She said the little girl's name was Elisha and that she was five years old. Elisha had come to Haley as soon as she was lost. Together they sang songs and played games, and Elisha acted as a guide to lead Haley down the bluff trail to the river through a very challenging ravine. The authorities had thought it was too difficult for a small child to manage this route wearing only a tee-shirt and flip-flops and so left it out of consideration.

While some children are known to have imaginary friends, this had never been the case with Haley. Nonetheless, Haley went on to describe her new playmate's hair and clothing and drew pictures of her. I began to wonder if there had been an incident with a lost child in that remote area before and if there was a possibility of a spirit connection. After checking with authorities to learn about any legends or stories, I discovered that a child had been murdered and buried two decades earlier quite near to where Haley had been found.

Fascinated by this information, I searched old newspapers and court records. [The grandmother was also a director of the local League of Women Voters.] Among these items in the possession of the authorities was a picture of the child's mother, along with other photos of a religious cult. The cult members were accused and convicted of killing the child [whose name was Elisha] because the leader of the group, considered to be the "prophet," had declared her possessed.

Evidence that Something Survives Bodily Death

My search for the mother led me to the man who had served as the mother's attorney. To my surprise, he had maintained contact with her, and he agreed to put us in touch with each other. The e-mails that followed were amazing to both of us. I learned that the month and very day that Haley was lost was the exact month and day that Elisha was buried. The name Haley gave for her friend was very close to a name Elisha had called herself. The hair and clothing styles Haley had drawn were distinctive of Elisha and the styles of the time at which Elisha had died. [Bell-bottoms and tie-died T-shirt.]

Haley also told us about a silver flashlight that Elisha had at night and that Elisha had refused to let Haley hold it. I asked the mother if her daughter had had a flashlight, and she startled me with the following account:

Elisha had a Raggedy Ann doll that she always slept with. [A woman in the cult] *took it away from her. I had a small silver flashlight that I kept in my room because Elisha was afraid of the dark. I had to work three jobs from early morning till late at night and I found out later that* [the woman] *would put Elisha in the room in the dark. After her doll was taken, Elisha began to sleep with the flashlight. I would wake up at night and find that she had it with her under the covers. She would cry when I would try to take it, and most of the time I let her have it.*

After thinking about this possibility of a spirit child, I have wondered if Elisha was, in fact, the lure to attract Haley away from the adults and off the right path, rather than the means to save her.

The canyon-trails part of this story has now been described in a privately published book, *The Search for Haley: An Insider's Account of the Largest Search Mission in Arkansas History*, by photographer and trail guide Tim Ernst.[11] Trail guide Emst was only slightly interested in the ghost-story aspect of this case. What motivated him to write his book was his investigation of what would be required for a little girl in flip-flops to get, without injury, from the top of the canyon to the river at the bottom.

That's the end of the Haley story, but it's not the end of Harold McCoy's exploits that year. In her recently published book *Extraordinary Knowing*, psychiatrist Elizabeth Lloyd Mayer tells the story of a lost-and-found harp that in its own way is as remarkable as the tale of Haley.[12] In December of 2001, Dr. Mayer's eleven-year-old daughter Meg gave a harp concert at a hall in Oakland, California. In the course of festivities after this Christmas concert, someone stole her valuable, hand-carved harp from its resting place backstage. The daughter was heartbroken over her own carelessness as well as the loss of her precious instrument.

Mayer writes, "For two months we went through every conceivable channel trying to locate the harp—instrument dealers, police, TV, Harp Society newsletters—nothing worked. . . . Finally a devoted friend suggested that I call a famous dowser—Harold McCoy, in Fayetteville, Arkansas," which was a thousand miles away. Mayer called McCoy and told him her story. After a few moments of reflection he told her the harp was still in Oakland. He suggested that she send him a street map of Oakland, which is a large industrial city on the east side of San Francisco Bay. Two days later, McCoy called to say, "I've got the harp located. It's in the second house on the right on D__ Street, just off L__ Avenue." Mayer found the house, but didn't know how to proceed in this very run-down neighborhood. And the police wouldn't help her to get a search warrant. After puzzling over what to do next, Mayer decided to post fliers within a two-block radius of the house. Two days later she got a call from a man who said that he had seen the flier and that his next-door neighbor had shown him the harp. After a series of circuitous phone calls the caller agreed to meet Mayer behind an all-night Safeway at 10:00 that evening. The harp was returned. And, as Mayer writes, "This changes everything."

A Posthumous Grandmaster Chess Game

Can you imagine a chess game between a living grand master and one who had died fifty years before? Who do you think would win? Well, it was a very close game. Twenty years ago, a famous chess game was apparently played between living and deceased chess grand masters. A German psychologist and a Swiss investor were involved in this remarkable example of survival. Dr. Wolfgang Eisenbeiss and Dieter Hassler published this grand master game from the beyond in the British *Journal of the Society for Psychical Research* in April, 2006.[13] The German trance medium Robert Rollans, who worked with the researchers, was asked to find psychically a deceased grand master who was willing and able to play a chess game with the living grand master Victor Korchnoi. Rollans was able to find the Hungarian grand master Geza Maroczy, who had died in 1950. The match was played for seven years and eight months, ending February 1993, shortly before the death of Rollans at the age of seventy-nine.

Shortly after the publication of the journal, I sent the reported final chess score to my brother-in-law—World Chess Champion Bobby Fischer—who was then living in Iceland, having been rescued from a Japanese jail by the kindness of the Icelandic government and the Icelandic Chess Federation. Bobby (since deceased) wrote to me saying, "I looked at the score, and anyone who can go fifty moves with Victor Korchnoi is playing at a grand master level." This case is of great interest to survival researchers because it shows that, in addition to personality and information, a medium can manifest a *skill at the highest level* of the deceased communicator. Grand master Maroczy provided, through the medium, all sorts of personal, intimate, and humorous information about his life and his interactions with the grand masters of his day, who included the Cuban José Raúl Capablanca and the Russian Alexander Alekhine (both world champions). Korchnoi said that

Maroczy played the same kind of intensely complicated middle game that he was famous for in the 1920s. In his prime, Maroczy had been the second strongest player in the world, just as Victor Korchnoi was. It was a hard-fought match. But, in the end, the living player won.

Dr. Vernon Neppe, who is a physician, survival researcher, and chess champion, wrote a careful analysis of this case: "A Detailed Analysis of an Important Chess Match: Revisiting the "Maroczy–Korchnoi Game.["14] Dr. Neppe's detailed investigation shows that there were no sufficiently strong chess computers in 1986 possibly available to stand in for Maroczy when the game started. Neppe points out that, of the thirty-one "esoteric" questions posed to Maroczy by the researchers, all thirty-one were answered correctly! However, in the opening moves of the game (move ten), Maroczy played a king move—which though strong and popular in his heyday has been refuted since his death. Outside of that one weak move, he made no significant errors. In the middle game, Korchnoi said that he was still uncertain of a win. This game is thought by Dr. Neppe and me to refute the super-psi hypothesis, that is, the idea of universal knowledge that I described earlier.

Myers's Cross-Correspondence Case

I want to return to the great nineteenth-century English scholar, F. W. H. Myers, who spent a good part of his life investigating mediumistic evidence for survival of human personality after the death of the body. His landmark book, *Human Personality and the Survival of Bodily Death*, gives many examples of spirit communications that sound surprisingly like long-distance phone calls from the dead. Nonetheless, he felt that the only way one could be certain that a spiritual communication could be definitely assigned to a previously alive person, rather than just to clairvoyance—or universal perception—on the part of the medium, would be for the spirit to communicate information that the medium could not possibly know, even psychically. (That's why the previously described postmortem chess game is so important.) Such a case would be the only way to falsify the so-called super-psi, clairvoyance hypothesis. After Myers died in 1901, he apparently carried out this experiment posthumously. The deceased Myers sent independent fragmentary messages to three well-known and widely-separated mediums in England, India, and the United States. The messages made sense only when they were combined and analyzed at the Society for Psychical Research in London. These celebrated communications are known as the "cross-correspondence cases." They are like three apparently meaningless pieces of a jigsaw puzzle that show a recognizable picture only when all three are put together. Many of these complex transmissions were drawn from Myers's extensive knowledge of classical Greek and Roman plays and poetry, as described in Francis Saltmarsh's fascinating analysis of this cross-correspondence material in his book *The Future and Beyond*.[15]

After a lifetime of research, Myers left a tremendously touching letter to be read and published after his death. In it, he summarizes some of his thoughts and hopes concerning survival. Myers writes as follows:

> I believe that we live after earthly death: and that some who read these posthumous confidences may be my companions in the unseen world. It is for this reason that I now address them. I wish to attract their attention and sympathy. I wish to lead men and women of like interests but of higher nature than my own to regard me as a friend whose companionship they will seek when they too have made their journey to the unknown home.[16]

Chapter 9

A True Change of Heart

Here is another intriguing tale: Claire Sylvia, the parent of a teenaged daughter, lived near Boston and taught high school drama. Claire was also an accomplished dance teacher and performer before a chronic lung disease damaged her heart and left her unable to breathe properly. She felt fortunate to receive a heart/lung transplant at Yale-New Haven Hospital in Connecticut in 1988, and she recovered swiftly from the operation. Because hers was the first heart/lung transplant in New England, the event generated much publicity on television and in the newspapers, and she was visited by many reporters while still in the hospital. On the third day after her surgery, a reporter asked, "Claire, now that you've had this miracle, what do you want more than anything else?"

She was more surprised than anyone to hear herself exclaim that what she most wanted at that moment was, "A beer!" In her book *A Change of Heart*, she describes her confusion over her response: "I was mortified that I had answered this sincere question with such a flippant response. I was also surprised because I didn't even *like* beer. At least, I never had before. But the craving I felt at that moment was specifically for the taste of beer. For some bizarre reason, I was convinced that nothing else in the world could quench my thirst.

"That evening, after the reporters had left, an odd notion occurred to me: maybe the donor of my new organs . . . had been a beer drinker. Was it possible, I wondered, that my new heart had reached me with its own set of tastes and preferences?"[17]

As Sylvia progressed on the road to recovery, she found that her energy level became almost frenetic at times. She felt much more assertive, even aggressive. Her lung capacity, physical exuberance, and libido became more robust than ever before, even after she fully recovered and began dancing again professionally. She began to seek out physically challenging forms of recreation, such as riding fast on a motorcycle and taking rigorous outdoor hikes. Her daughter and a friend chided that her formerly graceful gait had become swaggering and "lumbering, like a football player." Claire had always been a confirmed heterosexual, but now she began to find herself attracted to women whom she "as a woman, didn't feel were especially attractive," such as short blond ones, and to have dreams in which she was getting married to a woman.

In short, Claire Sylvia began to feel that she had taken on a new personality—that of a risk-taking, teenaged boy—along with her new heart and lungs. She believed that the traits she had inherited were those of a young man named Tim, who visited her in recurring dreams and whom she believed to be her organ donor. Her hunch became an obsession when she found herself craving the taste of green peppers and, of all things, chicken nuggets, which she had formerly considered to be revolting.

A psychic friend helped her to locate her donor's obituary "in the middle of the page of a Maine newspaper" and that led to her meeting with her donor's family. They confirmed that her donor had been a restlessly energetic young man who had died in a motorcycle crash with a *bag of chicken nuggets under his jacket*. He had loved green peppers and beer, had had a short blond girlfriend, and had possessed many of the same personality characteristics that Claire now felt mingling with her own. Over time, the parents and siblings of her teenaged donor welcomed Claire Sylvia into their family.

Sylvia's experiences led her to organize a support group for others in her area who had transplanted organs, and she discovered that many of them had similar sensations of inheriting another person's spirit, mannerisms, and preferences along with their donated organs.

Chapter 9

A Message in Russian from My Daughter

Another aspect of these communications that had interested Myers was *xenoglossy*, in which the medium brings a message from a dead person and speaks it in a foreign language to which she has never been exposed. I experienced such a case a week after the tragic death of my daughter Elisabeth from a brain tumor in 2002, when her husband Mark told me that he'd received a letter from a woman in Seattle. The writer, a nurse, had been one of the twenty spiritual healers in Elisabeth's successful experiment on distant healing. In this woman's dream, a few days after Elisabeth's death, Elisabeth came to her with an urgent message for her husband. But the Seattle nurse could not understand it at all. She thought the message was nonsense syllables. Elisabeth kept repeating them over and over, so that after awakening the woman could write them down phonetically.

At dinner, Mark opened the letter containing the message, which was two rows of English letters with each row arranged in four, three-letter groups—like a code. As he tried to read the message, I recognized the first group of syllables as the Russian words for "I love you." I didn't recognize the second group. A native Russian speaker has since told me that they say "I adore you" in idiomatic Russian. The Seattle lady claims not to know or have been exposed to Russian—or indeed to any language other than English. Elisabeth, of course, was a translator and fluent in Russian. We believe that this is just the sort of message that Elisabeth would send to establish that she is still present somewhere.

In the end, after decades of study, philosopher Stephen Braude concludes in his deeply analytical book *Immortal Remains* that the super-psi hypothesis requires what he calls a burden of "crippling complexity that tips the balance further in that direction [the direction of survival]."[18] This leads him to decide in favor of the proposition that some aspect of awareness or personality does indeed survive. And it's *not* just some kind of "super-psi"—a combination of particularly outstanding telepathy combined with clairvoyance—that would allow a medium to know everything about a deceased person. Nor would it be explained by one's venturing into Jung's *collective unconscious*. But, because he is a philosopher, Braude is required to conclude that "parsimony or simplicity, however pleasing, cannot be taken as a guarantee of truth."[19]

*The great strength of science is that it is rooted in actual experience.
The great weakness of contemporary science is that
it admits only certain types of experience as legitimate.*
—David Bohm

10

How It All Works:
The Physics of Miracles

For our finale, I would like to mention the hugely energetic and highly psychic Madam Helena Blavatsky, who in 1875 was a cofounder with Henry Steel Olcott of the Theosophical Society. Theosophy is rooted in the ideas of compassion for all beings, human self-transformation, and the investigation of the powers latent in humanity. Blavatsky was the author of numerous books, including *Isis Unveiled*, which connected Eastern mysticism and Western scientific speculation. She was one of the first writers in the West to give systematic study to so-called "planes of consciousness" and to investigate the unexplained laws of nature and humankind's esoteric powers. She taught that "There is no religion higher than the truth."

Under Blavatsky's inspired leadership, the great psychics Charles Leadbeater and Annie Besant at the Theosophical Society in India carried out their amazing microscopic psychic examination of the inner structure of many atoms of the periodic table. Annie Besant first published her initial psychic examination of the periodic table in an article entitled "Occult Chemistry" in the journal *Lucifer* in 1895.[1] I was able to read this rare publication at the New York Public Library. I show the journal's cover featuring Besant's article in figure 10.1.

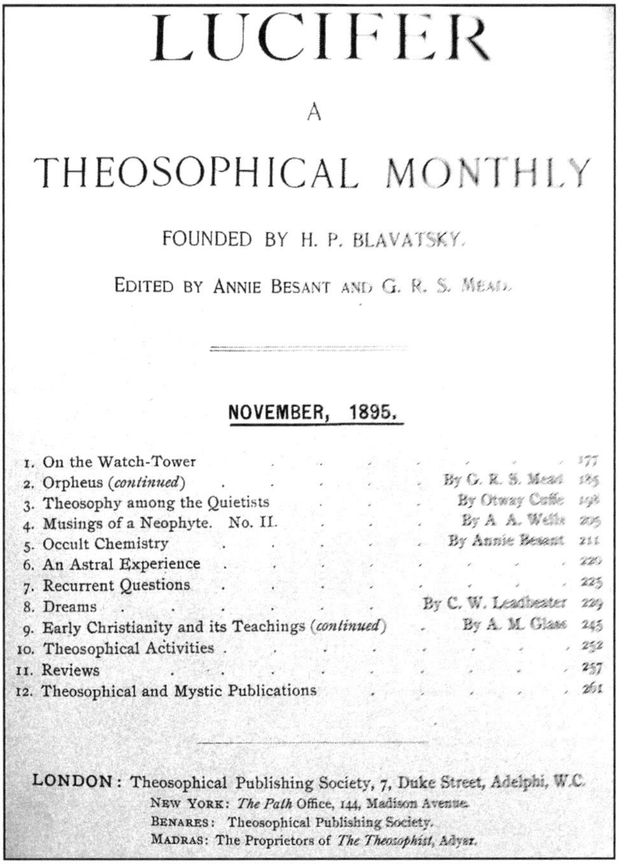

LUCIFER

A

THEOSOPHICAL MONTHLY

FOUNDED BY H. P. BLAVATSKY.

EDITED BY ANNIE BESANT AND G. R. S. MEAD.

NOVEMBER, 1895.

1.	On the Watch-Tower		177
2.	Orpheus (*continued*)	By G. R. S. Mead	185
3.	Theosophy among the Quietists	By Otway Cuffe	198
4.	Musings of a Neophyte. No. II.	By A. A. Wells	205
5.	Occult Chemistry	By Annie Besant	211
6.	An Astral Experience		220
7.	Recurrent Questions		225
8.	Dreams	By C. W. Leadbeater	229
9.	Early Christianity and its Teachings (*continued*)	By A. M. Glass	245
10.	Theosophical Activities		252
11.	Reviews		257
12.	Theosophical and Mystic Publications		261

LONDON: Theosophical Publishing Society, 7, Duke Street, Adelphi, W.C.
NEW YORK: *The Path* Office, 144, Madison Avenue.
BENARES: Theosophical Publishing Society.
MADRAS: The Proprietors of *The Theosophist*, Adyar.

Figure 10.1: 1895 publication of "Occult Chemistry" in *Lucifer* Magazine.

In 1907, these two prodigious psychics were the first to describe two of the three isotopic forms of hydrogen. Leadbeater psychically looked into a block of paraffin wax ($C_{25}H_{50}$—obviously loaded with hydrogen) and saw that there were two kinds of hydrogen: one with mass one (ordinary hydrogen) and the other with mass three (tritium), "discovered" by Ernest Rutherford in 1934. Leadbeater called this element *occultium*. His findings were published in 1907, in *The Theosophist*, six years before Frederick Soddy conjectured that there *might even be such a thing* as isotopes. Soddy received the Nobel Prize for his work on isotopes in 1921. The two psychic Theosophists summarized their work in an illustrated book called *Occult Chemistry*, first published in 1908.[2]

Leadbeater and Besant continued for many years to pursue their microscopic examinations of the elements. In 1932 they psychically discovered a new form of hydrogen with twice the number of constituent particles as normal hydrogen. They called this new element *adyarium*, for the city in India where the Theosophical Society was located. Only after they published their findings did they learn that Harold Urey had discovered what he called *deuterium* the previous year.

My introduction to this work was through sitting in the library of the Theosophical Society in New York City in 1956, when I was a member of the society and a graduate student in physics at Columbia. While there I was given an original copy of the 1908 *Occult Chemistry* by Dora Kunz, who was the president of the society at that time. Dora Kunz was a well-known psychic healer and cocreator with Delores Krieger of the Therapeutic Touch movement—which now has tens of thousands of nurse practitioners using her healing approach. Dora and I became friends, and I did some ESP experiments with her. She would unerringly locate small magnets that I had hidden around her spacious office, where she said she could see their fields as a direct visual sensation of color. This was just before I went to England to further study and to look for psychics at the venerable Society for Psychical Research in Adam and Eve Mews in London.

In the 1908 *Occult Chemistry* book, and from the very beginning in 1895, Leadbeater and Besant drew the smallest atomic constituents (protons) as triangular in form and as having a fundamental smallest element at each vertex, as I show in figure 10.2.

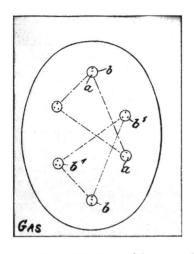 

Figure 10.2. Copy of the original 1909 drawing of a hydrogen or deuterium
atom by Charles Leadbeater (left), and contemporary drawing of a proton,
comprising two up-quarks and one down-quark (right), from *Wikipedia,* 2010.
Protons were discovered by Ernest Rutherford in 1918. Quarks were predicted
by Murray Gell-Mann in 1964 and found at SLAC in 1968.

Since the time of the Theosophists' work, physicist Dr. Stephen Phillips has written an intriguing book called *Extra-Sensory Perception of Quarks,* analyzing their perceptions and conjectures.[3] Phillips and I agree that the smallest elements of Besant and Leadbeater's tripartite atom function a lot like the quarks of modern physics. The standard model today describes protons as made of three quarks bound together. That quark analysis is the subject of Phillips's very interesting and provocative 1980 book.

It is evident to me from my studies of both Buddhism and Theosophy that we are encouraged to move our awareness into the spacious realm where omniscience is available and expected—whether looking at microdots, as Hella Hammid did at our SRI lab in California, or looking at atomic structure in Adyar, India. Of course, we cannot know *everything.* Though our awareness is nonlocal, our data-processing minds are only sequential and finite. The evidence is very strong, however, to support the idea that we can indeed know any-thing we wish to know—anything that actually has an answer.

The Physics of Psi

Sir Arthur Eddington was one of the premier astrophysicists in the early twentieth century. Shortly after the end of World War I, he car-ried out the eclipse observations in Africa that verified Einstein's general theory of relativity. His detailed astronomical photos from the field showed the apparent curvature of starlight passing near the gravitational field of the sun. He wrote extensively about the origin of the cosmos and also about his personal journeys into the peaceful meditative realms, which he describes as "glimpses of transcendent reality." Sir Arthur tells us:

> If I were to try to put into words the essential truth revealed by the mystic experience, it would be that our minds are not apart from the world: and the feelings that we have of gladness and melancholy and our other deeper feelings are not of ourselves alone, but are glimpses of reality transcending the narrow limits of our particular consciousness.[4]

This is a message from a man of limitless mind, who invites us to visit the nonlocal existence beyond space and time. The physics of nonlocality is fundamental to quantum theory. The most exciting research in physics today is the investigation of what physicist Da-vid Bohm calls quantum-interconnectedness, or *nonlocal correlations*. This idea was first proposed in 1935 by Einstein, Podolsky, and Rosen (referred to as EPR) as evidence of a "defect" in quantum theory. In their paper Einstein called this apparent quantum-interconnected-ness of entangled photons a "ghostly" (spooky) action at a distance.[5]

Nonetheless, it was later formulated in 1964 as a mathematical proof by John Stewart Bell, whose nonlocal (distant) correlations have now been experimentally demonstrated in Berkeley, Paris, Geneva, and Vienna.[6] The experiments show that two quanta of light, given off from a single source and traveling at the speed of light in opposite directions, can maintain their connection to each other. And when measured with polarizers, they behave as though they are a single entity. But the mathematical proof known as Bell's Theorem does not really have to be demonstrated in the laboratory. It is not a conjecture, a theory, or a supposition. Rather, John Bell gave us a *mathematical proof that our space-time reality is nonlocal*—whether we like it or not. The most incredible feature of Bell's Theorem is that our thoroughly local-looking world cannot be explained by any conceivable local reality. His proof published in 1964 completely supports Schrödinger's conjecture about entanglement from thirty years earlier. Schrödinger famously said that "entanglement was THE unique significance of quantum mechanics,"[7] and Bell gave a method for demonstrating both entanglement and nonlocality in the laboratory.

It appears that entangled photons are affected jointly by what happens to each twin, even many kilometers away. John Clauser, who, with Stuart Freedman at the University of California, Berkeley, was the first to demonstrate nonlocality in the laboratory,[8] recently described his impressions of these experiments to me. He said that similar "quantum experiments have been carried out with photons, electrons, atoms, and even 60-carbon-atom Bucky balls. It may be impossible to keep *anything* in a box anymore." Bell further emphasizes, "No theory of reality compatible with quantum theory can require spatially separate events to be independent."[9] That is to say, the measurement of the polarization of one entangled photon determines the polarization of the other photon at their respective measurement sites. In fact, the whole experimental apparatus—spanning many kilometers—determines the photons' joint polarization. That's why nonlocality is an experimental physicist's nightmare.

This surprising coherence between distant entangled entities that is called *nonlocality* by scientists such as Bell, Bohm, and Clauser continues to attract us. In writing on the philosophical implications of nonlocality, physicist Henry Stapp of the University of California at Berkeley states that these quantum connections could be the "most profound discovery in all of science."[10]

Entangled photons are now relatively easy to create by shining a laser with energetic, short-wavelength violet light into a nonlinear crystal. This will give rise to two new entangled lower-energy, deep red photons, which we can call A and B. (This process is known as *parametric down-conversion*.) If two more twin photons are similarly created, we can call them X and Y. Now, through the miracle of nonlocality, if photon A and photon Y are caused to become entangled, their *widely separated* twin brothers B and Y also become instantaneously entangled, even though they never came anywhere near one another. This reminds me of the situation in which my wife and I had a beautiful wedding in Santa Fe, causing my son in Washington, D.C. and my wife's son in Berkeley instantly to become stepbrothers—whether they liked it or not.

Furthermore, nonlocality is a property of both time and space reminiscent of data dealing with human identical twins—separated at birth and reared apart—who nonetheless show striking similarities in their tastes, interests, spouses, experiences, and professions beyond what one could reasonably ascribe to their common DNA. One famous set of twins reared far apart from birth were confusingly both named Jim. Although they never communicated, each twin married a woman named Betty, divorced her, and then married a woman named Linda—different women of course. When the twins finally met for the first time thirty-nine years later, it turned out that they were both firemen, and both had felt a compulsion to build a circular white bench around a tree in their back yard, just before they met at the twin studies organization at the University of Minnesota—at the twin cities. I can believe that there might be fireman genes, or music genes, but I don't believe that there are Linda genes or Betty genes. This looks to me like a nonlocal connection. Similarly, in ganzfeld telepathy experiments at the Rhine Research Center, Richard Braughton found that by far the most significant mind-to-mind connections in his two hundred pairs of participants were between mothers and one of their children.

David Bohm and "The Undivided Universe"

The view of many quantum physicists is that we live in nonlocal reality, which is to say that *we can be affected by events that are distant from our ordinary awareness.* That's the evidence. No one presently knows how ESP works. But I see a striking similarity between the nonlocal functioning of remote viewing in our SRI laboratory—independent of distance and time—and the descriptions of EPR (nonlocal) optical experiments in the physics laboratory. This is an alarming idea for an experimental physicist, because it means that laboratory experiments set up on an isolated table are subject to outside influences that may be beyond the scientist's control. Things like this are being seen in Anton Zeilinger's lab in Vienna as I write this in 2011. Within a year, things may get even worse. In fact, the data from precognition research strongly suggest that an experiment could, in principle, be affected by a signal sent from the future! As I mentioned before, David Bohm has called this important web of connections "quantum-interconnectedness." From my description of Daryl Bem's precognition experiments in chapter 7, you may remember his demonstration that briefly showing a word list to a person, a few seconds after a test, improves his memory of the words the first time he saw it! The future is improving the past. (Going over the test after the exam can improve your grade!)

A contemporary discussion of this interconnectedness has been presented by physicist David Bohm in his last book, *The Undivided Universe.*[11] This physics text has great contemporary credibility, because Bohm derives quantitatively correct answers to some of the most puzzling questions at the ragged edges of modern physics with his concept of *the implicate order and enfoldment.* A whole generation of physics students in the 1960s learned quantum theory from Bohm's outstanding graduate textbook of that title. Bohm provides a compelling model for all the data we have been examining. He does so through the use of a holographic model of the universe. This model is especially appealing for the psi researcher, because the defining property of a hologram is that every tiny piece of the hologram contains a complete picture of the whole.

In physics, quantum mechanical-wave functions predict and describe with perfect precision (ten decimal places in optics) what we will experience in our physical measurements. For Bohm, these wave functions make up a physical, four-dimensional, space-time hologram in which we are all embedded. The wave functions are solutions arising out of the Schrödinger equation, which is the quantum mechanical engine used to solve all problems in the quantum domain. However, these solutions are usually treated as merely mathematical models, so-called probability waves. In Bohm's interpretation, the quantum mechanical-wave functions are treated as having measurable effects through space and time. These wave functions describe what Bohm calls "active information," and this information has its own nonlocal existence.

If you look at a hologram on a photographic plate, the imbedded three-dimensional image is invisible. It is entirely dispersed in the optical interference pattern spread throughout the plate, even though these fringes cannot be seen or measured directly. Bohm calls this the *implicate*, or "enfolded," order in the holographic plate. The *explicate* order would be the three-dimensional picture that you see when you illuminate the hologram with a laser beam. The important idea here is that each of us has our mind in our own piece of the space-time hologram, containing all the information that exists or ever was. I believe there has never been a better description of Patanjali's *akashic* records from two millennia ago than Bohm's contemporary model. Imagine that you had a large sheet of postage stamps, where the whole sheet showed a picture of a flag and each small stamp showed a picture of the same flag. As you break off smaller and smaller pieces of the hologram, the three-dimensional field of view decreases along with the spatial resolution, but you still get the whole picture. It's as though you start with a big piece of *matzah*. No matter how small a piece you break off, you still have *matzah*.

Bohm says, "The essential features of the implicate order are that the whole universe is in some way enfolded in everything, and that each thing is enfolded in the whole."[12] This is the fundamental statement of a holographic ordering of the universe. It says that, like a hologram, each region of space-time contains information about every other point in space-time. And our data indicate that this information is available to consciousness. Bohm continues:

> All of this [quantum interconnectedness] implies a thoroughgoing wholeness, in which mental and physical sides participate very closely in each other. Likewise, intellect, emotion, and the whole state of the body are in a similar flux of fundamental participation. Thus, there is no real division between mind and matter, psyche and soma. The common term psychosomatic is in this way seen to be misleading, as it suggests the Cartesian notion of two distinct substances in some kind of interaction.[13]

This is Bohm's rejection of any kind of mind-body dualism. He considers physics to be comprehensive enough to embrace consciousness—and I strongly agree. Moreover, it is consciousness that comes to the fore to solve many of the so-called observational paradoxes in quantum mechanics:

> Extending this view [that you cannot separate the observer from the observed], we see that each human being similarly participates in an inseparable way in society and the planet as a whole. What may be suggested further is that such participation goes on to a greater collective mind, and perhaps ultimately to some yet more comprehensive mind, in principle capable of going indefinitely beyond even the human species as a whole.[14]

In the holographic universe of David Bohm, there is a unity of consciousness, a "greater collective mind," with no boundaries of space or time. Similarly, I believe that our psychic abilities offer us one way of experiencing this world of nonlocal mind or community of spirit. Remote viewing thus reveals to us a part of our spiritual reality, but it is only a tiny part of the total spiritual spectrum. So a short answer to the question, How is it that I can psychically describe a distant object? is that the object is not as distant as it appears. To me, the data suggest that all of space-time is available to your consciousness right where you are. You are always on the edge. Einstein, of course, was correct in his analysis showing a correlation between photons receding from each other at the speed of light. At that time, however, it seems that he was mistaken in his concern about the correlation violating relativity theory, because it does not appear (at this time) that entangled photons can be used for message sending—which was Einstein's main concern about quantum connections and nonlocality. But, as I mentioned, experimentalists are still working on the problem. Furthermore, I believe that arguing about the primacy of mind over matter has all the logical import of arguing about the primacy of chickens over eggs—they are both bad questions.

Therefore, it is the EPR analysis from Schrödinger in the 1930s, together with the contemporary experiments cited above, that give scientific support to the current view of nonlocal connectedness. However, I want to emphasize that I do not believe that the EPR-type of correlations are the *explanation* for mind-to-mind connections. In fact, it is very important to remember that we cannot use the apparent EPR connection for faster-than-light message sending, which was Einstein's concern. No such messages can be sent. But I think that the EPR experiments offer an unequivocal laboratory example of the nonlocal nature of our universe. Indeed, I believe that *it is the nonlocal nature of space-time that makes both ESP and EPR connections possible.*

ESP skeptics who don't know anything about physics are fond of saying that ESP violates the laws of physics. That is not true. Psychic abilities are neither supernatural nor nonphysical. To quote Professor Mark Fox in his 2010 Oxford University graduate text *Quantum Optics,*

> The non-locality implied by the quantum interpretation of the EPR experiments has no counterpart in the classical world. The measurement of the state of one photon instantly determines the results for the other one. . . . The implication is that microscopic systems that are non-local exist in nature. That is why *local* hidden variable theories do not predict the correct result." [In other words, Bell was right.][15]

I take his word *determines* to mean, in the Buddhist sense, "dependent co-arising" rather than "causes." That is, when we measure the polarization of entangled photons, the measurement at one measurement location is not independent of the measurement at the other end. That is the meaning of *nonlocality* from the many EPR experiments carried out over the past forty years. But physicists are still equivocating over whether this nonindependence is an example of a causal connection or dependent co-arising. For our purposes, the connections indicate that the universe provides surprising opportunities for nonlocal interactions. This nobody can deny.

The Eight-Space Model

I recognize that every model or world view is perishable and that one day it may be found that the system proposed below may not be the best model for psi. However, I am confident that two factors will remain: (1) that psi phenomena *are not a result of an energetic transmission*; and (2) *that they are an interaction of our awareness with a nonlocal hyper-dimensional space-time in which we live.* I believe that this space-time is complex in the mathematical sense and is the structure behind Bohm's holographic model. The result is that any two locations in the "real" plane, where we live and love, can be connected by a path of zero distance, drawn through the total volume of complex space-time. My colleague Elizabeth Rauscher, a theoretical physicist from UC Berkeley and Lawrence Berkeley National Laboratory, and I have worked for many years to create such a mathematical and physical model.[16] I will sketch out the elements in what follows. Again, all of what I am describing here is in agreement with Bohm's model.

The objective of our investigation has been to make use of the remote perception and precognitive database to deduce the relevant physical principles and laws governing paranormal functioning. One of the most common objections to the existence of psi is that it appears to be in conflict with the laws of physics because we have not yet found the mechanism for such information transfer. In our investigation we have attempted first to demonstrate the compatibility of psi phenomena with the laws and content of physics and then to develop a theoretical model that is descriptive of the nonlocal properties of psi. In our research we further present a detailed theoretical model describing the properties of psychic phenomena that we have demonstrated to be in agreement with the main body of physics. Specifically, we have examined the complex, eight-dimensional Minkowski space (named after the mathematician Hermann Minkowski and described shortly) that is consistent with the foundations of quantum mechanics, Maxwell's formalism and the theory of relativity.

The twentieth-century relativity theorist John Archibald Wheeler once wrote about our understanding of the world [including psi], "The answer will be found in the geometry, not in the fields."[17] That's the road we are traveling; this is not about "mental radio." Modern physics shows that the universe is nonlocal—especially for photons and elementary particles that remain correlated, even at great distances. In addition, the data from thirty years of remote-viewing research strongly show that the universe is nonlocal for psi—independent of distance and time—and for our awareness as well. This is exactly the Buddhist and Hindu teaching that there is no separation in consciousness. Your awareness fills all of space-time. *Atman* equals *Brahman*, as the Hindus have been saying for three millennia.

Our description for psi is a purely geometrical model formulated in terms of space and time coordinates—called a metric—in which each of the familiar three spatial coordinates and one temporal coordinate is expanded into its real and imaginary parts, making a total of six spatial and two temporal coordinates.[18] In figure 10.3, I show three views of the model space, recognizing that it is not easy to represent eight dimensions on a two-dimensional page. If you don't find the drawing helpful, just skip it.

In the illustration the future is up and the past is down. First, in the part of the figure labeled (a), we have a view of the eight-space manifold (coordinate system) in which a point P (the traveler) is separated from the origin in space and time. In (b), points P_1 and P_2 (the two observers) are separated in space but not in time. In (c), point P_1 at the origin is separated in time from distant point P_3, but a path can always be found to connect them.

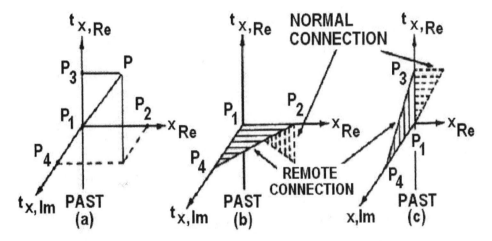

Figure 10.3. Showing the location of four points in the complex manifold. In figure (a), point P_1 is the origin, and P is a generalized point that is spatially and temporally separated from P_1. In figure (b), the points P_1 and P_2 are separated in space but synchronous in time. This could be a representation of real-time remote viewing. In figure (c), points P_1 and P_3 are separated temporally and are spatially contiguous. This represents a precognitive perception.

The metric of this complex eight-space is a measure of the manner in which one physically or psychically moves along a world line in space and time. This movement can be just as mundane as meeting a friend (1) tomorrow at 4:00 p.m. on the corner of (2) Forty-second Street and (3) Broadway on the (4) fifteenth floor—notice that there are *four* coordinates. Essentially, real-time remote viewing demands the ability of the individual's awareness to be contiguous with a specific target at a distant location. This ability to access information nonlocally requires that the *experienced distance* between you and the target is zero. Similarly, for precognition one is contiguous in *awareness* with the future event that is sensed. The complex eight-space described here *can always provide a path, or world line in space and time, that connects the viewer to a remote target, so that his awareness experiences zero spatial and/or temporal distance in the metric (or matrix).*

Here, we present a brief description of our eight-space model. The complex metrical space includes the three real dimensions of space and the usual dimension of time, and it also includes three *imaginary* dimensions of space and one *imaginary* dimension of time. These imaginary components of space and time are real quantities multiplied by the imaginary number $i = (-1)^{1/2}$. The interesting property of i is that $i^2 = -1$, a real number. Thus, in a complex space, *the square of an imaginary distance becomes a negative real distance squared.* In the eight-space, the real components comprise the elements of the space defined by Einstein and Minkowski. This is actually a four-dimensional representation of what we have been taught about right triangles in high school, which is the well-known Pythagorean theorem. That is, the square of the distance between the corners of the right triangle opposite the ninety degree angle (the hypotenuse) is equal to the sum of the squares of the other two sides, $h^2 = (a^2 + b^2)$. (Please tell me that you've seen this before!) This distance when measured in the complex Minkowski space is still represented by the squares of the sides of the now complex, hyper-dimensional triangle. This expanded space is constructed so that each real dimension is paired with its imaginary counterpart. In the complex space, for any hypotenuse defining the space-time distance between two points (such as you and your friend who both live on the real plane) we can always find an apex point in the complex manifold to make an angle of the triangle (off the real plane), such that the sum of the squares of the sides $x^2 + (iy)^2$ can be zero. That is, in the complex Minkowski space-time, *there can always be found a path of zero distance connecting any two points on the real plane.* If you have any questions, please take a look at my Web site, www.espresearch.com, where you can read the complete paper entitled "The Speed of Thought." And for those of you who are interested in the mathematics of space-time, I provide a more detailed explanation in the postscript below.

It appears that for consciousness there may or may not be any separation, depending on one's *intention*. We think it is evident that these abilities are fundamental to our understanding of consciousness itself. *In fact, psi functioning may be the means that consciousness uses to make itself known in the internal and external physical world and to our own awareness.* The main conclusion of our model is that there is no separation for consciousness in nonlocal complex space-time.

In the next chapter I will describe in detail the protocol we used at SRI for teaching remote viewing. And I will offer instructions to assist you in learning to do it yourself.

Postscript
For People Who Like Math

The evidence from four decades of laboratory experiments is overwhelmingly in support of the fact that we live in a nonlocal universe. It is the kind of space that Padmasambhava, Longchenpa, Schrödinger, Bohm, and Bell have envisioned. Dr. Elizabeth Rauscher and I have worked out one possible way of describing a model for nonlocal space-time that would support the data we see in remote viewing and precognition. This is not an *ad hoc* construction on our part. We are making use of a metric originally proposed by the German mathematician Hermann Minkowski that aided Einstein in describing a space that would elucidate the then new special theory of relativity.

Minkowski's great contribution to understanding relativity was the addition of a complex time dimension to the familiar three space dimensions. To create a space-like dimension out of time, Minkowski multiplied the time dimension "t" by "c" (the speed of light) and by "i" (the square root of -1). The four space-time dimensions are usually written as *x, y, z*, and the imaginary time dimension "ict" (the square root of -1, times the speed of light, times the time dimension).

We remind you from high school algebra that the long side of a right triangle *h* (with sides *a, b,* and *h*) is $h^2 = a^2 + b^2$. This is the well-known theorem of Pythagoras. In Minkowski space, the distance between two points is, similarly, $h^2 = a^2 + b^2 - (ict)^2$. And because "i" is the square root of "-1" squaring, it gives -1, and so we multiply $(ict)^2$ by an additional -1 to give a positive distance coordinate. Minkowski also invented the complex space-time triangle to measure distances in complex space-time, just as we are using it here (see figure 10.3).

In Minkowski space, each of these *four* distances is a complex quantity, having both a real and an imaginary component. This gives rise to what we call an "eight-space" model, since it has a total of *eight* real and imaginary dimensions. In physics the generalized distance is designated as "s." So that's what we use here. Your position in space is defined by three space coordinates, x, y, and z. To simplify the writing of the equation, we combine these three spatial dimensions into a single space coordinate $\chi = (x, y, z)$. And since we are describing how your consciousness experiences some distant place, we designate your location as χ_1 and your distant friend's location as χ_2. Remembering that we are in complex eight-space, each of our coordinates will have a real part, χ_{Re} and t_{Re}, and an imaginary part, χ_{Im} and t_{Im}. In the real part of this space-time, the *spatial* part of the separation between you and your friend is $\Delta s^2 = \chi_1^2 + \chi_2^2$. Finally, in the complex eight-space, there are four components to the total complex distance: there is the real distance, the imaginary distance, a real time distance, and an imaginary time distance. The total distance squared is the sum of these four distances squared.

A simple example would be the following: Imagine that you and I lived on a flat piece of graph paper with complex coordinates x and iy (i times y). If you lived at the origin (0, 0) and I lived at x, iy, the squared distance between us would be $x^2 + (iy)^2$. We remember that in the complex plane we always find $(iy)^2 = -y^2$. So the exciting result of all this is that if I moved from my location at iy to a new location (ix) where y = x, the distance between us would be $x^2 + (ix)^2$, which equals zero!

The equation below shows the total distance and how we can find a path of zero distance in the complex eight-space. In order to find a path of zero separation between you and your distant friend, your consciousness must expand to fill the eight-space and find the complex path whose terms all add to zero, which allows you to sense no separation at all.

$$\Delta s^2 = \left(x_{Re,2} - x_{Re,1}\right)^2 + \left(x_{Im,2} - x_{Im,1}\right)^2$$

$$-\left(t_{Re,2} - t_{Re,1}\right)^2 - \left(t_{Im,2} - t_{Im,1}\right)^2$$

In the above equation, the upper left diagonal term $\left(x_{Re,2} - x_{Re,1}\right)^2$ can be offset or "cancelled" by the lower right diagonal term $-\left(t_{Im,2} - t_{Im,1}\right)^2$ and the lower left diagonal term $-\left(t_{Re,2} - t_{Re,1}\right)^2$ is off-set by the upper right diagonal term $\left(x_{Im,2} - x_{Im,1}\right)^2$.

Because of the relative signs of the real and imaginary space and time components, and in order to achieve connectedness between the two observers, $\Delta s^2 = 0$, we must "mix" space and time. That is, we use the imaginary time component to affect a zero space separation. We identify $\left(x_{\text{Re},1} - t_{\text{Re},1}\right)$ with a subject receiver remotely perceiving information from a target $\left(x_{\text{Re},2} - t_{\text{Re},2}\right)$.

As I mentioned, the complete paper entitled "The Speed of Thought" is available at my Web site www.espresearch.com. Carry on!

The true value of a human being is determined primarily by the measure and the sense in which he has attained liberation from the self.

—Albert Einstein

11

Learning Remote Viewing:
Separating the Psychic Signal from the Mental Noise

For the past twenty years I have been teaching remote viewing to people all over the world. For me, it harkens back to my childhood passion for stage magic. But now I am doing real magic—and sharing it with all who care to learn. My view is that I am not actually teaching anything but rather giving people permission to make use of an ability they already have. I hung up my laser physicist's jacket and tie when I retired from Lockheed in 1997. Since then I have traveled to Italy, France, Scandinavia, New Zealand, and all over the United States to teach remote viewing. The Italians have been by far the most successful, perhaps because of their exuberance and openness.

As a result of our coauthored books,[1] Jane Katra and I were invited to teach remote viewing and healing workshops in Italy on four different occasions. In these weekend sessions, thirty to forty people would be introduced to their psychic abilities in many different formats, including photographs, slides, and little objects. At the end of the workshop the group was divided into pairs of people who would take turns being the viewer and then the interviewer. Each person was asked in turn to describe a picture of an outdoor scene in his or her sealed envelope. The interviewer would then have to choose which one of four possible pictures the viewer was trying to describe. The number of participants in the four workshops averaged twenty-eight each—all Italians. Twenty of them, on average, got the correct answer, when only one-fourth, or seven, would be expected by chance. The odds against such a result are one in a thousand for one occurrence. The odds against such an occurrence in all four workshops are millions to one against chance. This stunning and almost magical outcome is another reason for my belief in ESP. Jane and I published these results in the *Journal of Scientific Exploration*.[2]

The very important corollary is that I have never had such good results with American students in more than a dozen workshops with the same teaching materials. I taught many of these workshops at the beautiful, ocean-side Esalen Institute in Bug Sur, California. Even the famous hot tubs didn't help the students to match the Italians. Before the fourth workshop I taught in Italy, at the northern lakeside town of Arco, I asked several of the Italians why they thought they did so much better than their American counterparts. A woman stood up in the large plenary session and explained that "Italian women know that they are the most beautiful and the sexiest, so why shouldn't they also be the most psychic?" I guess that about sums it up: identity, self-esteem, and intention! Italian women don't live their lives worrying about whether they're doing it right, no matter what "it" might be. Fellini would not be surprised.

After those Italian workshops, however, I have finally carried out a workshop in the United States that was highly successful and statistically significant—forty-two correct out of sixty binary trials—again at odds of a thousand to one. This was in Killington, Vermont, in 2009, with sixty participants from the annual conference of the American Society of Dowsers. These were not stylish Italian women in little black dresses; instead, I had a room full of cheerful and well-fed men in suspenders and bib-top overalls who psychically look for, and find, water for a living.

Remote viewing is a *non-analytical* ability; people usually cannot psychically read, name things, or make numerical measurements. Dowsing, on the other hand, is principally *analytical*, reflecting what we think of as left-hemisphere functioning. The dowsers use pendulums and dowsing rods to give them precise information about the data that has already been accessed by their subconscious, nonlocal awareness. This is an instrumental process, not a practice of visualization like remote viewing. They can tell you how many yards the new well will be from your house and how many feet you have to drill before you hit water. The important observation I was able to make from this conference is that remote viewing and dowsing are complementary approaches to gaining conscious access to subconscious information. The folks at this conference consider remote viewing to be a kind of "deviceless dowsing."

Learning How to Do Remote Viewing

In this chapter I will elaborate on the very simple first steps you can take toward learning remote viewing as described in the pervious chapters. This skill is a two-person game—especially in the beginning. First of all you need to find a trusted friend who will work with you and hold deep hope for your success. I hope you all will be able to get this far. You the viewer will describe your mental impressions of the interesting little target object that your friend the interviewer has brought to you for a learning session. Your interviewer should have a collection of such interesting little objects and have put each of them into its own small brown paper bag. The object in the bag is your target to describe.

Chapter 11

Now, there is a very tricky policy decision to make before you start. When I teach remote viewing, I always like for the first two trials to include the possibility of a telepathic (mind-to-mind) channel between the interviewer and the viewer. This gives the viewer three possible paths for receiving psychic data: one is the telepathic connection with a *friend* who has the answer already in her mind; another is the direct clairvoyant connection to the *target object*; and the third is the *precognitive* channel from the *feedback* you will receive *after* you have finished your viewing and your friend puts the object into your hand. Then you get to read your own mind in the future! However, if your interviewer knows the target, there is always a possibility that she can subconsciously cue you as to the correctness of what you say or draw as you go along in a session. This would be a bad outcome, because you would only be learning to read your friend's breathing and tone of voice instead of anything about your own psychic and mental processes. Interestingly, if we go to the experts, we learn that Ingo Swann thinks that the early stages of remote viewing can be well advanced with an interviewer who knows the answer—as he argued when he taught the military at SRI. On the other hand, Joe McMoneagle says in his *Remote Viewing Secrets* that "all persons present should be blind to the target."[3] So, what to do?

To digress: in 2010 I was in Paris, attending the international meeting of the Parapsychological Association, where I received their Outstanding Career Award. At this meeting I spoke to the more skeptical researchers and told them how easy and natural psychic functioning is to elicit from interested participants, which is quite different from what many of these researchers had experienced.

At the end of my talk, a friendly young researcher, Claire Fouquet, asked me if I could show her how remote viewing works. The next day, she and her colleague took my wife and me to Chartres Cathedral—a site we had both longed to visit. Later in the afternoon, at a café, I told our delightful new friend Claire that I had brought something for her to view psychically and describe. This was, of course, not a double-blind experiment, but she obviously had no idea what I had brought from America for this informal trial. I am experienced enough, however, that I am confident I didn't subconsciously whisper the answer to her at our outdoor café. I simply turned over a paper placemat, gave her a pen, and said the magic words: "I have an interesting little object that I have brought for you to view. Please tell me about the surprising images that appear in your awareness. This object needs a description. Don't try to name it, or guess what it is; just tell me about your new and surprising impressions."

Claire's responses are shown in figure 11.1. The target had three components. It was a silver-plated, collapsible drinking cup with a little handle that folds up inside the cup. Because this cup is part of another experiment that I carry out in workshops, it happened to

Figure 11.1: Collapsible silver-cup target and drawings of remote viewer at a café in France. I knew the target and had it in my brief case. The viewer drew a representation of the silver dollar on the left, the cup in the center, and the alligator-skin box on the right.

have a silver dollar in the bottom of the cup. And the cup resides in a cylindrical, alligator-skin box with a tight-fitting top. I consider this to be a difficult and complex target. And I told Claire in advance that we had a complex target.

The first thing Claire drew was a little circle on the left of the main figure. She said, "I see something round and flat." I didn't comment but suggested that we take a little break and see if something else came into her awareness. (I had completely forgotten about the silver dollar in the cup.)

After the break, Claire said, "I see a shiny metal cylinder. It goes up and down!" She drew this and we took another little break. Then she made a third drawing of a cross-hatched little cylinder, which she said was also part of the target. This whole remarkably accurate description of an absurdly complicated target took about ten minutes. What could be easier than that?

My first rule for learning remote viewing is that *remote viewing should be fun*! I believe that the mind-to-mind channel I just described can work so excellently that it would be a pity to deprive yourself of the experience, especially in the early stages of learning remote viewing and dealing with mental images. But, after a couple of such trials, I believe you should work in a double-blind situation. You can do this by having the interviewer thoroughly mix up the bags holding each object, so that even she doesn't know what any one particular bag holds. Then take one of the bags and put it on the floor, out of sight. (In fact, all the bags should be kept out of sight, because people will tend to stare at the bags—as though they could see into them with X-ray vision as Superman does. This is not the way remote viewing works.) You are then ready to go for a double-blind trial. (In the remote-viewing experiments and operational trials at SRI, I *never* knew the target. All experiments were double-blind from the beginning.)

The Remote-Viewing Session

Your friend should now sit with you in a dimly lit room—each of you with pen and paper—and tell you that she has "an object that needs a description." If you come into the session with clearly formed initial impressions or images, it is very important that you write them down on the top of the paper and label them "initial images." Otherwise, they will follow you all through your session. In our army lingo we say you must debrief your initial images. Then draw a line under them to separate them from the rest of the transcript, recognizing that they may, or may not, have anything to do with the day's target.

You should then close your eyes, relax for a couple of minutes, and tell your friend about all your mental pictures relating to the object, *starting with the very first fragmentary shapes or forms.* The interviewer will start every session by asking the viewer to "Describe the surprising shapes and images that appear in your awareness." These first psychic bits are the most important shapes that you will see. You should make little sketches of these images as they come to view, even though they don't make sense and are not really objects. Naming and analysis are the principle enemies of remote viewing. (This has been known and understood since the eighth century, as I will describe later.) Your hand may make little movements in the air over the paper; notice them and describe what your subliminal mind is trying to tell you.

Good. Now, take a break and remember to breathe after each new picture comes into view. You should then look again at your internal mental slate. In this second look hopefully you will "see" or be given another image, or perhaps you will experience the same one again with additional information. As a viewer, *you are particularly looking for surprising and novel images that do not belong to your normal repertoire of mental impressions.* For the third viewing, consider that you will be holding the target object in your hand in a few minutes and ask yourself questions like the following: Does this object have a color or texture? Is it shiny? Does it have sharp edges? What could I do with it? Does it have movable parts? Does it have an odor? Is it heavy or light, wood or metal? Write down your answers, based on your feelings and mental pictures. You should continue this process until no new bits come to you. Ingo Swann calls this third phase "sensing the aesthetic impact." The whole process should not take more than ten to fifteen minutes. Remember, to be right, you have to be willing to be wrong. This is where the issue of trust between the two remote-viewing partners is so important. The good news is that through this process you can learn to give a surprisingly coherent description of a hidden object. The bad news is that you are exceedingly unlikely to ever know *psychically* exactly what the object is—because that kind of knowing requires analysis and naming. That can come later.

After you have described a number of different images, it is good to make a summary of all the things you have said. Try to distinguish between the images that you feel the most strongly about and those that more likely have originated from noise, memory, analysis, or imagination, or from things you saw earlier in the day. That is, you must go through your notes and try to separate out your most confident psychic bits from the analytical chatter. The remaining collection of bits will then be your final description of the target. Historically, ESP researchers have found that these confidence calls are often the best indication of correctness. If, though, you had been told in advance that your target would be one of two or more specific objects that were named for you, your difficulty in describing the correct one would be greatly increased, since you would have a clear mental picture of all the items in your mind. To separate out the psychic bits of information from the analytic overlay (mental noise), you have to go through the bit-collecting process many times. So we strongly recommend that you *don't work with targets known to you*. To the best of my knowledge, Ingo Swann is the only person who can reliably discrimi-nate among known targets. And he was able to be right 80 percent of the time in formal SRI experiments comprising fifty trials, in which he had to differentiate between two types of graph paper: rectangular cross-section paper and polar-coordinate paper!

After you have made your sketches and written down your impres-sions, your friend will show you the object. Your interviewer should go over with you all the correct things you saw in your session. You might then have the experience of saying, "I saw one of those, but I didn't mention it!" However, the rule in the remote-viewing game is that *if it didn't get down on the paper, it didn't happen*. So it is impor-tant to write down or draw *everything*, and eventually you will learn to separate the signal from the noise. You are now learning to sepa-rate the psychic signal and image from your memory, imagination, analysis, naming, guessing, and grasping. As I have said, these are all called analytical overlay (AOL). Above all, you want to refrain from naming and guessing. We often say that psi is like a musical ability; it is widely distributed in the population, and everyone has some abil-ity and can participate to some extent, even as the most nonmusical person can learn to play a little Mozart on the piano. On the other hand, there is no substitute for innate talent and practice. If all this sounds very simple, it is. My contribution here is to tell you how to get started and, most importantly, to give you permission to express and use your innate abilities and gifts. Based on four decades of ex-perience, I have no doubt that you can do remote viewing if you fol-low these instructions. No secret ingredient has been omitted. I wish you success and the feelings of excitement and awe that accompany it. After you have demonstrated for yourself that these intuitive abilities are indeed available, you may begin to wonder about other aspects of our nonlocal mind that can be explored. The true value of remote viewing lies in the fact that it puts us in contact with the part of our consciousness that is clearly unbounded by distance or time. Remote viewing allows us to become aware of our connected and interdependent nature. Its importance becomes particularly apparent when we share our knowledge with our friends. I believe that we are here to help one another expand our awareness and to enable one another to come in contact with our greater spiritual community.

Signal-to-Noise Ratio

We do not know how to increase the psychic signal as it appears in your awareness. But we have become very skillful in reducing the mental noise. Using radio, astronomers are now able to receive and analyze signals from stars that are billions of miles from earth—radiation from the very formation of our universe. Microwave masers (microwave amplification by stimulated emission of radiation, pronounced like *lasers* but with an "m") are able to amplify the signal without adding noticeably to the noise in which it is buried. To make this work, however, the astronomer must operate the detection system at a greatly reduced temperature in order to reduce the noise, since the instruments at normal room temperature would swamp out the extremely weak millimeter-wave signals. The important factor in detecting weak signals is to find a way to increase the ratio of the signal to the noise. (If the incoming signal has an energy of ten microwatts and the ambient noise is also ten microwatts, we would say that the signal-to-noise ratio is one—ten divided by ten—a very difficult situation for detection. If we can chill down the entire detection system and reduce the noise from ten to one microwatt, we will have increased the signal-to-noise ratio by a factor of ten; then we can do something.) In laboratory remote viewing we work with interesting but unknown targets instead of numbers and letters. Getting rid of the numbers and letters as a target is one way of reducing the mental noise.

Once, when I was teaching in Italy at the lakeside town of Arco, an architect was one of the remote viewers, and his target picture was the Parthenon. He created a detailed drawing of a classical building's plan view in which the columns of the temple have all been laid out flat, with their locations indicated by dots inside the rectangle of the base. This kind of dynamic activity is often seen in remote-viewing pictures. Fragmentation is common when a target has repeated elements, such as the stars and stripes of an American flag, a row of columns, or a string of beads.

Ingo Swann describes four degrees of distortion as he deals with this problem in his excellent book *Natural ESP*. He calls it *lack of fusion*:

> All parts are correctly perceived, but will not connect to form a whole.
> Some parts are fused, others are not.
> Fusion is only approximate.
> Parts are incorrectly fused; all parts are there, but put together in such a way to falsely create another image.[4]

Similarly, René Warcollier calls this phenomenon "parallelism," where similar geometric elements rearrange themselves. He discusses this and many other sources of mental noise in his 1948 ground-breaking book *Mind to Mind*. He describes the problem as follows:

> What seems to happen in the case of geometric figures is that movement is injected into what would otherwise be a static image. . . . It is almost as if we had for telepathy *no memory trace* of specific geometric figures, such as the rectangle and the circle. Instead we possess only angles and arcs. . . . There is a sort of mutual attraction between suitable parts, a kind of grouping which I call "the law of parallelism."[5]

In *Mind to Mind*, Warcollier gives many illustrations of this parallelism, or *lack of fusion* defect. Some of these are shown here in figure 11.2, where symbols are broken into angles and arcs. Warcollier and later Ingo Swann had great insight into the psychic perception problem. They both taught that the closer the viewer can get to raw, uninterpreted imagery and experience, the better. *Memory, analysis, and imagination are the enemies of psychic functioning.*

Figure 11.2: Some of the experiments described in René Warcollier's book *Mind to Mind* clearly demonstrate what he called *parallelism* and Ingo Swann called *lack of fusion*.

Engineer Warcollier also presents both theory and experiments of psi communication in *Mind to Mind*. He describes in detail why free-response experiments are almost always greatly superior to forced-choice trials, because they free the viewer from the mental noise of memory and imagination. Unfortunately, it took another twenty years for ESP researchers to take the ideas of this brilliant observer into account when designing their experiments. One of the most important things that we have learned in remote-viewing research is that analysis of target possibilities is the enemy of psi. If your only criterion for the existence of psi is how accurately a person can psychically read the serial number on your dollar bill or other such analytic information, then you'll conclude that there is no psychic functioning.

This concept was understood by the famous "muckraker" and writer Upton Sinclair, who, in his 1930 book *Mental Radio*, thoughtfully describes years of successful telepathic picture-drawing experiments that he carried out with his wife, Mary Craig. Craig was a heartful and spiritual woman who had a deep understanding, both intuitive and analytical, of the process of psychic perception. The following paragraphs contain her instructions condensed from a lengthy chapter in *Mental Radio*. We reprint them because her work demonstrates that she had mastered the art of mind-to-mind connection. In describing her technique for "the art of conscious mind-reading," she says:

> The first thing you have to do is learn the trick of undivided attention, or concentration . . . putting the attention on *one* object. . . . It isn't thinking; it is inhibiting thought.
>
> You have to inhibit the impulse to think things about the object, to examine it, or appraise it, or to allow memory-trains to attach themselves to it. . . . Simultaneously, [you] must learn to relax, for strangely enough, a part of concentration is complete relaxation . . . under specified control. . . .
>
> Also, there is something else to it—the power of supervising the condition. You succeed presently in establishing a blank state of consciousness, yet you have the power to become instantly conscious. . . . Also, you control, to a certain degree, what is to be presented to consciousness when you are ready to become conscious.[6]

In *Mental Radio*, Sinclair presents more than one hundred and fifty experiments involving picture drawing that he and Mary Craig had carried out. As she describes above, she developed great skill and insight into perfecting her technique for dealing with her mental images. In figure 11.3, I show eight representative picture pairs from Sinclair's ground-breaking book.

In an earlier chapter I mentioned that Einstein commented favorably on Sinclair's experiments in his preface to his friend's book. Einstein and Sinclair both lived in Princeton, New Jersey, at the time of these experiments, and Einstein had an opportunity to witness some of them. In his preface he wrote:

> The results of the telepathic experiments carefully and plainly set forth in this book stand surely far beyond those which a nature investigator holds to be thinkable. On the other hand, it is out of the question in the case of so conscientious an observer and writer as Upton Sinclair that he is carrying out a conscious deception on the reading world; his good faith and dependability are not to be questioned.[7]

Out-of-Body Experiences

Remote viewing is a safe and exhilarating activity that you can learn and practice at home with no fear of a bad experience. All you need is a friend to bring you little objects in a paper bag, while you practice visualizing as you learn to separate the fleeting psychic signal from the mental noise of memory, imagination, and analysis, as I have been describing. However, out-of-body (OOB) experiences can be another matter entirely. Since the publication of Robert Munroe's book *Journeys Out of the Body*, people have been asking me about the relationship between such an event and remote viewing.[8] Here is a brief summary:

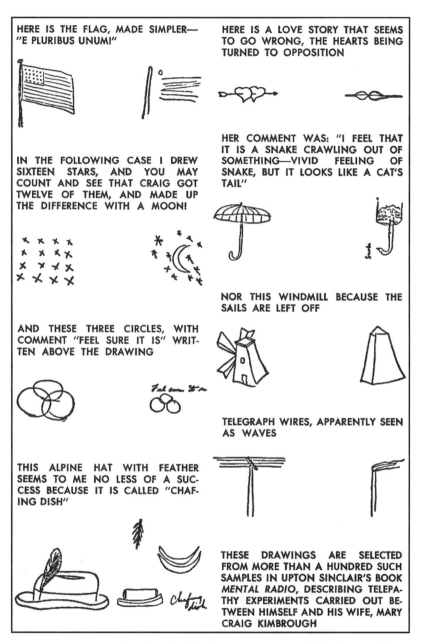

HERE IS THE FLAG, MADE SIMPLER—
"E PLURIBUS UNUM!"

HERE IS A LOVE STORY THAT SEEMS
TO GO WRONG, THE HEARTS BEING
TURNED TO OPPOSITION

IN THE FOLLOWING CASE I DREW
SIXTEEN STARS, AND YOU MAY
COUNT AND SEE THAT CRAIG GOT
TWELVE OF THEM, AND MADE UP
THE DIFFERENCE WITH A MOON!

HER COMMENT WAS: "I FEEL THAT
IT IS A SNAKE CRAWLING OUT OF
SOMETHING—VIVID FEELING OF
SNAKE, BUT IT LOOKS LIKE A CAT'S
TAIL"

NOR THIS WINDMILL BECAUSE THE
SAILS ARE LEFT OFF

AND THESE THREE CIRCLES, WITH
COMMENT "FEEL SURE IT IS" WRIT-
TEN ABOVE THE DRAWING

TELEGRAPH WIRES, APPARENTLY SEEN
AS WAVES

THIS ALPINE HAT WITH FEATHER
SEEMS TO ME NO LESS OF A SUC-
CESS BECAUSE IT IS CALLED "CHAF-
ING DISH"

THESE DRAWINGS ARE SELECTED
FROM MORE THAN A HUNDRED SUCH
SAMPLES IN UPTON SINCLAIR'S BOOK
MENTAL RADIO, DESCRIBING TELEPA-
THY EXPERIMENTS CARRIED OUT BE-
TWEEN HIMSELF AND HIS WIFE, MARY
CRAIG KIMBROUGH

Figure 11.3: Examples of eight telepathy experiments published in 1930 by
Upton Sinclair, with comments by the author.

Chapter 11

In a remote-viewing experience you quiet your mind and describe the surprising images that appear in your awareness—on your mental screen—in response to the question of the day, such as, "I have a target, or a hidden object that needs a description." You can describe and experience the color, shape, form, or weight of the object, or the overall architectural appearance of a target location. You can even go inside a distant building. But that's where it begins to merge with out-of-body occurrences.

Basically, there is a *continuum* from remote viewing to a full out-of-body experience with no discrete break between one and the other. In an out-of-body experience, you generally start with a simple remote viewing and then bring along with you your emotionality, sensitivity, and sexuality—to whatever degree you are comfortable. Unlike remote viewing, you definitely have the opportunity to scare yourself in an OOB experience because of the significant emotional commitment. In an OOB you have mobility of your point of view at the distant target beyond what you would experience in remote viewing. You also can have significant emotional interaction with a person at the target. (Bob Monroe describes such an interaction as leading up to his eventual marriage to the woman he was psychically visiting in an OOB journey.)

From my personal experience, OOBs are much more realistic, life-like, and cinematic than the more diaphanous, flickering in-and-out of most remote-viewing experiences. The OOB has a much higher and more detailed data rate (TV-like arrival rate of pictorial material) and is much more involving. Nevertheless, as a remote viewer becomes more experienced, his or her perceptions become increasingly stable.

I find that OOB experiences feel similar to lucid dreams in which you find that you are awake. Once you learn to have and recognize lucid dreams, you will never be overtaken by a nightmare because you will be able to be an active participant. Dr. Stephen LaBerge from

Stanford University received his PhD for his investigation into lucid dreaming and has been teaching the subject for the past twenty years.

My wife Patty and I took part in a ten-day "dream vacation" on the big island of Hawaii with LaBerge, where we learned to have lucid dreams. After a week of practice, I had an exhilarating flying dream in which I successfully flew out of my room and over the dark craggy bay and sparkly moonlit ocean next to the North Coast retreat center where we were staying. I also fulfilled my objective for the trip, that being to learn to control my occasional frightening nightmares, which I have not had since his workshop. However, it is important to remember that a lucid dream is not an OOB. What you see in the dream does not necessarily (or usually) exist on the physical plane, whereas OOBs will usually have a basis in reality.

The great Dzogchen Buddhist teacher Namkhai Norbu teaches in his little workbook *Dream Yoga and the Practice of Natural Light* that gaining control of your dreams prepares you for your journey through the *bardos*—that liminal period between lives where you have to deal with both peaceful and rather terrifying wrathful deities.[9] In my view, Dzogchen Buddhism is unquestionably the mind-training fast track to freedom, truth, and self-liberation.

I must say, we did not teach any methods for lucid dreaming or out-of-body experiences at SRI. We didn't want anyone to have a bad incident and complain to the management or the government that we had separated their consciousness from their body and they were unable to put themselves back together again.

In out-of-body experiences people also report powerful and quite realistic sexual experiences, including transgender ones. (You might have the surprising physical sensation of being a lover of *either* gender.) These occurrences may or may not be physical. That is, a remote sexual experience may manifest as an energetic encounter, like a remote kundalini experience, but associated with another distant person. Ingo Swann calls this "sexuality clairvoyance." For such an interaction to make sense, it is best conducted between consenting adults. Otherwise, it would be a kind of psychic rape. In his book *Psychic Sexuality*, Ingo Swann describes such distant sexual interaction. He writes, "The most familiar experience of telesthesia worldwide is that of sexual vibe sensing, which is a combination of clairvoyance and telesthesia as a transfer of sensations and motor impulses across distances."[10]

Psychic Sexuality is all about sex on the astral plane—across limitless space. And a volume for the truly adventurous is *The Confessions of Aleister Crowley,* where Crowley writes about his experiences with astral journeys.[11] But don't say I didn't warn you! The classic teaching manual on the subject is *The Projection of the Astral Body,* by Sylvan Muldoon and Hereward Carrington.[12] I recommend this 1929 monograph by a scientist and a psychic traveler to get an earlier perspective and good instruction on how to start your OOB career. I can personally attest to most of the above types of experiences, which have sometimes provided me with shocking but true information under totally satisfactory *double-blind* conditions. If that statement contains some ambiguity, so much the better. Since mental telepathy is well known to function quite independent of distance, none of these interactive opportunities should be at all surprising.

McKinley Kantor, Pulitzer Prize–winning author of a Civil War tale called *Andersonville,* wrote an OOB novel called *Don't Touch Me.*[13] I knew Kantor from when my father published *Andersonville* and Kantor's next book about the daily life of American Indians, called *Spirit Lake.* From conversations with him at parties, I learned of *Don't Touch Me* and came to believe that it is not entirely fiction but is rather at least partly based on his personal experiences in the war. In it he chronicles his trans-Pacific lovemaking with his passionate sweetheart who was living in the States while he was stationed with the US

Army in Korea. In the novel, she loved her boyfriend, Wolf, but the time difference made the long-distance relationship very problematic for her. Everything else he has written is very authentic, so I see no reason not to assume that this first-person narrative has some basis in fact. There are very powerful psychic forces acting to pull separated lovers together. On the other hand, these forces don't seem to exist as strongly for lovers who live in the same house and so are already continually bumping into each other.

Now my theory is that . . .
what is called supernatural is only a something
in the laws of nature of which we have been hitherto ignorant.
—Edward Bulwer Lytton

12

Naked Awareness:
Buddhist and Hindu Experience with Psychic Abilities

I am happy to have received some recent professional help in relating the psychic abilities we have seen in the laboratory to the religious and spiritual antecedents from two millennia past. My good friend Jeffrey Kripal, a professor of philosophy and religion at Rice University, has just published a very timely book, especially for me. It is called *Authors of the Impossible: The Paranormal and the Sacred*—just what I am writing about here. I had an opportunity to spend time with Jeffrey and several others at a week-long workshop at the Esalen Institute in 2008. We were discussing the relationship between super abilities (my special interest) and the super heroes who display these abilities in comic books (the powerful myths and heroic faces that provide the subterranean cohesion for the society).

In this 2010 book, Professor Kripal defines *psychical* as "the *sacred* in transit from a traditional religious register into a modern scientific one." For him, the psychical is always related to the "imaginal, the supernormal, and the telepathic." And the sacred is "the structure of human consciousness that corresponds to a palpable presence, energy or power, encountered in the environment." He describes this basic mystical experience, "as both f...ing scary, and utterly fascinating."[1] I couldn't agree more. The recurring question that I will be exploring throughout this chapter is, *Are psychic abilities sacred, or are they just abilities?*

So far in this book you have seen some of the best contemporary evidence for psychic abilities. But all this is not a twentieth-century invention. We have been exploring ESP for hundreds of years. "Any suitably advanced technology, whether mental or mechanical, is indistinguishable from magic," says Arthur C. Clark in the third of his Three Laws.[2]

Even for a genius like Isaac Newton, the Apple iPhone with its oracular capabilities would undoubtedly have appeared magical— much more so than the storied apple that fell from a nearby tree. Just because we do not yet understand psychic abilities and their relationship to science doesn't mean that they do not exist.

ESP allows us to have a direct experience of spacious awareness— transcending space and time. Many people find that their first introduction to such psychic abilities is exhilarating, even life changing. They instantly catch on to the idea that they themselves are obviously much more than just a physical body, as they learn to see into the distance and the future. This idea has been articulated in great detail for the past twenty-five hundred years in Buddhist and Hindu writings, particularly in the encyclopedic Buddhist meditation, *The Flower Ornament Scripture,*[3] and the inspirational Hindu volume, known as the *Yoga Sutras of Patanjali.*[4] In such ancient texts psychic abilities were studied, examined, and considered an important part of life; they weren't just deemed weird stuff and shuffled off into a supernatural or metaphysical corner as much of our society is wont to do.

Consciousness can be seen through the eyes of what Buddhists call "timeless or naked awareness," a dimension of consciousness that corresponds to our deepest and most *fundamental essence.* In this light, psychic abilities are neither New Age nor even a new idea. People have known for millennia that we have the ability to transcend space and time with our awareness and that timeless awareness is nonphysical and nonconceptual, i.e., presently ineffable. But we can learn to shift our way of being in the world from conditioned awareness—where we are held hostage by our clamoring ego and constant craving—to joyful living and spacious and timeless awareness.

This latter view of consciousness is the liberating objective of the Dzogchen Buddhist perspective, first described in the eighth century by the peerless Buddhist master Padmasambhava and still encouraged today by His Holiness the Dalai Lama. The quickest way to internalize this teaching is with regular meditation and through the conscious experience of our psychic nature. (Otherwise, it requires a hundred thousand prostrations!)

Nonduality Equals No Separation

Padmasambhava taught that when we give up seeing the world through our conditioning, we have an opportunity to experience our lives in liberation, freedom, and spaciousness. Known also as Guru Rinpoche, Padmasambhava was the historical figure who brought Buddhism from India to Tibet in the eighth century. In his inspiring and powerful book *Self-Liberation through Seeing with Naked Awareness*, he teaches that we tend to see the world through the lens of all our past sufferings, betrayals, societal instructions, and especially our ego.[5] He writes that when we finally give up this conditioned awareness in favor of pursuing a personal meditation of naked awareness—free of judgment, fear, and resentment—then we are on the path to timeless existence and liberation. This is a teaching of *nonduality* that is nonjudgmental and nonconceptual. If we give up naming and grasping, we see truly. This is the path to true freedom, spaciousness, and the end of suffering. And, as you recall, it is also exactly what I teach beginning remote viewers. The idea is that an experienced remote viewer will have found comfort and peace of mind in shifting his focus away from his own ego and its gratification to more spacious realms instead. Remote viewing is not a religion or spiritual path, but that doesn't prevent us from discovering that our ego and its defenses are principle sources of our suffering. We notice that gaining awareness of our *self* can definitely change our experience of the story of *who we think we are.*

My experience is that suffering ends when I identify with my free and spacious nature, rather than with what I see in the mirror in the morning. The new idea here is that learning remote viewing can indeed lead to naked or timeless awareness—experiencing the universe without *naming* or grasping, just as Padmasambhava describes in his book.

From thirty-five hundred years ago the Hindu Vedas teach us that our awareness, or self (*atman*), is *one with* and unseparated from ultimate transcendent reality, the physical and non physical universe, or *Brahman*. We need experience no separation from any aspect of the universe in consciousness. More recently, the great physicist Erwin Schrödinger, who perfected quantum mechanics, has written in his thoughtful monograph *What Is Life* that the teaching that *atman* equals *Brahman* is the greatest of all metaphysical principles. He goes on to write about nonseparation: "Consciousness is a singular of which the plural is unknown. There is only one thing, and that which seems to be a plurality is simply a series of different aspects of that one thing produced by a deception (the Indian Maya). The same illusion is produced in a gallery of mirrors."[6] You'll recall that psychic police commissioner Pat Price could see to Siberia from Menlo Park and that psychic artist Ingo Swann was able to describe the rings around Jupiter before a NASA rocket arrived to provide certainty and confirm his perception.

This nonseparation in awareness is the meaning of the nondual *yin/ yang* symbol, which signifies among other things that in every male there is some female; in every black, there is some white. This worldwide symbol of nonduality arises from China in the fourteenth century BC. In the arena of ESP, we are primarily concerned with nonlocal mind. Very often when you make a distinction or a judgment, you are making an error. This is of course not a plea to give up all discernment.

Figure 12.1. The yin yang symbol is recognized worldwide as the earliest representation of nondual thought.

This nondual ontology is completely apropos for psi itself. I assert that ESP does not occur outside the realms of physics or normal reality. I reject the idea of the dualistic description of psi and consciousness as being outside of any possible physical description, just as the Buddhists reject defining super-knowledge as supernatural. Many people—including those who should know better—are more comfortable saying that psychic phenomena are dualistic (meaning that mind and body are fundamentally different) than they are saying, "I don't understand what is going on." We must learn to understand and internalize the nondual nature of what *reality* comprises. To put it simply, psi is a manifestation of our and the universe's nonlocal (nondual) nature. The steadfastly nondual Buddhist logician Nagarjuna, of two millennia ago, never tired of reminding us that *most things are neither true, nor not-true.*[7] This is a high-level epistemological statement of our nondual nature. It is also contrary to Aristotle's famous teaching of the excluded middle, which teaches that *nothing* can be both true and not true. Sorry to say, Aristotle totally fails in the world of quantum mechanics. He taught that there is no middle ground. For example, a thing is either wood, or it's not wood. Of course, that makes a problem if the thing happens to be petrified wood. Similarly, we cannot usefully ask whether light is a wave or not a wave. However much we should wish it, that question has no answer. Light manifests both aspects; it is neither a wave, nor not a wave. Paradoxes appear when we are asking improperly formulated questions—questions that contain erroneous assumptions and paradoxes within themselves. Nagarjuna says that there cannot possibly be any paradoxes in nature; a seeming paradox only signifies our error in describing what we think we are looking at. Consciousness/mind is neither material nor nonmaterial; rather, it is multidimensional. Two thousand years after Nagarjuna, modern physicists would not say that Schrödinger's famous cat is neither alive nor not alive. They would equivalently say that the cat is in a *superposition state* of aliveness and not-aliveness—with exactly Nagarjuna's meaning. Schrödinger was well aware of Nagarjuna's four-valued logic from his life-long study of Vedanta.

This spacious view of our consciousness is described in the metaphor of Indra's Net, which is a *holographic* description of *nonlocal awareness* from 200 AD. (In modern physics, the defining property of the hologram is that every tiny piece of the hologram contains a complete picture of the whole. A holographic picture of a three-dimensional object is usually a glass photographic plate comprising an interference pattern that will restore a complete three-dimensional image of the object when it, or a little piece of it, is illuminated with a laser.

In a nonlocal universe such as ours, the accuracy of our psychic awareness is found to be independent of space and time. Such spatial and temporal independence is what we mean by the *nonlocality* of the space in which we live. The idea of *entanglement* of separated quantum particles that were once together is now well accepted by physicists. Schrödinger first described this idea in the late 1920s.[8] He saw it as *the* main difference between the new quantum theory and the old classical ways of describing nature. Entanglement has been elaborated upon by physicist David Bohm as "quantum-interconnectedness," which I described in chapter 10. In the Indra story, we are told that:

> Far away in the heavenly abode of the great god Indra, there is a wonderful net which has been hung so that it stretches out indefinitely in all directions. In accordance with the extravagant tastes of deities, there has been hung a single glittering jewel at the net's every juncture, and since the net itself is infinite in dimension, the jewels are infinite in number. If we now select any one of these jewels for inspection, we will discover that in its polished surface *there are reflected all the other jewels in the net, infinite in number. Not only that, but each of the jewels reflected in this one jewel is also reflecting all the other jewels,* so that the process of reflection is infinite.[9]

This description of Indra's Net is what nonlocality looked like to the Buddhists around the time of Christ. We are the jewels in the net.

The Ten Buddhist Super-Powers (or Acceptances)

Patanjali was a Hindu philosopher and grammarian also living at the time of Christ. In his *Yoga Sutras*, he describes how we can get in touch with our divine nature by learning to stop our ongoing mental chatter. The opening line of his famous sutras says that "*Yoga* (becoming one with God) is mind-wave quieting."[10] In other words, stopping the mental chatter leads one to the divine. In his writings on "powers," Patanjali shows in detail the way to experience telepathy, clairvoyance, precognition, intuitive diagnosis, and psychic healing.[11] These abilities are all available to the meditative and quiet mind. But Hindus and Buddhists both strongly urge that we should not get *attached* to them, as they can become stumbling blocks to one's spiritual path, as any attachment can. Meditation is the path.

The powerful Buddhist text known as *The Flower Ornament Scripture* describes telepathy and precognition in 100 AD. In its chapters called "The Ten Super-knowledges of the Buddha," this Buddhist compendium teaches that there is no paradox in precognition or in communicating with the dead, because past, present, and future are all infinite in extent and *dependently co-arising*. Thus, the future can affect the past—and, since our awareness is timeless and nonlocal, it should not be surprising that we can and do experience manifestations of the deceased or communications from the future in precognitive dreams. We are told also that telepathy appearing as mind-to-mind communication is to be understood as part of ordinary life; we are just not usually aware or attentive to its presence. All of the forms of super-knowledge are manifestations of the quiet and spacious mind and should be expected to appear in our lives as the natural outcome of nonlocal consciousness. *The Flower Ornament Scripture* does not consider any of these abilities to be supernatural; indeed, the idea is that nothing that appears in nature is supernatural.

In what follows, I will give you the flavor of the lyrical writing in this sixteen-hundred-page Buddhist transmission, written just a hundred years after the time of Christ. I present it not as scientific evidence for psi but rather to give you a feeling, and perhaps an experience, of the spaciousness of two millennia ago—the way of life that

Buddhist mediators and monks were experiencing. The following is from the *Flower Ornament Scripture: The Avatamsaka Sutra.*

Offspring of the Buddha, great enlightening beings have ten kinds of super-knowledge:

By means of the knowledge of others' minds, great enlightening beings know the difference of the minds of living beings in a world system: good minds, bad minds, minds that go along with birth and death. . . . This is called the great enlightening beings' first super-power of *accurate knowledge of others' minds.*

By means of the super-knowledge of the unobstructed pure celestial eye, great enlightening beings see sentient beings in worlds as many as atoms in untold Buddha-lands, dying in one place and being born in another. . . . They clearly see sentient beings with unobstructed eyes, seeing whatever deeds have been accumulated, whatever happiness or suffering they have experienced and whatever languages they speak. This is called the great enlightening beings' *super-knowledge of the celestial eye.*

By means of the super-knowledge of instant recall of past lives, the great enlightening beings are able to know the events of past lives of themselves, as well as the lives of persons in countless worlds, over countless eons . . . how long they lived and what Buddha works they performed. This is the great enlightening beings' third super-knowledge, *the spiritual faculty of knowing past lives.*

Great enlightening beings, by super-knowledge of the eons of the entire future, know the ages of the worlds as numerous as the atoms in untold Buddha lands. They also know the whole future of worlds as numerous as atoms. . . . This is called the great enlightening beings' fourth super-knowledge, *the power of knowing the ages of the entire future.*

There is also the super-knowledge of *the great celestial ear; the super-knowledge of going anywhere; the super-knowledge of dwelling without attachment, motion, or action; the super-knowledge of understanding the speech of all beings.*[12]

Chapter 12

To me it is clear that *The Flower Ornament Scripture* describes a spacious and unobstructed world in which we can experience the future, see into the distance, and diagnose and heal the sick. I equate all reference to "super-knowledges" with manifestation of psi. I hope that my Buddhist friends never tell me again that Buddhists aren't interested in psychic abilities. In what follows, you will see that the Hindu Patanjali is describing a similar world.

I have occasionally seen this world manifested through the eyes and activities of some of the world's great psychics, with whom I have been privileged to work. Western science had given us great accomplishments and shown us the far reaches of space. But it has shrunken our mental space down to the size of a coconut. I think it is past time for us to start questioning this reality and to claim the unobstructed reality that is available to us.

Patanjali taught that we obtain psi data by accessing the *akashic* records, which contain all information past, present, and future. One accesses it, he said, by "becoming it," with a *single-pointed focus of attention*. His writings provide us with a mental tool kit to accomplish this. Patanjali tells us that in order to see the world in our mind, we must quiet our "mental waves" (*chitta vritti* in Sanskrit). We have learned to call these waves *mental noise*.

While the Buddhists say that all our troubles come from making distinctions where in fact there are none, Patanjali taught that to be in control of our own consciousness we must learn to make distinctions among our mental states. As Shankara taught eight hundred years later in his masterwork, *The Crest Jewel of Discrimination*, the purpose of one's life is to learn to separate reality from illusion.[13] He was a pioneer in the nondual Hindu school of *Advaita Vedanta*—emphasizing nonseparation. That is, if we cannot control our own mind, how can we hope to control our interactions with the outside world? Patanjali described five states of mental functioning and made it clear

248

that we should always know which state we are in. He said we must discriminate among right thinking, wrong thinking (errors), sleeping or dreaming, remembering, and imagining. These states correspond precisely with our concept for learning to separate the psi signal from memory, analysis, and imagination—the principle sources of mental noise we encounter in remote viewing.

Duality and Nonduality

Since we are questioning reality, I feel that we have to take a little sanity break here concerning the nondual Buddhist view of no separation and the importance of separating reality from illusion. It's important to look at this apparent puzzle because I can just hear the philosophers saying, "You can't have it both ways: we either separate or we don't separate!"

The answer is simple: *Epistemology* is the stance we take in order to determine *how* we know a thing—how we know anything—and, most importantly, *how we determine what is true*. Shankara, together with most contemporary mental health professionals, thought it is very important firmly to find a way to separate reality from illusion, and they are right of course. For a physicist this is usually the path of empiricism.

Ontologically speaking, we develop our belief systems and try to make sense of the world we observe by using the epistemological tools we have chosen. If we look carefully, we observe that, by and large, *separation is an illusion*. I say that separation is an illusion because (unfortunately) most of the distinctions we make from our observations are based on false memories, misperceptions, errors of thought, and, above all, physiological projection, which is how we create our set of prejudices that color the way we experience almost everything. The *yin/yang* symbol is our reminder that the nondual view is usually the correct one. That's part of the reason why Buddhists tirelessly remind us that "separation is an illusion." Another part derives from the very important Buddhist idea of *emptiness,* referring to the observation that "everything we experience has only the meaning we give it." The thought of Buddhist emptiness often alarms people. The universe in not empty of cups, saucers, and stuff, but it is indeed empty and drained of meaning—apart from the meaning you assign. Experiencing emptiness, in the space between meditation and nonmeditation, is like experiencing simplicity itself.

My own ontological stance is that we live in a nonlocal world. That's what all the evidence seems to be saying as I write these words in 2010—but I could be wrong. Somebody might come up with a better model. Modern quantum physics is arguing for nonduality (particles can often be both here and there), and so is the compassion taught by all spiritual traditions that seek a peaceful world. A dualistic world is the one offered to us by the Calvinists' belief that society is made up of the divinely deserving rich and the undeserving poor. This particular dualistic ontology has failed repeatedly since the time of the French Revolution, even though certain individuals and societies keep trying to revive it. The nondual view says that we are all one in consciousness and that there is no separation. In the nonlocal and nondual world I am describing here, your connection to the tired and crabby woman at the cash register is even more than just a reflection of you—she *is* you. All you have to do to get the picture is to take a look at a recent laboratory photograph of entangled and overlapping particles.

Four hundred years after Padmasambhava, his teachings of spacious consciousness were expanded and made even more powerful by the peerless Dzogchen Buddhist dharma master Longchen Rabjam (aka Longchenpa). Many Buddhist students agree that his books teach and *directly transmit* the often luminous experience that our basic human nature is one of *timeless awareness*—an active awareness that fills the universe and our consciousness and is independent of time. He teaches that our experience of the *now* has no limits. In *The Precious Treasury of the Basic Space of Phenomena*, he says, "This work concerns the nature of mind, which is beyond cause and effect, effort and achievement, and which cannot be understood through inferior spiritual approaches."[14] To say that the workings of the mind are *beyond cause and effect* is another way of saying that the mind is timeless. He says in *The Way of Abiding*, "All phenomena of the world of appearances and possibilities . . . no matter how dynamic they seem to be, are none other than the display of naturally occurring timeless awareness."[15]

The Buddhist lama who wrote the introduction for the new translation of Rabjam's the *Basic Space of Phenomena* said that "This book is so powerful, that simply having it in your library results in a spiritual transmission." In it Longchenpa, writing in the fourteenth century, says:

> Mind itself—naturally occurring timeless awareness—has no substance or characteristics. . . . Naturally arising timeless awareness, being spontaneously present as the heart essence of *Dharmakaya* (the energetic experience of transcendence of the five senses), is free of conceptual or descriptive elaboration. . . . Not dependent on causes, incomparable timeless awareness gives rise to everything, and so there is no other source of phenomena. You are not bound by sensory appearances, but by fixation on them. . . . Sensory appearances and consciousness of them are of one taste in nondual unity.[16]

This model of psi functioning suggests that the information we access is always with us and therefore always available. It is not a new theory, but it seems to fit the data I've observed better than the information-transmission model (mental radio), in which one person sends a psychic message to another. In the eighth century, Padmasambhava wrote extensively on the nondual view that our awareness transcends all of space; his writing is a plea for the spacious and naked awareness that transcends our conditioning. In the thirteenth century, Langchenpa assumed that we have internalized this teaching and experience. His realization is that we ourselves are not only spacious but timeless as well. He was the first to create a whole practice out of the need to recognize that who we are is *timeless awareness*. It is my opinion that Dzogchen Buddhism is the fast track to spiritual awakening. It is not for the timid, however, because one has to surrender a lot of previously cherished outcomes.

Are Psychic Abilities Sacred?

As we learn to exercise our psychic abilities, ethical issues arise concerning these perceptual functions that are outside the understanding of modern science. Are psychic abilities sacred? Is it appropriate to think about using them for mundane purposes, such as making money in the stock market? Is healing sacred, and what does it have to do with our psychic capabilities?

Our psychic abilities allow us to experience mind-to-mind connections with each other, and many people regard these experiences as profoundly spiritual. There is no doubt that psi gives us a unique window on our nonlocal reality. It allows us to have contact with a kind of omniscience that none of our other senses makes available to us. Buddhist teachings would have us believe that psychic powers do indeed exist and that they can be used for beneficial purposes. However, if a person shows a special or obsessive interest in developing these powers, then he or she may not be ready to use them. In this tradition, ESP in all its forms is widely regarded as a stumbling block to be overcome on the path to enlightenment. One might well consider that using these abilities to spy on the Russians or to make money in the commodity market is a trivialization of a sacred gift. The reason I continue to give workshops to awaken student's awareness of their psychical abilities is that those who are ready will remain awake and excited by their new potential, while the others who are not ready will simply go back to sleep—no harm done. However, as with everything else in the world, there is no doubt that some individuals will attempt to use their newfound abilities for personal or antisocial purposes.

We often hear that psi is a weak and unreliable faculty. Arthur Koestler, in his pioneering book of 1956, *Roots of Coincidence*, spoke of the "ink fish phenomenon," wherein psi disappears in a murky cloud whenever you try to get too close to it.[17] This may have been true of available evidence in the 1950s and '60s. But current laboratory data, especially for remote viewing and Daryl Bem's precognition experiments at Cornell, show that psychic perception in the right experimental hands is robust and about to take its place alongside other perceptual modalities we know and trust. Now that the US government has declassified some of its highest quality ESP data, these results are beginning to find their way into mainstream scientific inquiry, rather than hovering at the edges of credibility in the tabloid newspapers and the movies.

Most healers believe that there is a spiritual aspect to what they do. This raises the important question of whether all psi functioning should be considered sacred. In the *Institute of Noetic Sciences Bulletin* physician Rachel Naomi Remen, medical director of the Commonweal Cancer Help Program in California, writes about the discrepancy between our "level of technology and the level of moral and ethical wisdom appropriate to the use of that technology."[18] About this discrepancy as it relates to the sacredness of psychic abilities compared with our other senses, she says:

Chapter 12

Our intuition informs us of the intangible, and may offer a glimpse of the great laws that govern the workings of the world. Yet, is the particular capacity by which we may experience an aspect of sacred reality necessarily sacred in and of itself? Is the eye which perceives holiness necessarily holy? In fact, can't any of our senses become a doorway to sacred experience?

Anyone who has seen the light pour through the great stained glass window at Chartres knows that vision can lead to sacred experience. Anyone who has heard the *Messiah* or the *Allegri Miserere* knows that hearing can evoke a powerful experience of the sacred, and anyone who has had really good sex knows the power of touch as a bridge to sacred experience. Yet seeing, hearing, and touch are simple human functions. Is psi a simple human function as well?[19]

Remen suggests that we consider psi as an expanded, rather than an exalted, human function. As such, it is subject to individual discretion as well as to human frailty. A sacrament can be any procedure or ritual that we use to contact our spiritual aspect. I believe that all our senses can be thought of as sacred in this regard; psi does not necessarily have a privileged position. It is how, and in what context, we choose to use any human capacity that seems important. And for what purpose? Serving which values?[20]

The word *siddhis* is used generally for the extraordinary powers acquired through the practice of yoga, but its real meaning is best expressed by the words *attainments* or *accomplishments*, concerned with the attainment of the highest states of consciousness. The study of psychic abilities is relatively new, but the knowledge of their existence has been described in the historic spiritual teachings of Hinduism, Buddhism, Islam, and in the Bible. According to all these paths of wisdom, we are spiritual beings residing as bodies and learning how to be human. We believe that the study of psi offers us insight into our spiritual nature as well as into the nonlocal dimension of consciousness uniting us all. It also offers us the opportunity to evaluate the same issues of integrity and responsibility that we confront in other aspects of our lives.

My favorite Indian sage Patanjali, a Hindu in the second century BC, instructed that "These [psychic] powers of the spreading or outgoing mind are injurious *to contemplation*" for an aspirant seeking enlightenment.[21] This is not because such powers are evil or even bad; it is because they are distracting for a person seeking unitive consciousness and the experience of inward illumination beyond all sensation.[22] He was concerned that our psychic abilities could potentially intensify a person's fascination with sensations, phenomena, and objects that can be a source of separation in daily life.

Patanjali also mentioned that psychic abilities may arise from causes other than the practice of yoga meditation. He agrees with the Buddhists that they are sometimes present at the time of birth and that they may also be produced by taking certain drugs, chanting mantras, or practicing austerities. Among the examples of *siddhis* or "psychic powers" that Patanjali said could be produced by diligent meditation practices are:

knowledge of past and future; understanding of the sounds made by all creatures; knowledge of past lives; knowing what others are thinking; prior knowledge of one's death; the attainment of various kinds of strength; perception of the small, the concealed, and the distant; knowledge of other inhabited regions; knowledge about the stars and their motions; knowledge of the interior of the body; control of hunger and thirst; steadiness; seeing the adepts in one's own interior light; general intuition; understanding of the mind; entering the bodies of others; lightness and levitation; brightness; control of material elements; control of the senses; perfection of the body; quickness of the body . . .[23]

Chapter 12

Most ancient sacred teachings emphasize the seductive distraction of psychic abilities, because they entice us to stray off the spiritual path with thoughts of using them to enhance our individual power or prestige. However, one of the goals of meditation that Patanjali had in mind was to bring a person out of normal everyday sensory awareness and into a nonlocal awareness of unity consciousness. I believe that for those of us who are actively involved with working, thinking, playing, and moving in the physical world, our psychic abilities have much to teach us about the illusion of our separate selves. The acceptance of the reality of our mind-to-mind connections can inspire others, as it has done for this author, to try to reach for our highest potentials as human beings.

Our psychic abilities become accessible when we are open-minded and share commonality of purpose and mutual trust with one another. Indeed, the revered Hindu teacher Shankara of the seventh century referred to psychic abilities as "powers of the unobstructed life."[24] I find the processes of achieving consensus and rapport with others to be worthwhile activities in themselves, in line with what Shankara called "the joy of harmony with the intent of our being."[25] What else might we discover as we remove the psychic barriers to our awareness of our connected natures? Exploring these states of nonlocal consciousness together with friends can give many richly rewarding experiences. The emergence of our psychic capabilities as we learn to focus our attention with mindfulness is a natural occurrence. As we discover more and more ways to apply our psychic abilities to real-world tasks, we will all have many opportunities to choose and choose again which of those applications of psi are ethical and appropriate for us.

Buddhist Masters of Enchantment

The *siddhi* traditions of yesterday and today tell us that, from the twelfth century to the present, visitors to Tibet have reported their experiences of seeing advanced *siddhi* meditators go into deep meditation, appear to float upward from their resting place, and then fill the room with light and blazing energy.[26] A good friend who is a psychiatrist recently told me of just such a shocking personal experience he had with the Dalai Lama. My friend was asked, at the end of a week-long therapeutic workshop, if he would like to see the Dalai Lama as he really is. The result of his affirmation was the experience of quietly sitting in meditation with His Holiness and suddenly having the room filled with a palpable energy, a blinding light, and the magical appearance of *Avalokiteshvara*—the Bodhisattva of Compassion. My friend was stunned and reports that his view of reality is permanently changed.

I have had two similar, but somewhat less energetic, experiences with practitioners of Advaita Vedanta. This is the form of self-enquiry taught by the Indian master Ramana Maharshi, the enlightened Indian saint who died in 1950.[27] Ramana's goal was to have us experience a flow of loving awareness as we meditate on the question of *who we might actually be* and *who is asking that question*. In each of my cases, I was with an awakened teacher and was suddenly and surprisingly filled with loving energy to such an extent that I was overcome with tears and almost fainted from the experience. I have seen people peacefully sitting in a *satsang* meditation meeting with my teacher Gangaji, and they suddenly fall to the floor, overcome with tears and laughter at unexpectedly experiencing this loving flow, which is who we truly are—as we shall see.

Chapter 12

Learning remote viewing can give you insight into your peaceful and timeless nature, but there is no substitute for sitting with an awakened, loving teacher. I wish you good luck in both endeavors.

It may come as a surprise to us, but, by studying our mind,
we discover our heart; by freeing our mind, we open our heart.
—Dzogchen, Ponlop Rinpoche

After eliminating the impossible, whatever remains,
no matter how improbable, is the truth.
—Sherlock Holmes

Epilogue
A Physicist's Proof of Psychic Abilities

In the preface I wrote that proof is defined as evidence "so strong that it would be logically or probabilistically unreasonable to deny the supported argument." On the basis of the evidence presented in this book, it would be unreasonable (in my opinion) to deny the existence of some kind of human ability to experience distant events. I hope you agree.

To prove something as *logically* true, it must be true by definition, as in "all children are younger than their biological parents." A counter truth to this statement could not exist. Similarly, in his 1944 book *What Is Life* the great physicist Erwin Schrödinger wrote, "Consciousness is a singular of which the plural is unknown. There is only one thing, and that which seems to be a plurality is simply a series of different aspects of that one thing produced by a deception (the Indian *Maya*). The same illusion is produced in a gallery of mirrors."

Schrödinger was right in his perfection of quantum mechanics in the 1920s known as the wave function. And he was right in 1944, a decade before DNA was discovered, when he described inheritance as driven by a "genetic code" of a small number of molecules strung together carrying information by their arrangement. These ideas are

Epilogue

also discussed in his little book *What Is Life*. They are not proof. But I am persuaded to accept Schrödinger's definition and his view of what we mean by consciousness as inherently singular with no separation, a situation that he considers to be self-evident.

Some of you may not revere Schrödinger as I do. But I hope you can agree with me when I say that by *empirical proof* I mean a demonstration whose occurrence is truly self-evident. With regard to psychic abilities, I have discussed at length two cases that I find convincing in this way:

The first occurred in 1974 when retired police commissioner Pat Price psychically identified Patricia Hearst's kidnapper from a large mug book consisting of hundreds of photos at the Berkeley Police Station. He then successfully told the detectives where to find the kidnap car fifty miles away.

The second was when in 1982 my little Delphi group psychically forecasted the changes in the price of silver successfully nine times in nine weeks, making $120,000, which was a lot of money at that time. As a trader on the floor of the Commodity Exchange told *NOVA*, which documented our exploits, "Doing anything nine times in a row in this volatile market is impossible!"

In the scientific literature, the highest premium is placed on *statistical* proof. Can one demonstrate the thing again and again? As I have recounted, in two now famous experiments conducted during our SRI program Pat Price and the photographer Hella Hammid were able accurately to describe where my colleague Hal Puthoff was hiding in the San Francisco Bay Area. Each remote viewer did exactly nine trials. In 1974, Price achieved seven first place matches, with a probability of 3×10^{-5} (odds of three in a hundred thousand). Two years later, Hella was even more successful in this psychic hide-and-go-seek game with a degree of success calculated at 2×10^{-6} (odds of two in a million). These experiments were published in the *Proceedings of the IEEE* in

Epilogue

March 1976. And in 1978, we carried out thirty-six similar remote-viewing trials with six army intelligence officers. They had an amazing nineteen first-place matches, when only six would be expected by chance. And their overall statistical significance was 3×10^{-5} (odds of three in a hundred thousand). Statistically, the six matches that would have been expected would amount to a batting average of 166. If the army officers had been baseball players, we would say that with their nineteen matches their team was batting better than 500—while the great Joe DiMaggio had a lifetime average of only 335! Such numbers support what we mean by statistical proof.

I conclude with these five demonstrations of psychic abilities because they were all entirely under my observation or control, and there is no way I could have been deceived. My purpose is to appeal to the authority of the scientific mind that so loves empirical data and strong statistical evidence. I sincerely hope that you find some aspect of this argument to be compelling.

NOTES

Foreword

1. Jessica Utts, "An Assessment of the Evidence for Psychic Functioning," quoted in Michael D. Mumford, Andrew M. Rose, and David A. Goslin, eds., *An Evaluation of Remote Viewing: Research and Applications* (Washington, DC: The American Institutes for Research, September 1995), 3-2; retrieved from www.lfr.org/LFR/csl/library/AirReport.pdf.
2. Ray Hyman, "Evaluation of Program on 'Anomalous Mental Phenomena,'" quoted in ibid., 3-42.
3. Jessica Utts, "The Significance of Statistics in Mind-Matter Research," *Journal of Scientific Exploration* 13, no. 4 (1999), 615–38.
4. Sarah S. Knox, *Science, God, and the Nature of Reality: Bias in Biomedical Research* (Boca Raton, FL: Brown Walker, 2010), 117.
5. Society for Psychic Research, quoted in Stanley Krippner, Harris L. Friedman, and Ruth Richards, *Debating Psychic Experience: Human Potential or Human Illusion* (Westport, CT: Praeger, 2009), 31.
6. See Benedict Carey, "Journal's Paper on ESP Expected to Prompt Outrage," *New York Times*, January 6, 2011; http://community.nytimes.com/comments/www.nytimes.com/2011/01/06/science/06esp.html, accessed October 16, 2011.
7. Olivier Costa de Beauregard, "The Paranormal Is not Excluded from Physics," *Journal of Scientific Exploration* 12 (1998), 315–20.
8. Henry Margenau, quoted in Lawrence LeShan, *The Science of the Paranormal: The Last Frontier* (Northamptonshire, UK: Aquarian Press; 1987), 118.
9. Jeffrey M. Schwartz, Henry P. Stapp, and Mario Beauregard, "Quantum Physics in Neuroscience and Psychology: A Neurophysical Model of Mind-Brain Interaction," *Philosophical Transactions of the Royal Society of Biological Sciences* 360 (June 29, 2005), 1309–27.
10. Thomas S. Kuhn, *The Structure of Scientific Revolutions*, 3rd ed. (Chicago and London: University of Chicago Press, 1996), x.
11. Ibid., 12.

NOTES

Introduction

1. Bernard Berelson and Gary Steiner, *Human Behavior: An Inventory of Scientific Findings* (New York: Harcourt, Brace & World, 1964), 126–27.
2. Russell Targ and Harold E. Puthoff, "Information Transmission under Conditions of Sensory Shielding," *Nature* 252 (Oct. 1974), 602–7.
3. Harold E. Puthoff and Russell Targ, "A Perceptual Channel for Information Transfer over Kilometer Distances: Historical Perspective and Recent Research," *The Proceedings of the Institute of Electronic and Electrical Engineers* 64, no. 3 (March 1976), 329–54.
4. Elizabeth Rauscher and Russell Targ, "Investigation of a Complex Space-Time Metric to Describe Precognition of the Future," in Daniel Sheehan, *Frontiers of Time: Retrocausation—Experiment and Theory* (Melville, NY: American Institute of Physics, 2006), 121–46.
5. Erik Larson, "Did Psychic Powers Give Firm a Killing in The Silver Market?" *Wall Street Journal* (Oct. 22, 1984).
6. Tony Edwards, Producer, "The Case of ESP," BBC Horizon, *NOVA*, 1983.
7. Anton Zeilinger, *Dance of the Photons: From Einstein to Quantum Teleportation* (New York: Farrar, Strauss, and Giroux, 2010).
8. Robert G. Jahn, "The Persistent Paradox of Psychic Phenomena: An Engineering Perspective," *The Proceedings of the Institute of Electronic and Electrical Engineers* 70, no. 2 (Feb. 1982), 136–68; Brenda J. Dunne and Robert G. Jahn, "Information and Uncertainty in Remote Perception Research," *Journal of Scientific Exploration* 17, no. 2 (2003), 207–41. The latter comprises a meta-analysis of two decades' research.
9. Marilyn J. Schlitz and William G. Braud, "Distant Intentionality and Healing: Assessing the Evidence," *Alternative Therapies* 3, no. 6 (Nov. 1997), 62–72.
10. William G. Braud, *Distant Mental Influence: Its Contributions to Science and Healing* (Charlottesville, VA: Hampton Roads, 2003).
11. Lance Storm, Patrizio Tressoldi, and Lorenzo Risio, "Meta-Analysis of Free-Response Studies 1992-2008: Assessing Noise Reduction Model in Parapsychology," *Psychological Bulletin* 136, no. 4 (2010), 471–85.
12. Deryl Bem, "Feeling the Future: Anomalous Retroactive Influences on Cognition and Affect," *Journal of Personality and Social Affect* (2010).

Chapter 1

1. Russell Targ and Harold E. Puthoff, *Mind Reach: Scientists Look at Psychic Abilities* (New York: Delacorte Press, 1977).

2. Harold E. Puthoff, recorded in private notebook, May 29, 1973.
3. Ingo Swann, *Natural ESP: The ESP Core and Its Raw Characteristics* (New York: Bantam Books, 1987).
4. Joseph McMoneagle, *Remote Viewing Secrets: A Handbook* (Charlottesville, VA: Hampton Roads, 2000).
5. Padmasambhava, *Self-Liberation through Seeing with Naked Awareness* (Ithaca, NY: Snow Lion Publications, 2000).
6. René Warcollier, *Mind to Mind* (Charlottesville, VA: Hampton Roads, 2001).
7. Quoted from Ingo Swann's Web site, http://www.biomindsuperpowers.com.
8. *Time* magazine, March 19, 1979, 96.
9. For pictures obtained by Voyager 2 of the ring and its placement within the crystal bands, see *Science News*, March 10, 1979, 149; July 14, 1979, 20.
10. I very much appreciate Dr. Edwin May's allowing me to describe the graph-paper experiment that has not yet been published in a scientific journal.

Chapter 2
1. Sheila Ostrander and Lynn Schroeder, *Psychic Discoveries Behind the Iron Curtain* (New York: Prentice Hall, 1970).
2. Arthur C. Clarke, *Childhood's End* (New York: Ballantine, 1953).
3. See T. D. Duane and Thomas Behrendt, "Extrasensory Electro-encephalo-graphic Induction between Identical Twins," *Science* 150 (1965), 367.
4. Utts, "An Assessment of the Evidence for Psychic Functioning," 32 (see foreword, n. 1).

Chapter 3
1. C. A. Robinson, Jr., "Soviets Push for Beam Weapon," *Aviation Week* (May 2, 1977), 17.
2. Russell Targ and Harold E. Puthoff, "Perceptual Augmentation Techniques," Final Report to the CIA (Menlo Park, CA: Stanford Research Institute, 1975), 9.
3. Targ and Puthoff, "Information Transmission" (see intro., n. 2).
4. Harold E. Puthoff and Russell Targ, "A Perceptual Channel for Information Transfer over Kilometer Distances" (see intro., n. 3).
5. *Chicago Tribune*, August 13, 1977.

NOTES

Chapter 4

1. See Robert G. Jahn and Brenda J. Dunne, *Margins of Reality: The Role of Consciousness in the Physical World* (New York: Harcourt, Brace, Jovanovich, 1987).
2. *The History of Herodotus*, trans. George Rawlinson, book 1, chaps. 1.40–1.45, http://classics.mit.edu/Herodotus/history.1.i.html.
3. H. W. Parke, *A History of the Delphic Oracle* (Oxford, England: Blackwell, 1939).
4. *The History of Herodotus*, chaps. 1.45–1.50.
5. Ibid.
6. Parke, *Delphic Oracle*.

Chapter 5

1. Russell Targ, Phyllis Cole, and Harold E. Puthoff, "Development of Techniques to Enhance Man/Machine Interaction," Final Report, NASA contract 953653 under NAS7-100 (1975).
2. Duane and Behrendt, "Extrasensory Electro-encephalographic Induction between Identical Twins" (see chap. 2, n. 3).
3. *San Francisco Chronicle*, 1971.
4. Robert A. Burton, *On Being Certain: Believing You Are Right Even When You Are Not* (New York: St. Martin's Press, 2008).
5. See Milan Ryzl, "Training the Psi Faculty by Hypnosis," *Journal of the American Society for Psychical Research* 41 (1962), 234–51.
6. See Guy Playfair, *Twin Telepathy: The Psychic Connection* (London: Vega, 2002).
7. See J. G. Pratt, J. B. Rhine, Burke M. Smith, and Charles E. Stuart, *Extrasensory Perception after Sixty Years: A Critical Appraisal of the Research in Extra-Sensory Perception* (Boston: Bruce Humphries, 1966).
8. See L. L. Vasiliev, *Experiments in Mental Suggestion* (Charlottesville, VA: Hampton Roads, 2002).
9. Russell Targ and Keith Harary, *The Mind Race: Understanding and Using Psychic Abilities* (New York: Villard, 1984), 252–53.
10. Ostrander and Schroeder, *Psychic Discoveries*, 28 (see chap. 2, n. 1).
11. Ibid.

Chapter 6

1. Paul Smith, *Reading the Enemy's Mind: Inside Star Gate, America's Psychic Espionage Program* (New York: Forge, 2005).
2. Targ and Harary, *The Mind Race* (see chap. 5, n. 9).
3. Ostrander and Schroeder, *Psychic Discoveries* (see chap. 2, n. 1).

Chapter 7

1. Ludwig Wittgenstein, *Tractatus Logico-Philosophicus* (London: Routledge and Kegan Paul, 1922).
2. Upton Beall Sinclair, *Mental Radio* (Charlottesville, VA: Hampton Roads, 2000).
3. William Cox, "Precognition: An Analysis, II," *Journal of the Association of Staff Physician Recruiters* 50 (1956), 99–109.
4. Gertrude Schmeidler, "An Experiment in Precognitive Clairvoyance: Part 1, The Main Results," and "Part 2, The Reliability of the Scores," *Journal of Parapsychology* 28 (1964), 1–27.
5. See Stephan A. Schwartz, *Opening to the Infinite* (Buda, TX: Nemoseen Media, 2007).
6. Larson, "Did Psychic Powers Give Firm a Killing" (see intro., n. 5).
7. Russell Targ, Jane Katra, Dean Brown, and Wendy Wiegand, "Viewing the Future: A Pilot Study with an Error-Detecting Protocol," *Journal of Scientific Exploration* 9, no. 3 (1995), 367–80.
8. Charles Honorton and Diane Ferari, "Future-Telling: A Meta-analysis of Forced-Choice Precognition Experiments," *Journal of Parapsychology* 53 (December 1989), 281–308.
9. Dean Radin, *The Conscious Universe: The Scientific Truth of Psychic Phenomena* (San Francisco: Harper Edge, 1997).
10. Braud, *Distant Mental Influence*, xxxv (see intro., n. 10).
11. Zoltán Vassy, "Method for Measuring the Probability of 1 Bit Extrasensory Information Transfer between Living Organisms," *Journal of Parapsychology* 42 (1978), 158–60.
12. Bem, "Feeling the Future" (see intro., n. 12).
13. Harold E. Puthoff and E. C. May, "Feasibility Study on the Vulnerability of the MPS System to RV Detection Techniques," Stanford Research Institute Internal Report, April 15, 1979; revised, 2 May 1979; Harold E. Puthoff, *Journal of Scientific Exploration* 10, no. 1 (1996), 63–76.

NOTES

Chapter 8

1. See Tom Harpur, *The Uncommon Touch: An Investigation of Spiritual Healing* (Toronto: McClelland & Stewart Inc., 1994), 38–73.

2. Vasiliev, *Experiments in Mental Suggestion* (see chap. 5, n. 8).

3. Henry P. Stapp, "Harnessing science and religion: Implications of the new scientific conception of human beings," *Research News and Opportunities in Science and Religion* 1, no. 6, (February 2001), 8.

4. Douglas Dean, "Plethysmograph Recordings as ESP Responses," *International Journal of Europsychiatry* 2 (1966), 439–46.

5. See William G. Braud and Marilyn J. Schlitz, "Consciousness Interactions with Remote Biological Systems: Anomalous Intentionality Effects," *Subtle Energies* 2 (1993), 1–47; "On the Use of Living Target Systems in Distant Mental Influence Research," in L. Coly, ed., *Research Methodology: A Reexamination* (New York: Parapsychology Foundation, 1991).

6. All the references to the work of William G. Braud can also be found in his recent book, *Distant Mental Influence* (see intro., n. 10).

7. William G. Braud, "Direct Mental Influence on the Rate of Hemolysis of Human Red Blood Cells," *Journal of the American Society for Psychical Research* (January 1990), 1–24.

8. _____. *Distant Mental Influence*, xviii (see intro. n. 10).

9. William G. Braud and Marilyn J. Schlitz, "Psychokinetic Influence on Electro-dermal Activity," *Journal of Parapsychology* 47 (1983), 95–119; William G. Braud, D. Shafer, and S. Andrews, "Reactions to an Unseen Gaze (Remote Attention): A Review, with New Data on Autonomic Staring Detection," *Journal of Parapsychology* 57 (1993), 373–90.

10. See Marilyn J. Schlitz and Steven LaBerge, "Autonomic Detection of Remote Observation: Two Conceptual Replications," Institute of Noetic Sciences (1994).

11. Targ and Puthoff, *Mind Reach* (see chap. 1, n. 1); Targ and Puthoff, "Information Transmission" (see intro., n. 2).

12. See Daniel J. Benor, *Healing Research*, vol. 1 (Munich, Germany: Helix Verlag, 1992).

13. Fred Sicher, Elisabeth Targ, Dan Moore, and Helene Smith, "A Randomized Double-Blind Study of the Effect of Distant Healing in a Population with Advanced AIDS," *Western Journal of Medicine* 169 (December 1998), 356.

14. Ibid., 361.

NOTES

15. Ibid, 356.

16. Randolph C. Byrd, "Positive Therapeutic Effects of Intercessory Prayer in a Coronary Care Unit Population," *Southern Medical Journal* 81, no. 7 (July 1988), 826–29.

17. William S. Harris, et al., "A Randomized, Controlled Trial of the Effects of Remote Intercessory Prayer on Outcomes in Patients Admitted to the Coronary Care Unit," *Archives of Internal Medicine* 159 (Oct. 25, 1999), 2273–78.

18. The effect size measures the efficiency or strength of the phenomenon under investigation and is equal to the number of standard deviations (Z) from chance that you observe, divided by the square root of the number of trials (N) you did in order to get that much significance.

19. John A. Astin, Elaine Harkness, and Edward Ernst, "The Efficacy of 'Distant Healing': A Systematic Review of Randomized Trials," *Annals of Internal Medicine* 132, no. 11 (June 2000), 903–10.

20. Schlitz and Braud, "Distant Intentionality and Healing" (see intro., n. 9); Elisabeth Targ, "Evaluating Distant Healing: A Research Review," *Alternative Therapies in Health and Medicine* 3, no. 6 (November, 1977).

21. Larry Dossey, M.D., "Healing Research: What We Know and Don't Know," *Explore* 4, no. 6 (November/December 2008), 147.

22. See O. Carl Simonton, *The Healing Journey* (New York, Bantam, 1992).

23. The Commonweal Cancer Help Program may be reached at P.O. Box 316, Bolinas, California 94924.

24. See Jeanne Achterberg, *Imagery in Healing: Shamanism and Modern Medicine* (Boston: Shambhala, 1985); Jeanne Achterberg, O. Carl Simonton, and Stephanie Simonton, "Psychology of the Exceptional Cancer Patient: A Description of Patients Who Outlive Predicted Life Expectancies," *Psychotherapy: Theory, Research, and Practice* 14 (1977), 416–22.

25. See H. J. Eysenck, "Health's Character," *Psychology Today* 22 (December 1988), 28–32; H. J. Eysenck, "Personality, Stress, and Cancer: Prediction and Prophylaxis," *British Journal of Medical Psychology* 61 (1988), 57–75.

26. See D. Spiegel, H. C. Kraemer, J. R. Bloom, J. R. Gottheil, and E. Gottheil, "The Effect of Psychosocial Treatment on Survival of Patients with Metastatic Breast Cancer," *Lancet* (October 1989); also David Spiegel, *Living Beyond Limits* (New York: Random House, Times Books, 1993).

27. See William Nolan, *Healing: Doctor in Search of a Miracle* (New York: Random House, 1974).

28. Lewis Thomas, quoted in Brendan O'Regan and Caryle Hirshberg, *Spontaneous Remission: An Annotated Bibliography* (Sausalito, CA: Institute of Noetic Sciences, 1993), 1. See also Thomas's *The Youngest Science: Notes of a Medicine Watcher* (New York: Viking Press, 1983), 205.

Chapter 9

1. See Burton, *On Being Certain* (see chap. 5, n. 4).
2. William James, in F. W. H Myers, *Human Personality and Its Survival of Bodily Death,* ed. Suzi Smith (New Hyde Park, NY: University Books, 1961).
3. ibid.
4. See Gary Dore, *What Survives? Contemporary Explorations of Life after Death* (Los Angeles: Tarcher, 1990).
5. Reuters News Service, January 31, 1998.
6. See Alan Gauld, *Mediumship and Survival: A Century of Investigations* (London: Paladin/Granada, 1983).
7. Ian Stevenson, *Twenty Cases Suggestive of Reincarnation* (New York: American Society for Psychical Research, 1966).
8. _____, *Where Reincarnation and Biology Intersect* (Westport, CT: Praeger, 1997).
9. _____, *Children Who Remember Previous Lives: A Question of Reincarnation* (Charlottesville: The University Press of Virginia, 1987).
10. Almeder, Robert, "A Critique of Arguments Offered against Reincarnation," *Journal of Scientific Exploration* 11, no. 4, (1997).
11. See Tim Ernst, *The Search for Haley: An Insider's Account of the Longest Search Mission in Arkansas History* (Pettigrew, AR: cloudland.net, 2001).
12. See Elizabeth Lloyd Mayer, *Extraordinary Knowing: Science, Skepticism, and the Inexplicable Powers of the Human Mind* (New York: Bantam, 2007).
13. Wolfgang Eisenbeiss and Deiter Hassler, "An Assessment of Ostensible Communications with a Deceased Grandmaster as Evidence of Survival," *Journal of the Society of Psychical Research* 70.2 (April 2006).
14. Vernon Neppe, "A Detailed Analysis of an Important Chess Match: Revisiting the Maroczy–Korchnoi Game," *Journal of the Society of Psychical Research* 71.3 (2007), 129–47.
15. See Harold Francis Saltmarsh, *The Future and Beyond: Paranormal Foreknowledge and Evidence of Personal Survival from Cross Correspondences* (Charlottesville, VA: Hampton Roads, 2004).

16. F. W. H. Myers and Eveleen Myers, *Fragments of Prose and Poetry* (London: Longmans Green, 1904).

17. Claire Sylvia, *A Change of Heart: A Memoir* (New York: Little Brown & Co. 1997); this summary first appeared in Jane Katra and Russell Targ, *The Heart of the Mind: Using Our Mind to Transform Our Consciousness* (Novato, CA: New World Library, 1999).

18. Stephen Braude, *Immortal Remains: The Evidence for Life after Death* (London: Rowman and Littlefield, 2003), 283.

19. Ibid., 305.

Chapter 10

1. Annie Besant, "Occult Chemistry," *Lucifer: A Theosophical Monthly* (November 1895).

2. C. W. Leadbeater and Annie Besant, *Occult Chemistry: Clairvoyant Observations of the Chemical Elements* (London: Dodo Press, 1908).

3. Stephen M. Phillips, *Extra-Sensory Perception of Quarks* (Wheaton, IL: Quest Books, 1980).

4. Sir Arthur Eddington, quoted in Alan H. Batten, "A Most Rare Vision: Eddington's Thinking on the Relation between Science and Religion," *Journal of Scientific Exploration* 9:2 (Summer 1995), 231–34.

5. A. Einstein, B. Podolsky, and N. Rosen, "Can a Quantum Mechanical Description of Physical Reality Be Considered Complete?" *Physical Review* 47 (1935), 777–80.

6. J. S. Bell, "On the Einstein, Podolsky, Rosen Paradox," *Physics* 1 (1964), 195–200.

7. Schrödinger, as quoted by John Clauser in a private communication at the twenty-fifth anniversary meeting of the Fundimental Fysiks Group, 2000.

8. S. Freedman and J. Clauser, "Experimental Test of Local Hidden Variable Theories," *Physical Review Letters* 28 (1972), 934–41.

9. Bell, "On the Einstein, Podolsky, Rosen Paradox," 200.

10. Henry P. Stapp, in Robert Nadeau and Menas Kafatos, *The Nonlocal Universe: The New Physics and Matters of the Mind* (New York: Oxford University Press, 1999).

11. See David Bohm and Basil J. Hiley, *The Undivided Universe: An Ontological Interpretation of Quantum Theory* (New York: Routledge, 1993).

12. Ibid., 382.

13. Ibid., 386.

14. Ibid.
15. Mark Fox, *Quantum Optics: An Introduction* (New York: Oxford University Press, 2010).
16. See Elizabeth A. Rauscher and Russell Targ, "The Speed of Thought: Investigation of a Complex Space-Time Metric to Describe Psychic Phenomena," *Journal of Scientific Exploration* 15, no. 4 (2001), 331–54.
17. John Archibald Wheeler, *Geometrodynamics* (New York: Academic Press, 1963).
18. See ibid. and also Elizabeth A. Rauscher and Richard L. Amaroso, *The Moons of Pluto: Solving Maxwell's, Schrödinger's, and the Dirac Equation in Complex Minkowski Space* (Singapore: World Scientific, 2010).

Chapter 11

1. See Russell Targ and Jane Katra, *Miracles of Mind: Exploring Nonlocal Consciousness and Spiritual Healing* (Novato, CA: New World Library, 1998) and Jane Katra and Russell Targ, *The Heart of the Mind: How to Experience God without Belief* (Novato, CA: New World Library, 1999).
2. Russell Targ and Jane Katra, "Remote Viewing in a Group Setting," *Journal of Scientific Exploration* 14, n. 1 (2000), 107–14.
3. McMoneagle, *Remote Viewing Secrets*, (see chap. 1, n. 4).
4. Swann and Puthoff, *Natural ESP* (see chap. 1, n. 3).
5. Warcollier, *Mind to Mind* (see chap. 1, n. 6).
6. Sinclair, *Mental Radio*, 116 (see chap. 7, n. 2).
7. Ibid., xi.
8. See Robert Monroe, *Journeys Out of the Body* (Garden City, NY: Doubleday, 1971).
9. See Namkhai Norbu, *Dream Yoga and the Practice of Natural Light* (Ithaca, NY: Snow Lion Publications, 1992).
10. Ingo Swann, *Psychic Sexuality: The Bio-Psychic "Anatomy" of Sexual Energies* (Rapid City, SD: Ingo Swann Books, 1999), 158.
11. See Aleister Crowley, *The Confessions of Aleister Crowley: An Autohagiography* (London: Penguin Books, 1979).
12. See Sylvan J. Muldoon and Hereward Carrington, *The Projection of the Astral Body* (London: Rider and Paternoster House, 1929).
13. See MacKinlay Kantor, *Don't Touch Me* (New York: Random House, 1951).

NOTES

Chapter 12

1. Jeffrey Kripal, *Authors of the Impossible: The Paranormal and the Sacred* (Chicago: University of Chicago Press, 2010), 9–11.
2. Arthur C. Clarke, *Profiles of the Future: An Inquiry into the Limits of the Possible* (New York: Harper & Row, 1962).
3. See Thomas Cleary, trans., *The Flower Ornament Scripture*, translation of the *Avatamsaka Sutra*, 2 vols. (Boston and London: Shambhala, 1993).
4. See Patanjali, *Sutras*, in Swami Prabhavananda and Christopher Isherwood, trans., *How to Know God* (Hollywood, CA: Vedanta Press, 1983; reprint, 2007).
5. See Padmasambhava, *Self-Liberation* (see chap. 1. n. 5).
6. Erwin Schrödinger, *My View of the World* (Woodbridge, CT: Ox Bow Press, 1983), 87–89.
7. See Jay L. Garfield, *The Fundamental Wisdom of the Middle Way: Nagarjuna's Mulamadhyamakakarika* (New York: Oxford University Press, 1995).
8. See Amir D. Aczel, *Entanglement: The Greatest Mystery in Physics* (New York: Four Walls Eight Windows, 2002).
9. Francis H. Cook, trans., *The Jewel Net of Indra: The Avatamsaka Sutra* (Philadelphia: University of Pennsylvania, 1977).
10. Patanjali, *How to Know God?* 14.
11. Ibid., 183.
12. Cleary, trans., *The Flower Ornament Scripture*, 870–75.
13. Shankara, in *Shankara's Crest Jewel of Discrimination*, Swami Prabhavananda and Christopher Isherwood, trans. (Hollywood, CA: Vedanta Press, 1975).
14. Longchen Rabjam, *The Precious Treasury of the Basic Space of Phenomena* (Junction City, CA: Padma Publications, 2001).
15. _____, *The Precious Treasury of the Way of Abiding* (Junction City, CA: Padma Publications, 2001).
16. _____, *A Treasure Trove of Scriptural Transmission: A Commentary on the Precious Treasure of the Basic Space of Phenomena* (Junction City, CA: Padma Publications, 2001), 54–56.
17. Arthur Koestler, *The Roots of Coincidence* (New York: Random House 1972).
18. Rachel Naomi Remen, "Is Psi Sacred?" *Noetic Sciences Review* 35 (Autumn, 1995), 34.
19. Ibid.

NOTES

20. Many of the ideas described in this subsection, "Are Psychic Abilities Sacred," were previously explored in a somewhat similar fashion by this author and Dr. Jane Katra in our coauthored 1998 book, *Miracles of Mind*, 135 (see chap. 11, n. 1).

21. Patanjali, *Sutras*, in Swami Prabhavananda and Christopher Isherwood, trans., *How to Know God* (Hollywood, CA: Vedanta Press, 1983; reprint, 2007), 187.

22. Ibid, 204.

23. Alistair Shearer, trans., *Effortless Being: The Yoga Sutras of Patanjali* (London: Unwin, 1989).

24. Shankara, in *Shankara's Crest Jewel of Discrimination*, 23.

25. Ibid.

26. See Keith Dowman, trans., *Buddhists Masters of Enchantment: The Lives and Legends of the Mahasiddhas* (Rochester, VT: Inner Traditions, 1998).

27. See David Goodman, *The Teachings of Sri Ramana Maharshi* (London: Arkana/Penguin Books, 1985).

Glossary

Causality: Two events A and B are said to be causally related such that A causes B, if whenever B occurs, A occurs (usually first). Causes can be *necessary* or *sufficient* or both. We would say that A is *necessary* for B, e.g., the train *never* moves unless the electricity is turned on. A is not necessarily *sufficient*, however, inasmuch as, in this case in which A is the electricity, many other elements must all be working properly for the train to move. On the other hand, a pistol shot to the head is almost always sufficient for a person to be dead.

Clairvoyance: Clairvoyance is the direct perception or experience of a contemporaneous distant object or event that is *not known* to any other person.

EEG: EEG is a graphical record of electrical activity of the brain (brain waves) produced by an electroencephalograph.

Entanglement: Photons or other systems are said to be entangled when a perturbation of one causes a change in the state of the other, even when the two are physically isolated and insulated from each other. Entanglement implies a nonlocal connection.

ESP: Extrasensory perception (ESP) involves the direct reception or experience of information not gained through the recognized physical senses but rather sensed with the mind. ESP is considered a kind of direct knowing without any intermediate processes.

Naked awareness: Naked awareness is awareness that is free of ego, attachment, conditioning, or any other mental obstruction or obscuration that prevents you from experiencing the world as it really is—spacious, infinite, and empty of meaning.

Nonlocality: In classical physics, *nonlocality*, meaning action at a distance, is a direct influence of one object on another distant object. In quantum physics, the term *nonlocal* means that correlations exist between distant systems (usually photons) that cannot be described by any local theory. Such a form of nonlocality does not allow superluminal (faster than light speed) communication. It does not violate special relativity.

Glossary

Precognition: Precognition is the direct experience or knowing of an event that has not yet occurred. It pertains to knowing the future.

Psi: From the Greek, Ψ (*psi*), the twenty-third letter of the Greek alphabet; the term *psi* derives from the Greek, "psyche" or "soul." It is used synonymously with ESP.

Psychokinesis (PK): Psychokinesis is the alleged ability of a person to affect the physical state of a distant object. The best evidence pertains to psychokinesis on living systems, such as distant healing.

Remote Viewing (RV): Remote viewing is a protocol developed at Stanford Research Institute in the 1970s to allow people to learn to describe and experience objects and events blocked from ordinary perception—often at great distances. It is a kind of ESP.

Retrocausality: Retrocausality pertains to a future event affecting the past. If I dream tonight about an elephant trampling my garden and then tomorrow morning I see an escaped elephant trampling my garden, I would say that last night's dream was caused (retrocausally) by today's elephant. On the other hand, it is important to note that a future event can never *change* the past. An example would be for me to go to the past and kill my grandmother so that she could never gave birth to my mother. That kind of change cannot occur.

Telepathy: Telepathy pertains to one person directly knowing or experiencing the thoughts of another person from whom their ordinary perception is blocked. It is loosely equivalent to mind reading.

Bibliography

Achterberg, Jeanne. *Imagery in Healing: Shamanism and Modern Medicine.* Boston: Shambhala, 1985.

————, Simonton, O. C., and Simonton, S. "Psychology of the Exceptional Cancer Patient: A Description of Patients Who Outlive Predicted Life Expectancies." *Psychotherapy: Theory, Research, and Practice* (1977): 416–22.

Almeder, Robert. "A Critique of Arguments Offered against Reincarnation." *Journal of Scientific Exploration* 11, no. 4, (1997).

————. *Death and Personal Survival: The Evidence for Life after Death.* Lanham, MD: Rowman and Littlefield, 1993.

Austin, John A., Elaine Harkness, and Edward Ernst. "The Efficacy of 'Distant Healing': A Systematic Review of Randomized Trials." *Annals of Internal Medicine* 132, no. 11 (June 2000): 903–10.

Batten, Alan H. "A Most Rare Vision: Eddington's Thinking on the Relation between Science and Religion." *Journal of Scientific Exploration* 9, no. 2 (Summer 1995): 231–34.

Bell, J. S. "On the Einstein, Podolsky, Rosen Paradox," *Physics* 1 (1964): 195–200.

Bem, Deryl. "Feeling the Future: Anomalous Retroactive Influences on Cognition and Affect." *Journal of Personality and Social Psychology* (December 2010).

Benor, Daniel J. *Healing Research.* Vol. 1. Munich, Germany: Helix Verlag, 1992.

Berelson, Bernard, and Gary Steiner. *Human Behavior: An Inventory of Scientific Findings.* New York: Harcourt, Brace and World, 1964.

Bessant, Annie. "Occult Chemistry." *Lucifer: A Theosophical Monthly* (November 1895).

Bohm, David, and Basil J. Hiley. *The Undivided Universe: An Ontological Interpretation of Quantum Theory.* New York: Routledge, 1993.

Braud, William G. *Distant Mental Influence: Its Contributions to Science and Healing.* Charlottesville, VA: Hampton Roads, 2003.

Bibliography

_____. "Direct Mental Influence on the Rate of Hemolysis of Human Red Blood Cells." *The Journal of the ASPR* (January 1990): 1–24.

Braud, William G. and Marilyn J. Schlitz. "Consciousness Interactions with Remote Biological Systems: Anomalous Intentionality Effects." *Subtle Energies* 2 (1993): 1–47.

_____. "On the Use of Living Target Systems in Distant Mental Influence Research." In Lisette Coly, ed. *Psi Research Methodology: A Re-examination.* New York: Parapsychology Foundation, 1991.

_____. "Psychokinetic Influence on Electro-Dermal Activity." *Journal of Parapsychology* 47 (1983): 95–119;

Braud, William G., D. Shafer, and S. Andrews. "Reactions to an Unseen Gaze (Remote Attention): A Review, with New Data on Autonomic Staring Detection." *Journal of Parapsychology* 57, no. 4 (1993): 373–90.

Braude, Stephen. *Immortal Remains: The Evidence for Life after Death.* London: Rowman and Littlefield, 2003.

Burton, Robert A. *On Being Certain: Believing You Are Right Even When You Are Not.* New York: St. Martin's Press, 2008.

Byrd, Randolph C. "Positive Therapeutic Effects of Intercessory Prayer in a Coronary Care Unit Population," *Southern Medical Journal* 81, no. 7 (July 1988): 826–29.

Clarke, Arthur C. *Childhood's End.* New York: Ballantine, 1953.

Clary, Thomas, trans. *The Flower Ornament Sutra*, translation of the *Avatamsaka Sutra.* Boston and London: Shambala, 1993.

Cook, Francis H., trans. *The Jewel Net of Indra: The Avatamsaka Sutra.* Philadelphia: University of Pennsylvania, 1977.

Cox, William. "Precognition: An Analysis, II," *Journal of the Association of Staff Physician Recruiters* 50 (1956): 99–109.

Dean, Douglas. "Plethysmograph Recordings as ESP Responses." *International Journal of Europsychiatry* 2 (1966): 439–46.

Dore, Gary. *What Survives? Contemporary Explorations of Life after Death.* Los Angeles, CA: Tarcher, 1990.

Dossey, Larry, M.D. "Healing Research: "What We Know and Don't Know." *Explore* 4, no. 6 (November/December 2008): 341–52.

Dowman, Keith. *Buddhists: Masters of Enchantment.* Rochester, VT: Inner Traditions, 1988.

Bibliography

Duane, T. D. and Thomas Behrendt. "Extrasensory Electro-encephalographic Induction between Identical Twins." *Science* 150 (1965): 367.

Edwards, Tony. "The Case of ESP." BBC Horizon, *NOVA*, 1983.

Einstein, A., B. Podolsky, and N. Rosen. "Can a Quantum Mechanical Description of Physical Reality Be Considered Complete?" *Physical Review* 47 (1935): 777–80.

Eisenbeiss, Wolfgang, and Deiter Hassler. "An Assessment of Ostensible Communications with a Deceased Grandmaster as Evidence for Survival." *Journal of the Association of Staff Physician Recruiters* 70.2, no. 883 (April 2006).

Ernst, Tim. *The Search for Haley: An Insider's Account of the Longest Search-Mission in Arkansas History.* Pettigrew, AR: Cloudland, 2001.

Eysenck, H. J. "Health's character." *Psychology Today.* 22 (December 1988): 28–32.

————. "Personality, Stress, and Cancer: Prediction and Prophylaxis. *British Journal of Medical Psychology* 61 (1988): 57–75.

Fox, Mark. *Quantum Optics: An Introduction.* Oxford: Oxford University Press, 2010.

Freedman, S., and J. Clauser. "Experimental Test of Local Hidden Variable Theories." *Physical Review Letters* 28 (1972): 934–41.

Gauld, Alan. *Mediumship and Survival: A Century of Investigations.* London: Paladin/Granada, 1983.

Goodman, David. *The Teachings of Sri Ramana Maharshi.* London: Arkana/Penguin Books, 1985.

Harpur, Tom. *The Uncommon Touch: An Investigation of Spiritual Healing.* Toronto: McClelland and Stewart, Inc.,1994.

Harris, William S., et al., "A Randomized, Controlled Trial of the Effects of Remote Intercessory Prayer on Outcomes in Patients Admitted to the Coronary Care Unit." *Archives of Internal Medicine* 159 (Oct. 25, 1999): 2273–78.

Honorton, Charles, and Diane Ferari. "Future-Telling: A Meta-analysis of Forced-Choice Precognition Experiments." *Journal of Parapsychology* 53 (December 1989): 281–308.

Jahn, Robert G.. "The Persistent Paradox of Psychic Phenomena: An Engineering Perspective." *Proc. IEEE* 70, no. 2 (Feb. 1982): 136–68.

Bibliography

Jahn, Robert G., and Brenda J. Dunne. *Margins of Reality: The Role of Consciousness in the Physical World*. New York: Harcourt Brace Jovanovich, 1987.

Katra, Jane, and Russell Targ. *The Heart of the Mind*. Novato, CA: New World Library, 1999.

Koestler, Arthur. *The Roots of Coincidence*. New York: Random House, 1972.

Kripal, Jeffrey. *Authors of the Impossible: The Paranormal and the Sacred*. Chicago: University of Chicago Press, 2010.

Larson, Erik. "Did Psychic Powers Give Firm a Killing in the Silver Market?" *Wall Street Journal*, Oct. 22, 1984.

Leadbeater, C. W., and Annie Besant. *Occult Chemistry: Clairvoyant Observations of the Chemical Elements*. London: Dodo Press, 1919.

Longchen Rabjam. *The Precious Treasury of the Basic Space of Phenomena* and *The Precious Treasury of the Way of Abiding*. Junction City, CA: Padma Publishing, 2001.

Mayer, Elizabeth Lloyd. *Extraordinary Knowing: Science, Skepticism, and the Inexplicable Powers of the Human Mind*. New York: Bantam, 2007.

McMoneagle, Joseph. *Remote Viewing Secrets: A Handbook*. Charlottesville, VA: Hampton Roads, 2002.

Mumford, Michael. *An Evaluation of Remote Viewing: Research and Applications*. Washington, D.C.: American Institutes of Research, 2005.

Myers, F. W. H., and Eveleen Myers. *Fragments of Prose and Poetry*. London: Longmans Green, 1904.

————. *Human Personality and Its Survival of Bodily Death*. Edited by Suzi Smith. Hyde Park, NY: University Books, 1961.

Nadeau, Robert, and Menas Kafatos. *The Non-Local Universe: The New Physics and Matters of the Mind*. Oxford: Oxford University Press, 1999.

Neppe, Vernon. "A Detailed Analysis of an Important Chess Match: Revisiting the Maroczy–Korchnoi Game." *Journal of the Society of Psychical Research* 71.3 (2007): 129–47.

Nolan, William. *Healing: Doctor in Search of a Miracle*. New York: Random House, 1974.

O'Regan, Brendan, and Caryle Hirshberg. *Spontaneous Remission: An Annotated Bibliography*. Sausalito, CA: Institute of Noetic Sciences, 1993.

Bibliography

Ostrander, Sheila, and Lynn Schroeder. *Psychic Discoveries Behind the Iron Curtain.* Englewood Cliffs, NJ: Prentice Hall, 1970.

Padmasambhava. *Self-Liberation through Seeing with Naked Awareness.* Ithaca, NY: Snow Lion Publications, 2000.

Parke, H. W. *A History of the Delphic Oracle.* Oxford: Blackwell, 1939.

Patanjali, *Sutras,* in *How to Know God.* Translated by Swami Prabhavananda and Christopher Isherwood. Hollywood, CA: Vedanta Press, 1983.

Phillips, Stephen M. *Extra-Sensory Perception of Quarks.* Wheaton, IL: Quest Books, 1980.

Playfair, Guy. *Twin Telepathy: The Psychic Connection.* London: Vega, 2002.

Pratt, J. G., J. B. Rhine, Burke M. Smith, and Charles E. Stuart. *Extrasensory Perception after Sixty Years: A Critical Appraisal of the Research in Extra-Sensory Perception.* Boston: Bruce Humphries, 1966.

Puthoff, Harold E. "Feasibility Study on the Vulnerability of the MPS System to RV Detection Techniques." Stanford Research Institute Internal Report, April 15, 1979; revised May 2, 1979.

Puthoff, Harold E., and Russell Targ. "A Perceptual Channel for Information Transfer over Kilometer Distances: Historical Perspective and Recent Research." *Proc. IEEE* 64, no. 3, (March 1976): 329–54.

Rabjam, Longchen. *The Precious Treasury of the Basic Space of Phenomena.* Junction City, CA: Padma Publishing, 2001.

Radin, Dean I. *The Conscious Universe: The Scientific Truth of Psychic Phenomena.* San Francisco: Harper Edge, 1997.

Remen, Rachel Naomi. "Is Psi Sacred?" *Noetic Sciences Review* 35 (Autumn 1995): 34.

Rauscher, Elizabeth A., and Richard L. Amaroso. *Orbiting the Moons of Pluto: Complex Solutions to the Einstein, Maxwell, Schrödinger, and Dirac Equations.* Singapore: World Scientific, 2010.

Rauscher, Elizabeth A., and Russell Targ, "The Speed of Thought: Investigation of a Complex Space-Time Metric to Describe Psychic Phenomena." *Journal of Scientific Exploration* 15, no. 4 (2001): 331–54.

————. "Investigation of a Complex Space-Time Metric to Describe Precognition of the Future." In *Frontiers of Time,* by Daniel Sheehan. Malville, NY: American Institute of Physics, 2006.

Bibliography

Saltmarsh, Harold Francis. *The Future and Beyond: Paranormal Foreknowledge and Evidence of Personal Survival from Cross Correspondences*. Charlottesville, VA: Hampton Roads, 2004.

Schlitz, Marilyn, and William Braud. "Distant Intentionality and Healing: Assessing the Evidence." *Alternative Therapies* 3, no. 6 (November 1997).

Schlitz, Marilyn, and Steven LaBerge. "Autonomic Detection of Remote Observation: Two Conceptual Replications." Sausalito, CA: Institute of Noetic Sciences (1994).

Schmeidler, Gertrude. "An Experiment in Precognitive Clairvoyance: Part 1, The Main Results" and "Part 2, The Reliability of the Scores." *Journal of Parapsychology* 28 (1964): 1–27.

Schrödinger, Erwin, *My View of the World*. Woodbridge , CT: Ox Bow Press, 1983.

Schwartz, Stephan A. *Opening to the Infinite*. Buda, TX: Nemoseen Media, 2007.

Shankara, in *Shankara's Crest Jewel of Discrimination*. Translated by Swami Prabhavananda and Christopher Isherwood. Hollywood, CA: Vedanta Press, 1975.

Patanjali, *Sutras*, in *How to Know God*. Translated by Swami Prabhavananda and Christopher Isherwood. Hollywood, CA: Vedanta Press, 1983.

Sicher, Fred, Elisabeth Targ, Dan Moore, and Helene Smith. "A Randomized Double-Blind Study of the Effect of Distant Healing in a Population with Advanced AIDS." *Western Journal of Medicine* 169 (December 1998): 356–63.

Simonton, O. Carl. *The Healing Journey*. New York: Bantam, 1992.

Sinclair, Upton Beall. *Mental Radio*. Charlottesville, VA: Hampton Roads, 2002.

Smith, Paul. *Reading the Enemy's Mind: Inside Star Gate, America's Psychic Espionage Program*. New York: Forge, 2005.

Spiegel, David. *Living Beyond Limits*. New York: Times Books/Random House, 1993.

Spiegel, David, Helena C. Kraemer, Joan R. Bloom, and Ellen Gottheil. "The Effect of Psychosocial Treatment on Survival of Patients with Metastatic Breast Cancer." *Lancet* 2 (October 1989): 888–91.

Bibliography

Stapp, Henry P. "Harnessing Science and Religion: Implications of the New Scientific Conception of Human Beings." *Research News and Opportunities in Science and Religion* 1, no. 6 (February, 2001): 8.

Stevenson, Ian. *Children Who Remember Previous Lives: A Question of Reincarnation.* Charlottesville: The University Press of Virginia, 1987.

————. *Twenty Cases Suggestive of Reincarnation.* New York: American Society for Psychical Research, 1966.

————. *Where Reincarnation and Biology Intersect.* Westport, CT: Praeger, 1997.

Storm, Lance, Patrizio Tressoldi, and Lorenzo Risio. "Meta-Analysis of Free-Response Studies 1992-2008: Assessing Noise Reduction Model in Parapsychology." *Psychological Bulletin* 136, no. 4 (2010): 471–85.

Swann, Ingo, and Harold E. Puthoff. *Natural ESP: The ESP Core and Its Raw Characteristics.* New York: Bantam, 1987.

Sylvia, Claire. *A Change of Heart: A Memoir.* New York: Little Brown & Co. 1997.

Targ, Elisabeth. "Evaluating Distant Healing: A Research Review." *Alternative Therapies in Health and Medicine* 3, no. 6 (November 1977).

Targ, Russell, Phyllis Cole, and Harold E. Puthoff. "Development of Techniques to Enhance Man/Machine Interaction." Final Report, NASA contract 953653 under NAS7-100 (1975).

Targ, Russell, and Keith Harary. *The Mind Race.* New York: Villard, 1994.

Targ, Russell, and Jane Katra. *Miracles of Mind: Exploring Nonlocal Consciousness and Spiritual Healing.* Novato, CA: New World Library, 1998.

————. "Remote Viewing in a Group Setting." *Journal of Scientific Exploration* 14, no. 1 (2000): 107–14.

Targ, Russell, Jane Katra, Dean Brown, and Wendy Wiegand. "Viewing the Future: A Pilot Study with an Error-Detecting Protocol." *Journal of Scientific Exploration* 9, no. 3 (1995): 367–80.

Targ, Russell, and Harold E. Puthoff. "Information Transmission under Conditions of Sensory Shielding." *Nature* 252 (October 1974): 602–7.

————. *Mind Reach: Scientists Look at Psychic Abilities.* New York: Delacorte, 1977.

Thomas, Lewis. *The Youngest Science: Notes of a Medicine Watcher.* New York: Viking, 1983.

Bibliography

Vasiliev, L. L. *Experiments in Mental Suggestion*. Charlottesville, VA: Hampton Roads, 2002.

Vassey, Zoltán. "Method for Measuring the Probability of 1 Bit Extrasensory Information Transfer between Living Organisms." *Journal of Parapsychology* 42 (1978): 158–60.

Warcollier, René. *Mind to Mind*. Charlottesville, VA: Hampton Roads, 2001.

Wood, Ernest. *Yoga*. Baltimore: Penguin, 1962.

Wittgenstein, Ludwig. *Tractatus Logico-Philosophicus*. London: Routledge and Kegan Paul, 1922.

Suggested Reading: Studies in Consciousness

Some of the twentieth century's most profound metaphysical texts are out of print, hard to find, and unknown to most readers; yet they are still of importance. Their insights into the dynamic world of metaphysics and parapsychology are still valuable and vital. The publishing house Hampton Roads has made many of these texts available again through their Studies in Consciousness series, which covers such perennially exciting topics as telepathy, astral projection, after-death survival of consciousness, psychic abilities, long-distance hypnosis, and more. In addition to authoring or co-authoring eight books, I have had the privilege of co-publishing the following dozen books with Hampton Roads, with the great support and encouragement of Frank DeMarco, a co-owner of the firm. I encourage you to familiarize yourself with these wonderful books (in which I have no financial interest). For simplicity's sake, only the years of the original publication and the latest Hampton Roads reprint is given.

Distant Mental Influence: Its Contributions to Science and Healing, by William Braud, 2003. A new book describing pioneering research on how the thoughts of one person can affect the physiology of a distant person. Preface by Larry Dossey, M.D.

Dream Telepathy: Experiments in Natural ESP, by Montague Ullman, Stanley Krippner, and Alan Vaughan, (1973) 2002. This pioneering and highly successful telepathic study was conducted at Maimonides Hospital in the 1960s. Preface by Stanley Krippner and Montague Ullman.

Experiments in Mental Suggestion, by L. L. Vasilliev, (1963) 2002. Includes his famous experiments in long-distance hypnosis. Preface by Arthur Hastings; introduction by Anita Gregory.

An Experiment with Time, by J. W. Dunne, (1927) 2001. Detailed reports of a scientist's precognitive dream journal and theories. Preface by Russell Targ.

Suggested Reading

The Future and Beyond: Paranormal Foreknowledge and Evidence of Personal Survival from Cross Correspondences, by Francis Saltmarsh, (1938) 2004.

Human Personality and Its Survival of Bodily Death, by F. W. H. Myers, (1906) 2001. Myers's landmark work in the theory of psychology, psychic research, and survival. Preface by Jeffrey Mishlove; edited and with an introduction by Suzi Smith.

Mental Radio, by Upton Beall Sinclair, (1930) 2001. Carefully conducted ESP experiments by the famous muckraking writer and his psychic wife. Preface by Albert Einstein.

Mind at Large: IEEE Symposia on the Nature of Extrasensory Perception, by Harold E. Puthoff, Charles Tart, and Russell Targ, eds., (1979) 2002. Preface by Russell Targ.

Mind Reach: Scientists Look at Psychic Abilities, by Russell Targ and Harold E. Puthoff, (1977) 2005. The first book describing remote viewing research at Stanford Research Institute. Preface by Margaret Mead.

Mind to Mind, by René Warcollier, (1948) 2001. Detailed description of psychic capabilities and the sources of mental noise limiting such perception. Preface by Ingo Swann.

The Secret Vaults of Time: Psychic Archaeology and the Quest for Man's Beginnings, by Stephan A. Schwartz, (1978) 2005. A comprehensive account from antiquity to the present time, describing the use of psychic abilities to aid classical archaeology.

Thoughts through Space: A Remarkable Adventure in the Realm of the Mind, by Sir Hubert Wilkins and Harold Sherman, (1951) 2004. True psi adventure involving a downed plane in the arctic. Preface by Ingo Swann.

Index

BOLD indicates figures and illustrations.

Index

Index

Index

Dore, Gary, 177

Dossey, Larry, 150, 170

dowsers and dowsing, 136, 185

  remote viewing and, 188, 220–21

Do You See What I See: Memoirs of a Blind Biker (Targ), 76

dreams, precognitive, 128–33

Dream Yoga and the Practice of Natural Light (Namkhai Norbu), 235

duality and nonduality, 207, 249–52

Duane, T. D., 99

Duke University, 96, 127, 169

Duncan, Helen, 178–80

Dunn, Brenda, 6–7

Dzogchen, Ponlop Rinpoche, 258

Dzogchen Buddhism, 235, 250

E

Eddington, Arthur, 201

Edwards, Tony, 134

effect size, 169

eight-space model, 209–13, **211**

Einstein, Albert

  on being sheep, 104

  interest in ESP, 126

  on liberation from self, 218

  Minkowski space and, 212–13

  on miracles, 66

  on nonlocality, 7

  on prejudices, 38

  quantum-interconnectedness and, 201, 207–8

  on Sinclair, 233

  on time, 124

  worldview of, xviii

Eisenbeiss, Wolfgang, 189

Elisha (ghost child), 186–87

emotions, 143, 171

emptiness, 250

Enlightenment, 109

entanglement, 7, 202, 245

EPR (Einstein, Podolsky, Rosen), 201, 204, 208–9

Erhard, Werner, 89

Esalen Institute, 39, 220, 239

ESP (extrasensory perception). *See also* paranormal phenomena; psi; psychic abilities

  acceptance of, xiv–xv

  classes of experiments, 6–8

  cognitive styles and, 83

  evidence for, 4, 12–13

  general ESP, 34

  naming problem in, 33–36

  occult chemistry and, 197–201

  passive recipient in, 157–59

  plane and train loads and, 127–28, **128**

  proof of, xi–xix

ESP-teaching machine, 14, 39, 42, **91, 93**

  features of, 89–93

EST Foundation, 89

evidence, xxi, 4, 12–13. *See also* proof

excluded middle, 244

experimentation

  experimental series in, 21

  factors in, 138–39

Index

Index

viewing random locations, 69–71, **72,** 262

Harary, Keith, 117, 133

Harman, Willis, 41–42

Harris, William, 168

Harvard Prayer Study, 169

Hastings, Arthur, 63

Hauk, Jack, 164–65

healing
distant, 151–52
intentionality in, 166–67

Healing: Doctor in Search of a Miracle (Nolan), 171

Healing Research (Benor), 166

Hearst, Patricia, 6, 14, 57–59

hemolysis experiments, 160–61

Herodotus, 84–86

Hodgson, Richard, 180

Hofstadter, Douglas, xv–xvi

Holmes, Sherlock, 260

hologram, 205–6, 244

Honorton, Charles, 137–40

Horizon (television program), 134

House Committee on Intelligence Oversight, 56

Human Behavior: An Inventory of Scientific Findings (Berelson and Steiner), 3, 9

Human Personality and Survival of Bodily Death (Myers), 176, 190–91

Hutchinson, Anne, 109

Hyman, Ray, xii, xiii

hypnosis, 96–97, 152
distant, 154–57

Hyslop, James, 180

I

Icelandic Chess Federation, 189

IEEE. *See* Institute of Electronic and Electrical Engineers

illusion, 2–3, 249

Immortal Remains (Braude), 194–95

implicate order, 206

Indra's Net, 244–45

information-transmission model, 251–52

"ink fish phenomenon," 253

Institute for Advanced Study, 117

Institute for Transpersonal Psychology (ITP), 8, 63

Institute of Electronic and Electrical Engineers (IEEE), 79

Institute of Noetic Sciences Bulletin, 253

Institute of Noetic Sciences (IONS), 8, 89, 142, 159, 169, 172

Institute of Transpersonal Psychology (ITP), 159

intention, in healing, 152–53

intercessory prayer, 169

interconnectedness
of consciousnesses, xviii, xix
nonlocality and, 3
in physics, 201–4, 204–8

International Herald Tribune, 127

International Remote Viewing Association (IRVA), 23, 26, 136

Index

intervention paradox, 128–29
IONS. *See* Institute of Noetic Science
iPhone app, 14, 93
IRVA. *See* International Remote
   Viewing Association
Isis Unveiled (Blavatsky), 197
ITP. *See* Institute for Transpersonal
   Psychology

J
Jahn, Robert, 6–8, 79
James, William, 176, 180
*Journal for the Society for Psychical
   Research,* 189
Journal of Scientific Exploration
   (Almeder), 183–84, 220
Journeys Out of the Body (Munroe),
   233
Jung, C. G., xxviii
Jupiter, rings of, 20, 30–33, **33**, 243

K
Kamensky, Yuri, 97
Kantor, McKinley, 236
Katra, Jane, 135–36, 165, 219
Kelvin, Baron, xvii
Kerguelen Island, 27, **28**, 29
Khayyam, Omar, 129
Kingsley, Ben, 109
Knox, Sarah S., xiv–xv
Koestler, Arthur, 253
Korchnoi, Victor, 189–90
Kress, Ken, 21, 51, 56
Krieger, Dolores, 199

Kripal, Jeffrey, 239
Krucoff, Mitchell, 169, 170
Kubert, Dan, 11, 12
Kuhn, Thomas, xvii
Kunz, Dora, 199

L
LaBerge, Stephen, 162–63, 234
LaBerge, Walter, 105
lack of fushion defect, 230, **230**
Laetrile, 170
Langley-Porter Neuropsychiatry
   Institute, 102
Larson, Erik, 134
Lawrence Berkeley National
   Laboratory, 209
Lawrence Livermore Laboratory,
   118, **119**
Leadbeater, Charles, 197–98
Legion of Merit award, 15
Leigh, Vivian, 11–12
Leningrad Institute for Brain
   Research, 97, 154
Life magazine, 68
Life Science Division (LSD) of CIA,
   43, 56
Limitless Mind (Targ), xxii
Longchen Rabjam (Longchenpa),
   213, 250
LSD. *See* Life Science Division
lucid dreaming, 234–35
Lucifer magazine, 197, **198**
Lucky, Robert, 77
Lytton, Edwar Bulwer, 238

Index

Index

Gravity Probe B mission, 20
telepathy experiments and, 90,
93–96
National Institutes of Health (NIH),
8
National Security Agency (NSA), 20,
25, 49–50
Natural ESP (Swann), 26, 229
Nature, 5, 60
Naumov, Edward, 98
Neppe, Vernon, 190
neuroscience, xvi
Newark College of Engineering, 158
Newton, Isaac, 240
Newton's Laws, 126–27, 160, 240
New York Times, 169
"Nightline" television show, 47
Nikolaev, Karl, 97–99
Nolan, William, 171–72
nonduality, 241–45, **243**
nonlocal correlations, 201
nonlocality, 3, 7, 245
physics and, 16, 125
nonlocal (unobstructed) awareness,
21–22, 29, 79, 153, 244
Nova (television series), 6, 134–35,
262
NSA. *See* National Security Agency

O
Observer, The (newspaper), xiv, xix
"Occult Chemistry" (Besant), 197,
198
Occult Chemistry (Leadbeater and
Besant), 199

Office of Technology Assessment,
148
Olcott, Henry Steel, 197
Omega Institute, 21
*On Being Certain: Believing You Are
Right Even When You Are Not*
(Burton), 94, 175
OOB. *See* out-of-body (OOB)
experiences
Opening to the Infinite (Schwartz),
133
Oppenheimer, J. Robert, 88
Oracle at Delphi, **84,** 84–86
organ donation, 192–93
Ostrander, Sheila, 40–41, 121
out-of-body (OOB) experiences,
232–37

P
P., Dr. (anonymous researcher),
121–23
Padmasambhava, 30, 213, 241, 250
paradigms, xvii, xix
parallelism, 229–30, **230**
paranormal phenomena, xiv–xv,
xvi. *See also* ESP (extrasensory
perception)
Parapsychological Association (PA),
13, 76, 158, 222
parapsychology, 3
Parke, C. W., 85, 86
PASS button (in ESP testing), 89–91
Patanjali, 206, 245–46, 248, 255
Pell, Clayborne, 45, 56
Pellew, George, 180–81

Index

Index

psychokinesis (PK), 153, 164

psychology, parapsychology and, 3

psychotronic research, 41

Puthoff, Harold. *See also* Stanford Research Institute
cofounding SRI, 19, 41–43
as physicist, 117, 262
report by, 56–57
role in remote viewing, 9, 63

Q

quantum-interconnectedness, 201, 204–8, 245

Quantum Optics (Fox), 208

R

Rabjam, 251

Radin, Dean, 142

Raja yoga, 98

Ramana Maharshi, 257

Random Number Generation Perturbations protocol, xiii

random-number generator, 36, 60, 138, 145

Rauschner, Elizabeth, 209, 213–16

Reading the Enemy's Mind (Smith), 115

Redwood City Marina, 63

reincarnation, 181–84

reinforcement, 89–91

relaxation, 160, 169

"Relaxation Response," 169

Remen, Rachel Naomi, 253–54

remote viewing (RV). *See also* associative remote viewing

AIR assessment of, xii–xiii, xxii

associative, 134

by author, 10, **10**

of Backfire bomber, 115–16

Buddhism and, 3

of Chinese atom-bomb test, 25–26

at Delphi, **84,** 84–86

of distant targets, 27–32

distortion in, 229

encouragement of, 108–9

as experimental protocol, xiii, 6–7

interviewers in, 121–23

of MX missile locations, 147–49

of objects in cans, 73–75, **74**

in police work, 50

preparation for, 221–25

of random locations, 60–65, **62, 64,** 69–71

of rings of Jupiter, 20, 30–33, **33,** 243

session, 225–28

of Soviet submarine, 115

of Soviet weapons factory, 50–57

teaching, 23, 26–27, 219–21

as unobstructed awareness, 4

Remote Viewing Secrets (McMoneagle), 26–27, 222

Rende, John, 133

Resurrection (film), 110

retroactive priming, 146

Retrocausal Conference, 123

retrocausality, 8–9

Index

Index

Index

Index

About the Author

Russell Targ is a physicist and author, a pioneer in the development of the laser and laser applications, and a cofounder of the program established in the 1970s and 1980s at Stanford Research Institute (SRI) to investigate psychic abilities. SRI is a research and development think tank in Menlo Park, California.

Called *remote viewing*, Targ's work in the psychic area has been published in *Nature*, the *Proceedings of the American Association for the Advancement of Science* (AAAS), and *The Proceedings of the Institute of Electronic and Electrical Engineers* (IEEE).

Targ has a bachelor's degree in physics from Queens College and did graduate work in physics at Columbia University. He has received two National Aeronautics and Space Administration awards for inventions and contributions to lasers and laser communications. In 1983 and 1984 he accepted invitations to present remote-viewing demonstrations and to address the USSR Academy of Science on this research.

He is author or coauthor of seven books dealing with the scientific investigation of psychic abilities and Buddhist approaches to the transformation of consciousness, including *Mind Reach: Scientists*

About the Author

Look at Psychic Ability (with Harold E. Puthoff, 1977, 2005); *Miracles of Mind: Exploring Nonlocal Consciousness and Spiritual Healing* (with Jane Katra, 1998); and *Limitless Mind: A Guide to Remote Viewing and Transformation of Consciousness* (2004). He also wrote an autobiography, *Do You See What I See: Memoirs of a Blind Biker*, in 2008.

As a senior staff scientist at Lockheed Missiles and Space Company, Targ developed airborne laser systems for the detection of windshear and air turbulence. Having retired in 1997, he now writes books on psychic research and teaches remote viewing worldwide. His website is www.espresearch.com.